AN EMPIRE
OF THE EAST

AN EMPIRE OF THE EAST

Travels in Indonesia

NORMAN LEWIS

JONATHAN CAPE
LONDON

First published 1993

1 3 5 7 9 10 8 6 4 2

© Norman Lewis 1993

Norman Lewis has asserted his right
under the Copyright, Designs and Patents Act 1988
to be identified as the author of this work

First published in the United Kingdom in 1993 by
Jonathan Cape
Random House, 20 Vauxhall Bridge Road, London SW1V 2SA

Random House Australia (Pty) Limited
20 Alfred Street, Milsons Point, Sydney,
New South Wales 2061, Australia

Random House New Zealand Limited
18 Poland Road, Glenfield,
Auckland 10, New Zealand

Random House South Africa (Pty) Limited
PO Box 337, Bergvlei, South Africa

Random House UK Limited Reg. No. 954009

A CIP catalogue record for this book
is available from the British Library

ISBN 0-224-03230-5

Typeset by Deltatype Ltd, Ellesmere Port, Cheshire
Printed in Great Britain by Clays Ltd, St Ives PLC

To Claudia and Gawaine, and also to Louis,
reluctantly left behind on grounds of extreme youth

CONTENTS

PREFACE

INDONESIA IS SPREAD in a vast archipelago across 3,000 miles of the southern seas. Its population, creeping towards 200 million, is uniquely diverse in its composition of 300 ethnic groups speaking some 250 languages; each inhabited island possessing a different history and culture from the next. Eisenhower first conferred imperial status upon this island agglomeration when speaking of what he called 'the rich empire of Indonesia'. He demanded that nothing should be allowed to interfere with its unification process, for 'a strong Indonesia would provide the essential barrier to the spread of communism in the East'. Whether they liked it or not, the components of what had been until 1949 the Dutch East Indies were to be surrendered to Javanese rule. West Papua, promised self-determination, became Irian Jaya under the Indonesia flag. As late as 1975 the United States and Australia joined forces in the manoeuvres following which East Timor, a Portuguese colony, was invaded and occupied.

Both these takeovers have encountered local resistance protracted over many years, while an unending struggle conducted by the central power against the separatists in Aceh (Sumatra) has added to the hundreds of thousands of lives lost in insurgencies. While the absorption of West Papua into the empire was accepted by the world as a *fait accompli*, the United Nations has protested on numerous occasions against the illegal occupation of East Timor. In February 1983 a UN Commission on Human Rights expressed 'deep concern over continuing human rights violations in the territory of East Timor' and in the same month Amnesty International found that extra-judicial executions and disappearances have become a central part of the Indonesian government's repertoire. The capture of the rebel leader Xanana Gusmao led in 1993 to his trial and sentence to life imprisonment. With that the Indonesian government declared that the eighteen-year resistance was at an end. Yet almost simultaneously British Aerospace announced a deal signed secretly for the supply of twenty-four Hawk combat jets to Indonesia – aircraft described in promotional literature as well suited to ground attack. The *Independent*'s headline on 11.6.93 concluded that these 'may be used on Timor rebels'.

Little of these unhappy events is likely to impinge in any way upon the experiences of the average Western visitor to the country. Indonesia aims to present itself above all as a democracy of the kind we understand, and at five-yearly intervals the nation goes into a paroxysm of excitement over elections which infallibly return Golkar, the President's party, to power. Innovations in the electoral process have included Golkar's advance notice of the overall majority it expects to get, which is always correct, and its choice of the leaders of the parties – destined to a crushing defeat – which will oppose it. Sometimes enthusiasm for President Suharto's cause is carried to extreme lengths. Thus, in the 1987 election, called by the President the country's 'festival of democracy', the island of Kalimantan is reported as having scored a possible world's record turnout of 508% of the registered voters. 'Once again,' Suharto is said to have commented, 'the nation has applauded the success of our policies.'

Despite the cultural attractions of Java and its bustling modern cities at the heart of the Empire, many Western travellers will wander away in search of the graciousness of the East Indies of old. This in its gentle decline is most likely to be found in the outer islands where sheer distance has preserved it from our times. There are few places anywhere with reserves of human warmth and generosity to equal those of these island people of slender means and little ambition, although too often labelled by the government *suka terasing* (isolated and backward).

In all probability Indonesia can still offer the greatest variety of primitive scenes and entertainments of any country on earth. Upon these the State casts a cold entrepreneurial eye. The real test of acceptability is whether or not these lighthearted affairs can be detached from the life of the people and converted to marketable folklore for the benefit of the nascent tourist business. Tourism is seen as a major industry of the future but there is a lack of realism about the forms it is likely to assume. A few hundred square miles of the incomparable rainforest of Sumatra used to house more rare animals than all the zoos put together, and was surely the most precious of national assets. But the trees among which the animals hide are going even faster than those of Brazil, and soon there will be no trees and no animals.

'So what comes next?' I asked a man who had just turned a half-million acres of a forest in Aceh into cement sacks.

'Personally I've nothing to worry about,' he said. 'The big money's in tourism these days. From now on it's golf courses. This is going to be the paradise of Japanese golfers.'

But can there really be enough golfers in Japan – or even the whole world – to fill this terrible gap?

SUMATRA

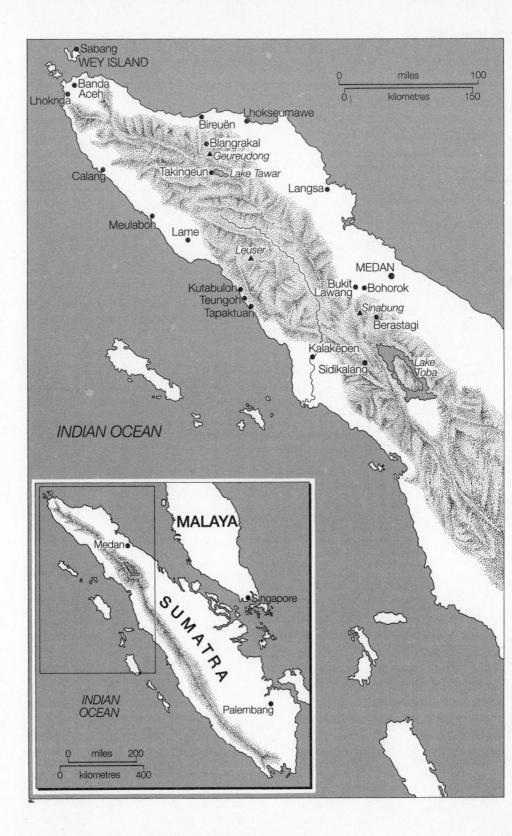

ONE

IN EARLY 1991 I embarked on a series of journeys in Indonesia. The choice offered by an archipelago of 13,000-odd islands is overwhelming, and a traveller setting out in youth, with the intention of leaving none unvisited, would find himself trapped in the bailiwick of old age before completing such an odyssey. Change in Indonesia is rapid and sometimes depressing. Today's luxuriant forest is tomorrow's bare hillside, and today's mountain tomorrow's copper mine. I was at pains to avoid areas that had succumbed to tourist influences, for mass tourism is the great destroyer of customs and cultures, and the purveyor of uniformity. There are astonishing resemblances between Spain's Costa del Sol and Thailand's Phuket.

For me the places holding the greatest interest were those that had withstood the standardising processes of the Indonesian government, thus retaining an individualism that it was hard to believe could survive. Among those were Aceh in North Sumatra with a culture and history entirely separate from the Javanese one the government seeks to impose. East Timor was a former Portuguese colony which, having resisted an Indonesian takeover, had become the scene of this century's most ferocious small war. In Irian Jaya Stone-Age Papuans continued to resist absorption into the national amalgam. Fresh news awaited the visitor to all of these destinations, but apart from their special interest, urgency was the spur.

That Aceh should have been chosen for the first of these peregrinations was largely fortuitous. My son Gawaine and his friend Robin – both refugees from the stresses of life in the City – were taking a six-month therapeutic break in South-east Asia, and now they suggested we join forces. At this time almost all the islands of Indonesia were plunged into the season of rains. Only North Sumatra, projecting well across the Equator, offered a climatic exception. Travel elsewhere in the archipelago could be difficult indeed, but Aceh was dry – offering the benefits of uncomplicated journeyings if, and when, compelled to leave the beaten track. Enthusiasm for the project was general. We would refresh ourselves with new simplicities, relax among village people, drink boiled water, eat rice flavoured with chillies, and travel among basketed chickens and parcelled-up piglets by village bus. And so we flew to Medan, capital of North Sumatra, where the practicalities were to be tackled.

A minimum of prosaic information would be required: we needed to supply ourselves with local maps, find out where buses went, decide on routes, enquire as to the availability of accommodation at the end of the journey, collect whatever schedules and timetables might exist. With this object in view, our first visit was to the office of NATRABU, the government tourist board, where we were questioned by a series of smart girls, recalling the air-hostesses whose melting sympathy and charm so frequently advertised a short while back on British television quite certainly contributed to the success of the national airline.

We explained that we hoped to travel by bus from Medan to Banda Aceh on the island's northernmost tip, returning after various side-trips by the west coast. This part of the journey we expected to be by far the most interesting, for the road – much of it in poor condition – passed through what sounded like the least-visited part of the island, where the coastal villagers lost their animals to tigers coming down by night from the mountains. In the rainy season stretches of this route were impassable for weeks on end, and an oldish guidebook spoke of cars and buses having to be rafted across three of the rivers. Some difficulties had arisen here, we read, through problems of transmigration and the understandable resentment of Sumatrans to see newcomers, whom they considered as foreigners settled on their land. Finally there were the reports of an insurrection in Aceh province by separatists, although little news of this was permitted to appear in the Indonesian press.

The three beautiful secretaries at NATRABU considered our project, expressing at first limited enthusiasm and encouragement and then the invasion by doubt, with the wonderfully subtle expressions and delicate finger gestures suggesting the genesis of a Balinese dance. Part of Indonesian protocol on such occasions prohibits the bringing of bad tidings – in this case conveyed in the use of the word impossible, either in Indonesian or English translation. 'Sometimes difficulties are arising,' said the spokeswoman, holding the telephone through which unsatisfactory news had been received as though she had just gathered a lotus. 'Maybe there are buses to Langsa,' she said. Langsa was seventy miles away up the easy east coast road.

'And after that?'

'We are waiting for answers to our questions. Soon we shall know. You see, perhaps today is bus, but tomorrow no. Maybe you are in Langsa and they say you this bus must go back. What will you do?' In spite or because of the possible predicament, all three girls burst into laughter, trilling their merriment in a most musical fashion.

The office was the personification of the orient of our day, glutted with electronic equipment among shining spaces. All the aparatus in sight seemed to have been designed to disguise its actual function. A TV set succeeded in looking like a jousting helmet, and a shutter like the door of Ali Baba's cavern dropped over the computer in its wall niche when not in use. Of the past nothing remained but a small girl who kneeled to polish foot by foot the already gleaming floor.

The spokeswoman detached herself from her friends and glided back to where she had placed us under an air-conditioning vent which blew breeze over us with the sound of distant prayer. 'We could hire a car for you,' she said.

We shook our heads. 'Not a car,' I said.

'What will you do, then? Walk?' She went through a mime of an exhausted pedestrian dragging himself down the road under the sun. All the girls laughed happily again, and we did our best to show amusement too. Groaning, I dragged my hand across a sweat-soaked brow, and the effort to enter into the spirit of the joke delighted them. Amazingly, the highly developed Indonesian sense of humour is of the slapstick kind, running to false noses and Chaplinesque moustaches. 'They like to look on the funny side of things,' said a booklet on how to make friends and influence people in Indonesia. The author instanced the case of a friend who had scored a social success at a party by taking out his false teeth and holding them in his hands to snap convivially at fellow guests.

By now we had the girls on our side, but with all the goodwill in the world, they couldn't make the buses run. It was clear that it was a car or nothing. 'We are making special deal for you,' the spokeswoman said, 'but' – she hesitated, and her smile increased in brilliance – 'it is necessary to take a guide.'

'Why?'

'Because you cannot find your way. Some new roads are not on map. The car is no problem. For the guide I do not know. Maybe we find one, maybe we don't. I can telephone.'

She went away to phone and came back shaking her head. 'I try them all. They don't want,' she said.

'Did they say why?'

'They tell me distance is very far. They do not want to leave their family. I think their wives are saying them don't go.'

'So what can we do?'

'Well, now I try another company. These guides have no work to do. Maybe one will come.'

This time she was joyously successful, with a gain of face as the bringer of good news. 'This is very good man, but very poor. When there are tourists he is water-skiing instructor, but now no tourists and he must take work. He will come. This man's name Mr Andy.'

'Mr who?'

'Real name you will not be able to speak, so he has taken short name. Many people are doing this, because short names are more suitable for us.'

We called back an hour later to meet Mr Andy, a small, neat man in a carefully pressed denim suit with meticulous repairs over the trouser knees where wear and tear had gone too far. He had a kind and sensitive face embellished with an army-style moustache, which in view of the extreme passivity of his expression seemed out of character. His glittering eyes were devoid of malice, and the impression he gave was of a responsible citizen occupied with a struggle to maintain the decency of his poverty. He could have been in his late thirties and for some reason the name he had chosen for himself could not have been more inappropriate.

The girls had retired to the rear of the office and from a diffused image of them through a glass screen appeared to be involved in the gentle gymnastics of what I supposed to be a Sumatran dance. 'You are wishing to go for water-skiing to Lake Toba?' Mr Andy asked. 'On this lake I am chief instructor Albatross Club.'

'No,' I said. 'We're going north to Aceh.'

'Ah, Aceh, you say?' His moustache flickered. 'In Aceh only Lake Tawar is good. You may enquire if Hotel Takingeun have boat for hire.'

'We don't want to go water-skiing.'

He smiled moving only the corner of his lips, as we were to learn he always did, as a matter of politeness, to conceal emotion of any kind. In this case he was resigning himself to a disappointing situation. 'What is purpose of your visit?' he asked.

'To look at the place. We wouldn't expect problems in driving from Medan to Banda Aceh, but we're told the west coast road is bad and we need a guide. The people here tell us you're just the man.'

'Ah,' he said. 'Yes. How long will we be away?'

'At this stage I don't know. Are you sure you want to take this on?'

A change had come over him. He straightened himself, and there was a briskness in his manner I had not seen before. For a moment he reminded me of a man I had known who had suddenly come to terms with the fact that he was about to go to prison, and I knew I was witnessing a case of resignation.

'I can take it on,' he said.

'And we can start tomorrow?'

'Tomorrow. What time shall I come?'

'Well, let's make it early. Say seven.'

Parting company with Mr Andy, we walked over to the main post office and picked up letters at the poste restante. One from London contained a *Financial Times* cutting which reported that the Indonesian government had sent in five battalions to crush a rebellion in Aceh. The newspaper spoke of the worst violence in years. If this were the case it seemed extraordinary that I should be allowed simply to pick up a hire car and drive it into an area of some sensitivity.

By coincidence a front-page editorial in the English language *Indonesian Times* caught my eye on a news-stand. It was headed – as might have been expected – *Incorrect reports on security in Aceh*, and the gist of what followed was that any such reports were the baseless inventions of the foreign media, produced with the intention of harming Indonesia's image. No more convincing evidence of trouble could have been offered than that from Jakarta's point of view the situation in Aceh was serious enough to have jolted the Indonesian press out of its normal silence in all such matters. This very long and puffed-out article provided absolutely no information on the subject of current happenings. There was nothing to bite on. The Indonesian people, who have lived for some thrity years in a news blackout, shy away like deer from any discussion into which politics enters. No-one we spoke to in Medan admitted to any idea of what was going on in the north.

There was also a letter from my daughter Claudia – a medical student who would be working and travelling for a year in Indonesia – dealing with her adventures on the island of Sumba. Her letters were an ideal complement to my own experiences in these islands, and it was hoped that we would be able to meet and travel together to East Timor, at some point during these travels.

Claudia and her friend Rod, also a medical student, had been engaged in a project with homeless street children in Java, and at the termination of this were visiting a number of islands where their principal concern was the predicament of the original inhabitants. In many cases these were threatened by the loss of their land, and under pressure to abandon traditional religions, dress, housing and means of subsistence, thereby becoming available as the labour force of logging, mining and plantation industries that were moving in. In Sumba the enemy was mass tourism, and as this letter shows the processes of deculturation involved were much advanced.

> Well, we finally made it to the Pasola, and stayed in a house where a funeral was going on. The people were no longer Merapu but converted to Christianity and we heard some had been forcibly baptised. The only difference this appears to have made is they don't keep priceless ikats (traditional dyed fabrics) symbolising the Merapu religion in the rafters any more and they don't kill a horse to carry you off to heaven. In the one we saw they were not even allowed to inject the corpse to preserve it – so when they showed us grandma wrapped up in an ikat in the sitting position, she had a lot of bubbling red exudate coming out of her nose and mouth. They said tomorrow she'd be black and smelly, so they'd keep her covered up. We gave a donation to help her on her way, and so she'd protect us and give us a long and prosperous life. We also brought gifts of sugar, and were given local betel which we bravely tried but didn't enjoy too much, but caused a lot of merriment as we inexpertly spat it out. Three pigs were swiftly killed by a knife in the chest, then we got to eat pig fat served with blood soup – Mum enak! Yesterday the second day of the funeral saw the end of a cow and a buffalo, then off to the ancient grave with a massively heavy stone top. There were cries of 'Wooohhh' as they levered it up, then pushed her in. The Pasola was wonderful –far, far more exciting than expected. Full details in my next.

Next morning Mr Andy was waiting for us at the reception exactly on time. If possible he seemed to be even smaller and neater than on the previous day, and there was evidence of some further needlework on the doubtful areas in his denims. He was clutching a small wallet containing, it was to be supposed, the essentials of travel, and his moustaches were lifted slightly by his unrevealing smile as we came into sight. The car, delivered to the forecourt, was a seemingly new Toyota of robust appearance, with enormous tyres, a high ground clearance, and bearing a self-satisfied maker's claim about the construction of its body. The agreement was that the two boys would take turns to drive. Gawaine got in behind the wheel, I settled myself beside him, and Robin and Andy climbed up into the back. We drove to a filling station to top up with petrol and the man at the pumps asked Andy where we were bound for, and when Andy told him he laughed and drew his hands across his throat. Taking this to be a joke we paid little attention, but the menace it concealed revealed itself and grew until in the end it cast a shadow over the journey.

The road northwards from Medan to Banda Aceh, capital of the province, keeps close to the sea, and a wide coastal plain, now virtually cleared apart from recent plantations of rubber and coconut palms, is described in one of the guidebooks as boring. This was far from being the case, for much of it is flanked by rice paddies, and there a few livelier and more varied scenes of farming activity then those concentrated in these sparkling wetlands, and nowhere softer colours and more indulgent light. Rice farmers everywhere enjoy and pride themselves upon their orderly existence, and orderliness is inseparable from the efficient production of their crop. The water in which they work can only be kept under control by exact practice and comformity with natural laws, and this enforces tidiness. One never sees a rice field with a ragged boundary, and paddies are firmly geometrical and fitted into their surroundings in a lively mosaic of shapes that increases rather than detracts from the charm of the landscape. Monotony is avoided by variation from field to field in the growth of the rice seedlings: some barely pricking through the water's surface while others already display the viridian brilliance of full growth. The trimness of the paddies is accentuated by that of the little thatched shelters where tools are kept, and from which the farmers operate the devices they hope will scare away the birds. These are waders of the most elegant kind: delicately stepping storks, herons and egrets. The familiar coolie hats of the East are normally worn by the rice farmers here in Aceh, although as we drove north more and more wore black witches' hats, miraculously kept in place as they bent over their work, which added a stylish and dramatic note to the scene.

We spent a morning dawdling through this pleasant landscape. Until 1870 the great eastern plain of Sumatra had been covered with the densest of jungles, but with the discovery that the Deli tobacco grown in tiny clearings was probably the finest in the world, plantations on the old American model were introduced. By the end of the century the number of persons contracted to work on these equalled half the population of Holland, and for all the legalistic quibbles they were hardly distinguishable from slaves. It was the Eastern equivalent of the Industrial Revolution, perhaps rather worse. Van Stockum's invaluable *Traveller's Handbook to the Dutch West Indies* (1920), regards the plantations with benign interest. 'These industries brought much prosperity to the district, and they necessitated the importation of Chinese and Javanese labourers who work under contract and are very well looked after, owing to the combined efforts of the employers and the government. The labour legislature and the welfare work are highly developed in this plantation district.'

Such self-deluding pictures of a tropical near-Arcadia were damaged by the disclosures of a young Hungarian planter, Ladislao Szekely, whose book *Tropic Fever* was to arouse a frenzy of protest in Dutch colonial circles. Szekely, puffing on an English opium-filled cigarette, was present at the arrival of a new coolie transport. The coolies, including women and children, had been tricked by the recruiting officers of the Coolie Importing Company into accepting a silver coin and putting a fingerprint on a contract form. The victims were then seized and led away. 'On the boat the sailors had beaten the coolies and taken away their young wives. Coolies who had worked well for the company were waiting at Deli to take their pick of the women left over.'

The first part of the book is a catalogue of horrors. Families are torn from the jungles and split up, the women being not only separated from their menfolk but from their children. All names are changed, cancelling previous identities. There are scenes of unending violence. On Szekely's first day in the jungle a suspected thief is taken in a tiger trap, and the corpse of a coolie who had died in the night is flung as a matter of course through the nearest barrack-room window. Batak tribesmen with a notable propensity for cannibalism are hired to track down would-be escapers. Persuaded by a superior, Szekely buys a coolie's wife for ten guilders – although up to this point he appears as full of shame.

Then suddenly all this record of atrocity is put out of mind. The mood changes so dramatically that a suspicion dawns that perhaps the author has suffered a kind of breakdown causing him to throw in the towel and call for someone holding opposite opinions to finish the book. So far we have been reading an account of a Sumatra version of the outrages of Putamayo, but now the view is through different eyes. Szekely, at twenty-six, has become a Tuan Besar (big man), sanctioned by the Board of Directors to clear more and more forest for plantations, and living in a kind of forest suburbia. 'In front of my house was a large garden with carefully tended flower beds . . . four gardeners worked the grass mower from morning to night.' There are tennis courts and golf courses for the Europeans and football for the natives. 'I gazed upon the gentle, friendly landscape. Only six years had passed since our first axe-blow brought about a new life here.' In the next two weeks 500 coolies would be arriving. He finishes on a note of quiet satisfaction.

We lingered happily in a pleasant environment of work in these days easily performed; of buffaloes ploughing through shining mud with women following to tuck in the seedling rice plants. Farmers with time on their hands fished a little, with unimpressive results. There was always a child in sight flying a home-made kite. Eventually the matter of food came up. Andy knew this area and recommended a restaurant at Langsa. 'Here food very clean,' he said. 'You will enjoy.'

The restaurant turned out to be what at first appeared as a substantial double-fronted shop, an impression heightened by a modest display in both windows of cooked foods of various kinds, all these exhibits appearing more as crudely made plastic imitations than the real thing.

We went in and found ourselves in the Victorian surroundings of what could have been a family restaurant in the back street of an English country town. The walls bore massive, fly-spotted mirrors in heavy frames carved from dark, expensive-looking wood, and the dining area contained nine circular tables with marble tops, each of them some seven feet across. Having seated us at one of these, two waiters went off together to a cupboard under the back of one of the windows, opened it, and came back carrying between them a tray holding twenty-five dishes of food which they proceeded to arrange on our table. We prodded with our forks at the items on offer, identifying what might have been lamb or goat, the unmistakable limbs of chickens wrapped in yellow, parchment skin, a short black length of rubber imitation of bowel, segments of fish, and octopus tentacles. It was all cold, rock-hard, and caked with what had once been a reddish sauce, recalling an unimaginative museum exhibit illustrating, perhaps, articles of food recovered from a Celtic settlement. Within minutes of our arrival four customers sitting at the nearest of the enormous tables got up and prepared to leave. They too had been confronted with twenty-five plates and their disturbing contents, and we had been in time to watch their fumblings in search of last-minute titbits before their departure. The waiter picked among them, and added several obviously popular dishes to those we already stared down at disconsolately. 'Were all these things cooked some days ago?' I asked Andy.

'Oh, yes. Cooked once, twice a week. Very long time cooking. This way is keeping fresh.'

As it was quite impossible to bite into these victuals there was no opportunity, even had we desired to do so, to test their flavour, and in studying them, appetite had leaked away. Since no more food might be forthcoming for some hours, if at all that day, it seemed reasonable to stoke up with rice. A bowl of this was brought, but large mosquitoes, evidently attracted in a dry place to moisture when food was newly prepared, stuck like festive embellishments about its surface where they had weakened, then expired. Even Andy was not tempted by this offering. 'Rice is eating for farmers,' he explained. 'Make you no can do shit.' Otherwise he ate heartily and with evident relish, tearing at the dry and often withered segments of meat, the corrugations of skin and shattered bones, with small but powerful jaws. Experience might have taught him that this was the last such feast he would enjoy on the journey.

We were entering an area which appeared to be increasingly Muslim fundamentalist the further we travelled. Every village was dominated by its mosque, its size and architectural pretensions clearly reflecting the prosperity or otherwise of the local rice farmers. Some of the mosques were showy, domed pavilions; others, where crops may have been normally poor, were no more than a dome added by way of an afterthought to a normal house. The domes were of all sizes and shapes: inflated Moghul with accompanying towers, Slavic onion, Hollywood fantasy, Tartar. Some, in the case of the richer villagers, were very vulgar. Religious outcry broadcast by loudspeakers was a feature of this region, and it would have seemed that the normal call to prayer was liable to extension by a lengthy discourse in Arabic, or possibly a reading from the Koran.

These villages were spotless and rather austere. Each one had its school, and we passed several of them shortly after midday when studies came to an end. Pupils streamed from them by the hundred and our attention was drawn particularly to the girls in their fundamentalist uniforms, rubicund faces enveloped in spotless white wimples, with medieval-looking capes, and grey skirts reaching to within inches of the ground. A few among these, perhaps prefects, wore dark blue skirts instead of grey. All were stunningly immaculate, and it was amazing to see that, despite these constraining outfits, the girls clambered into the back of the minicabs waiting to collect them with great agility. It was an illustration of the versatility of human beings, who can so easily adapt themselves to the trappings designed for another environment and another age. Further on, in reflection perhaps of less stringent fundamentalist views, schoolgirls in the longest of long skirts had taken to bicycles. In another area, clearly even more relaxed, the skirts still as long as ever, were pink, and in a few cases the daughters of the rich had been allowed to pretend ignorance of orthodox prohibition of luxurious display by fringing the edge of their wimples on the forehead with trinkets of gold.

The road north from Langsa was full of surprise and colour. We passed over a terracotta river and round the verge of a swamp in which the mangroves brandished their black, surrealistic shapes. From this swamp a seepage spread inky plumes among neighbouring paddies. At this time of day heat-waves disguised the ingredients of this picture. In the halation it was hard to distinguish the white shapes of the peasants, knee deep in the paddies, from those of the cranes fishing a few yards away.

Evening stole up on us. We pressed on, besieged by hunger, to Lhokseumawe, a coastal settlement overshadowed by a vast oil refinery with the traffic under the severe discipline of police-manned road-blocks, and a one-way system that took the driver for a glum tour of the town before releasing him again into the main coastal road. One of the locals directed us to a Chinese restaurant where we settled to a succession of ingenious and imaginative dishes, only distracted by karaoke singing – a current fad in Indonesia which is not easy to avoid.

Andy had gone off to eat in an Indonesian place. When we picked him up later, as arranged, he took us to the Lido Graha Hotel, where he knew someone in the management who would give us a room. There was something about this vast barracks of a place that matched the architecture of the refinery and the industrial mood of the town. We were the only guests, so they had turned all the lights off to save money, and we had to feel our way along the passages leading to the rooms.

Apart from the reception the only place where there was a light was the bar. Here we were joined by Santana Mehta, an Indian from Bangalore who was in Lhokseumawe as part of a course he was doing on hotel management. He had aquiline features with fine, melancholic eyes, wore a blazer with a foulard scarf tied round his neck, and had spent a year in Sunderland that had left him overbrimming with nostalgic memories. 'I had a whale of a time,' he said. 'Darts every Saturday night in the Marquis of Granby and Sunday fooling around in boats with the girls on the River Wear.'

'Indonesia is OK,' Mehta agreed, 'but they don't do things the way we do them in England.' In England Mehta had been popular, one of the boys. Here he seemed to be held at arm's length – handicapped, he readily agreed, by the fact that although he understood the language he could not twist his tongue round the long, unfamiliar words well enough to speak it. In this wry fashion he found his isolation funny. Not even the manager's dog accepted him, he said. 'I am so kind to that dog. Much as I try my persuasion that we should go for a walk, he will not associate with me. I am suspecting that it is my smell that he does not like.'

Sumatra's monotheism worried him. He had little patience for a religion that ordered people to get out of bed at dawn to pray and do gymnastics on the floor. 'In Bangalore we are paying our respects to so many gods. If there is a party at a temple we are going to that temple.' He found it easier to get along with the British class society which in some way resembled the situation back home, rather than Islamic democracy which he did not understand. Puritanism shocked him. 'Take my advice not to invite ladies to your room in this hotel. Now the police are saying that they are prostitutes and they will shave their heads. You are foreigners, but otherwise they may punish you for adultery.'

Happily enough, Andy, whose faith at least kept him out of bars, was not present at this conversation. He had put a gloomy interpretation on the presence of road-blocks in the town, and now Mehta brought up the matter of rumoured insurrection. The army was in action, he said, in the mountains nearby. He knew no more than that, but had seen military helicopters over the town earlier that day.

A large swimming pool had been built in a pseudo-garden setting on the hotel's roof, and having learned of this we had arranged to take an early dip before leaving next morning. Arriving on the scene we found that despite possibly weeks of non-use the pool had been looked after to the extent that it was not only splendidly clear, but exuded a reassuring whiff of chlorine. But, possibly on the day of our arrival, it had been showered from the sky by many thousands of small black beetles, and these had formed an unbroken encrustation on the water, several inches in width, all around the rim. In addition there were islands of beetles floating here and there on the surface.

Under pressure of surplus energy, the young enjoy complexity in their sports. The hotel supplied a beach ball which Gawaine and Robin, standing at opposite ends of the pool, hurled across the water at each other, the game consisting of leaping into the air to kick the ball as far as possible before plunging into the pool. This exercise was pleasurably complicated by the need to avoid the rafts of beetles.

Athletic excess encouraged their attack on the hotel's set breakfast. This included spiced porridge, chopped octopus, cold chicken pieces in curry, giant strawberries and an assortment of cakes. Mehta came in, wearing the most crisply laundered shirt I had seen since Delhi, hailed us genially, seated himself at the next table and swivelled in his chair. He bent across to inspect our breakfast with a hint of the misgivings of an aviary eagle over some dubious titbit thrown into its cage. 'What is this food they are bringing us?'

'It calls itself an Indian-style breakfast,' I told him.

'This is not Indian,' Mehta said. 'It is pure imitation. They have caught me with this before. All spices and very deleterious for stomach juices. In your country I am eating one kipper for breakfast every day. It is enough. Someone must ask these people to desist from their imitations of Indian food.' He paused to look up at a weasel-faced man with eye-shades and a heavy gold bracelet hanging from his wrist who had just slid through the door. After a glance in our direction he withdrew. Mehta had lowered his voice. 'Guess profession,' he said.

'Police spy, would you say?'

'Spot on,' Mehta replied. 'He is checking to see no ladies are under table. He is living in hopes one day will be taking lady for hair to be shaven. The town is full of these silly men. So what is your immediate programme? Will you be leaving us?'

'We're going north,' I said. 'Probably get as far as Banda Aceh, and call it a day.'

Mehta lowered his voice, pulling with a finger at the corner of an eye in a cautious but unfamiliar gesture. 'May I give you piece of advice? Take it easy.'

'Any trouble expected, then?'

'I am recipient of many rumours,' Mehta said. 'Now there is one that hostages have been taken. Seven oilmen working with their explorations on road you will be following.'

'We're tourists, not oilmen. Nobody will bother with us.'

'Well, let us hope that is so,' Mehta said, 'and that you will arrive safely at your destination.'

'Do you suggest checking with the police?' I asked.

'Oh no, dear boy. That is one thing you must learn not to do. Keep profile low. In Indonesia that is golden rule.'

TWO

WEST OF LHOKSEUMAWE, in the direction of Banda Aceh, a change of climate suddenly drained the colour from the landscape. The paddies were empty, awaiting the rains. Behind the bare, iron scrollwork of the mangroves the sea had whitened over the sand, and here the fishermen, just offshore, used rakish black feluccas with black sails. For these people, said Andy with good-natured contempt, black was lucky. They prayed in the mosque but were not in reality true Muslims for they put out offerings to spirits and sea-monsters on their beached boats, and at the entrance to their huts. From this point on, westwards and northwards, the people were a strange lot. 'They eat things we do not eat,' he said, 'for example the heads and feet of chickens. Also some parts of the body they are leaving unwashed.'

At Bireuën, a few miles further on, we took the road going south leading to Lake Tawar and the not wholly explored Gayo range of mountains. Lake Tawar itself was the great inducement, for the guidebook said of it that, despite its spectacular scenery, it had remained undiscovered by tourism and could expect to receive only 100 visitors annually. All at once we were in another world. We had driven 200 miles through paddyfields along the shore, through many pleasant villages with kite-flying boys, Muslim girls on bicycles, old men with their long religious beards, rice-farmers with children's butterfly-nets splashing after tiny fish, and overbearing policemen on Japanese motorcycles – people in fact busying themselves in every corner of the landscape. Now we had passed the last little girl dragging her buffalo, and easily avoiding the occasional horn-thrusts in her direction, and the people had gone. The green and silent world of the jungle was closing in.

Suddenly, and strangely, it was cooler, and the odours of grass and sap, of acrid blossom, of earth and weedy decay were in the nostrils. Back on the coast road the only trees had lined up in plantation rows, identical in shape, height and colour, and as repetitious as a wallpaper pattern. Here they were spread in graceful disorder over the low hills at the back of the plain. Someone had built a mosque and then abandoned it. Its tin dome was streaked with rust, and tipped to one side like a drunkard's hat. To the delight of the boys the narrowing road had developed sharp bends, a corrugated surface and perilous potholes that offered an excuse for the display of driving skills. The roadside markets of the small coastal towns had been glutted with fish and innumerable varieties of fruit. The only village in the first ten miles on the road to Lake Tawar could offer no more than fruit bats, their wings tied with auspicious red twine, hanging upside down by the claws, their eyes subjecting the prospective buyer to a sad but penetrating gaze. They were offered very cheaply –the largest of them costing less than the equivalent of 5p – and would be turned into stews believed in Indonesia to be the most effective treatment for asthma. Even Andy believed in the value of this remedy, although he rejected as pagan superstition the popular consumption of their flesh as a remedy for defective eyesight.

It was immediately after leaving Blangrakal that we were exposed for the first time to the vivacity and exuberance of the Indonesian rainforest. We were passing under the flanks of the 10,000-foot peak of Mount Geureudong, of which we caught an occasional glimpse through the trees, where the entrances to the jungle were guarded by a phalanx of leaves like great interlocking shields. Placed behind them were enormous ferns which provided a defence for trees soaring possibly to 150 feet. Tucked into niches of this rampaging vegetation were tiny villages constructed almost entirely of corrugated iron, and here and there their occupants had quietly done away with a tree or two and crammed a minute paddyfield into the space, in which men with thin, sallow tropical bodies groped incessantly in the mud. Bundles of birds with white faces and long yellow bills had been trapped in these mini-swamps and were offered at the roadside, although the villagers showed no interest in them and there was no passing traffic. The area had somehow managed to avoid official scrutiny, for clandestine logging quite clearly went on in a small way. When we stopped to examine an orchid we discovered a pile of tree trunks, their peach-coloured wood laid bare by the axe, inefficiently concealed among the ferns. This bootlegging of wood was a dangerous business for the small people who practised it, for they risked long terms of imprisonment if caught. Great multi-national timber firms were clearing Indonesian forests at the rate of tens of thousands of acres a day. A hill tribesman living by the traditional slash-and-burn system, by which a fresh patch of an acre or two was cleared annually and cultivated for ten years or so before being returned to the jungle, might be sent to prison for ten years.

There were twenty or thirty miles of this impeccable forest, after which the road passed out of the steep hillside and down into an open valley where deforestation had taken place in past times, leaving a tangle of weeds, buffalo grass and secondary growth extending back to the distant mountains. Even as we passed, a woman swinging an enormous axe cut down a seedling large enough to supply a little firewood, and further on, where the forest cover had taken over, again a tree had been felled and left lying to be dragged away under cover of darkness.

Coming into Takingeun it seemed conceivable at first glance that it did in fact receive only 100 visitors a year, for at this time of political crisis it came close to being a ghost town. *Welcome*, in Indonesian, said a banner stretched across the street, but there was no-one about but a few children, and the losmen which had been recommended to us was closed. The view of Lake Tawar was of extreme charm. It was five or six miles across, eternally placid according to all accounts, and enclosed in a coronet of low, pointed mountains which were mantled as if in velvet of the deepest green. At regular intervals little triangular valleys opened out on the lake. These were walled in by slopes which gave out a close-cropped, burnished appearance, as did the glades revealed in openings in the trees. This supremely tropical vista reflected the harmony and spaciousness of a landscape that has escaped interference. Fishermen from invisible villages were out in flotillas of canoes. The lake is said to contain large numbers of small fish, valued not only for their flavour but for their stimulation of the sexual urge. We watched the nearest canoe in action, consisting of putting down the net, then driving the fish into it by splashing the surface of the shallow water with a paddle. The result, so far as we could see, was unpromising, yet two or three fairly minute fish were caught in an operation taking a few minutes. With five or six hours out on the lake it all added up.

The Hotel Renggali had been built upon a spit of land just above the water. In this part of the world people like to put up notices and it came as no surprise that the hotel should have displayed at its entrance a large banner worded in English: WELCOME TO ACEH THE SPIRITUAL DESTINATION OF THE EAST. The building harmonised with its grandiose surroundings in a way that such intrusions so rarely do. It was faintly reminiscent of childhood fairy tales in which castles may be emptied of their inhabitants by a spell, for there were no signs of life in the vicinity of the hotel. A longish wait followed at the reception before there were stirrings in the remote interior of the building, and a clerk who might have been reluctantly aroused from sleep came on the scene.

This hotel came close to being a magnificent shell. We were shown to splendid rooms, admired the astonishing panoply of mountains, forest and water through windows cunningly contrived to embrace half the curve of the horizon. The door closed softly behind the porter and silence fell again. Everything about the Renggali impressed: the thick pile of its carpets, the furniture of dark, richly grained wood with its metal inlay based probably on Persian models of Islamic calligraphy, the antique panels carved and painted with ethnic designs decorating the lounge, the music room in which a row of instruments, most of them unfamiliar, awaited on a podium the arrival of performers instinct told us would never appear.

The hotel had its wonderfully landscaped, empty gardens arranged in terraces and lawns through close-clipped hedges and shrubberies in blossom, which attracted a cloud of butterflies as they descended to the lake. Waiting at the water's edge was the canoe mentioned in a leaflet picked up at the reception, to conduct guests in the mood for a dip in the lake to areas where it was safe to swim. Why safe when all the lake within easy reach was so shallow? The leaflet explained. Although devout Muslims, the locals also contrived to be animists and they refused to allow visitors to risk their lives in parts of the lake under the domination of local spirits. It was after reading this leaflet that Andy told us he preferred not to sleep in a hotel bedroom that night but would lock himself in the car.

We took a walk along the lakeside to visit the nearest of the villages. These were the busiest, liveliest of places, reflecting once again a local appetite for road signs in Indonesian, *subsidence, hairpin bend, falling rock, danger, proceed with caution,* which they had purloined for use as a form of decoration together with advertisements of all kinds: for car batteries, soft drinks, detergents, and above all those for Rinso. The village streets were full of small, strutting Lowry figures, coming and going in all directions, with men holding cockerels clipped and ready for the combat under their arms, women hanging up washing, herds of goats directed by their owners purely by arm signals and ginger dogs. Inevitably these people grew rice, and here the paddies' sparkling attraction was intensified by the use of hundreds of brilliantly coloured flags planted in the mud or suspended from lines to keep the birds away. Small mosques were built in each village by the villagers themselves. The domes were what really counted in these buildings and they were made from scales of metal hammered out in local forges.

Despite the Acehnese reputation for social exclusiveness and taciturnity the whole population of a village turned out when we passed through to wave and shout something that we hoped was applause.

Surprisingly another guest arrived the next day to break the spell of the hotel's emptiness. 'Don't even attempt to pronounce my name,' he said. 'To my friends I am Anatole. Where are you from? England? Well of course one glance was sufficient. I hope you will be staying over the weekend. It is a relief to have someone to talk to. Here it is hard not to feel cut off. I am in the logging business. This is a nice place to relax and the security is good, but let us face it, it is a little dull.'

Anatole's father had been a diplomat and he had spent several of his formative years in Paris and London. He had black, gleeful eyes, his youthful appearance betrayed only by the tufts of grey over the ears. He stood as erect as a soldier on parade, but his hands were constantly in motion. I noticed about him, as I had done before in the case of upper-class Indonesians who ate frequently and well, a faint odour of the spices employed in their food. My impression of him was that he suffered from a lifelong struggle to use up energy. There was no time when all parts of his body were at rest. He had placed himself at this moment close to a table scattered with antique bric-a-brac, and constantly shifted the position of various objects. Thoughts breaking into the stream of consciousness provoked shallow bursts of action. He broke off in mid-sentence to dash to the window, from which he returned with a frown and a shake of the head. 'Boat still not fixed,' he muttered. 'As I was saying,' he went on, 'this is a great place to go to earth for a few days. By the way, I just saw your man down there. He was running round in a circle. Anything wrong with him?'

'He finds that it helps with the nerves,' I told him. 'He picked up some talk about hostage-taking and I think it worried him.'

'Tell him he has no value as a hostage,' Anatole said, with a sudden explosion of laughter. 'Anyway he's quite safe while he stays here. You must have heard of the GAM. The so-called Aceh Liberation Front. They're the people who are causing the trouble, but it's quiet in this season. Could be something going on round Meuseugit. That's past Banda, where the road gets squeezed in between the mountains and the sea. They just killed a few loggers working on one of our concessions. Here we're well placed. Trouble is it's coming to an end. We don't clear-cut in this area, and unless there's an upturn in the price of timber and we have to come back for what we've left, we'll be saying goodbye.'

'What happens next?'

'Indah Kiat might take me on. They have a 150,000-hectare concession south of here. This is a clear-cut and replacement with a eucalyptus project. It's very attractive but I'm sold on this place and I'd like to stay here. I'm thinking of moving into tourism.'

'What about the GAM?'

'They'll have vanished by then.' He tried to wink like a Westerner, but had to use the corner of his mouth as well as an eye. 'From now on the only thing that matters in the East is Japan. It's only three hours away, and given the right appeal the Japanese will come here in droves.'

'Will you be leaving them any trees?'

'It doesn't matter one way or the other. There's a lot of claptrap talked about forests. You can leave a forest a half-mile deep and no-one will notice the difference. If they want animals we can even put them in at the maximum utilisation rate; in the case of deer, for example, of fifteen per hectare.'

I found myself guided to the window, embracing a prospect of two-thirds of Lake Tawar, and as he came closer I again caught the faint whiff of cinnamon and cardamums. There were fifteen or twenty canoes in sight, several of them with their nets down and fishermen splashing in the water with their paddles. Five small mountains almost as regular in shape as pyramids came into this view. It was early morning, the light was bluish and the densely forested little mountains were veiled in ultramarine shadows, although their colouration would alter continually throughout the day, from bluish tones to a glowing russet-red according to the position of the sun. In a calm, stealthy fashion this view was changing all the time. Almost overhead a curdling of small clouds appeared, then vanished. Down in the nearest of the paddies the rice farmers were changing the position and colour of the flags. 'Beautiful, isn't it?' Anatole said. 'Sooner or later this is going to be the Acapulco of South-east Asia. Well, not quite Acapulco because it isn't by the sea. As it is, nobody produces anything. They grow rice and they eat it. They catch fifty cents' worth of fish a day. While gold awaits to be shovelled from the earth.'

He snapped his fingers loudly, a sound which I realised could signify frustration as well as enthusiasm, and frustration in this case was in response to the spectacle of the large speedboat by the hotel's steps leading down to the water. 'Nothing wrong with it that couldn't be fixed in five minutes,' he said, 'but they can't get a mechanic to come up from Medan.'

Before leaving the hotel I wanted to clear up a point. The guidebook warns the reader to check with the locals before going on early-morning and late-afternoon walks from Takingeun or Lake Tawar, because that is the time when the tigers 'which constitute a great danger' come down to feed. It is to be supposed that they are particularly numerous in the area, for 'if you get off the road', the book says, 'you see their tracks'. Having failed in many visits to countries where tigers abound to view any of these splendid animals, I was excited by news of their prevalence round

Takingeun. I discussed the likelihood of a sighting with the hotel manager. 'There are no tigers,' he said. 'If you find one footprint bring me to see it. I have lived here all my life and this is something I have not seen.'

THREE

WE DROVE INTO Banda Aceh, birthplace of Muslim fundamentalism, early in the afternoon, and found ourselves under a dome from Byzantium, holding half the sky in its burnished curve. A taped voice from the minaret offered salvation in a language nobody understood. We parked outside a supermarket and were joined in a moment by a Mitsubishi Shogun from which descended a stately fundamentalist matron, shrouded from the world almost in the style of Iran. She was followed by her three fundamentalist girls, small demure faces cowled in the manner of a medieval jousting casque to cut off side-vision. Getting out of our car, Gawaine and Robin, tall, fair and ruddy, passed briefly through their narrowed vision and were lost to sight, when from one of them came, in such a context, the most extraordinary sound to be heard in all Asia – a wolf whistle.

We began a rather perfunctory exploration of the place discouraged by the heat and also by the lack of any identifiable centre to the town. At this time one longs for the inner sanctum of calm often provided by the cathedral cities of Europe, from which the stresses of commercialism have usually been banned.

Banda Aceh was part of the modern Orient, vociferous, full of lively hucksters and tiring to the visitor. There were mosques galore, for Banda presented itself as a fortress of the unsullied practice of the religion. The atmosphere in the way of social and religious matters resembled that of Franco's Spain immediately after the last war, when women were followed by plain-clothes policemen with rulers intent on measuring their décolletage, and the obsession with covering the body was so great that even a male in shorts was legally obliged to conceal his kneecaps. As in Spain of old, many forms of censorship were rampant, including one by which so much could be cut out of films that in the end some ran to barely half their intended showing time. Aceh had become a Special Autonomous Territory, enforcing Islamic law, and although apprehended robbers do not lose a hand, sentences are said to be severe.

It was in Banda Aceh that the food problem came to a head. Delicious as Indonesian food can be in the restaurants of London or Jakarta, in

Indonesian provincial towns it is deplorable. As we had already discovered, meat, after marination in an assortment of chilies and spices, would go into the oven for several hours, to prepare it for a potential wait of days before it finally reached the table, and strange as it might seem, many Indonesians appeared to have developed a taste for the result. The Chinese, here as in all parts of the world, produced food that was uniformly edible and often exquisitely cooked, not only in restaurants but in roadside stalls. We tried to persuade Andy to join us in these often sumptuous meals, but he firmly resisted on the grounds that the Chinese ate pork. When we promised him that we would support him in abstaining from pork, he reasonably objected that in a Chinese restaurant everything goes into the same wok. Nor was he completely happy to be taken to an Indonesian restaurant, where, feeling continually under a menace, he would have to eat by himself. This being the case there were days when all four of us fell back on biscuits and stale cake, supplemented on occasion by a plateful of rice.

In Banda the problem was half-solved. By all accounts it possessed the best Chinese restaurant – the Tropicana – in this part of Sumatra, and by incredibly good fortune, the usual unpromising Indonesian eating house with a trayful of withered scraps on display in a showcase was just across the road. Andy was comfortably settled in this, close to the window where he could be kept under supervision, while we made for the Tropicana. This place of gastronomic adventure occupied two floors, and in it the Chinese had gathered in their families and their clans by their hundreds round enormous tables. Having run the gauntlet of the roaring television on the ground floor we escaped to an upper room where a karaoke singer struggled for an audience in the pounding surf of chatter and the competition of music turned up beyond the limits of amplification from numerous hidden sources.

Despite their reputation for exclusiveness as a race, the Chinese here were friendly and genial and a family instantly squeezed closer together to make room for us at a table. The waiter could do nothing with our English, but another was found who had spent most of his life in the States, and he began a fearful listing of dishes, beginning with pig's stomach stewed in blood.

'What else have you got?'

'You want something fancy – shark's fin, birds' nests, pork in snakes gall – you go for alligator? Shit, we got everything.'

'How about barbecued ribs?'

'Sure, if that's what you want. We gotta total of three hundred and sixty-five dishes on the menu here. One for every day of the year.'

'Barbecued ribs would be great.'

Among the many things that fascinated – and in this case mystified us – about our environment were collections of stickers, stuck apparently at random at the table's edge. These, printed simply with the word ALLAH, were in sight everywhere. There had been some re-arrangement of the seating of our Chinese neighbours, apparently to allow a family member to show off his American English. 'Hullo, there. You guys from out of town? I'm Lok Lee. In the trucking business here. Anything you want to know?'

For a start we wanted to know about all the advertisements for Allah in this stronghold of a race regarded by the Indonesians as unbelievers. 'We get a lotta Muslims guys come in here,' Lok Lee explained. 'On their feast days it's something you have to see. Hell, there's so many of them sonofabitches you can't get served. They order items they're not supposed to eat. Maybe pork under a different name. You inderstand me? They buy these stickers at the mosque. That's so Allah will look the other way.'

Two birthday parties were being held in this enormous room, and Lok Lee was off to join one of them. The Chinese have a crow-like avidity for the collection of foreign ceremonies for incorporation in the mixed bag of their own social pleasures, and birthday parties lead in popularity, adding in this case their separate lively contributions to general uproar.

'Happy birthday,' they began, and within seconds all those present in the large room happily joined in, chanting resoundingly in what they believed to be English.

'Ep-pi bir-deh to you,
Ep-pi bir-deh to you.
Ep-pi bir-deh Ho Fok Long.
Ep-pi bir-deh to you.'

The Chinese family shifted what may have been another candidate into position next to us.

'Where you go tomorrow?' he asked.

This man had certainly never been to America, but he was doing his best.

'We haven't made up our minds yet,' I told him.

'Why – ah you no go Weh?' he asked. He bared large yellow teeth in a persuasive smile. 'Why – ah you no stay here today and tomorrow go Weh?'

At first I had been afraid he was trying to get rid of us, but the rather fawning smile convinced me that this was not so.

'Where's Weh? I've never heard of it.'

'Weh one island in sea. Weh very good place.'

'What's it got to offer?'

'Weh is OK for do what you like. Banda very much hassle. Too much policemen, too much say prayers. Weh no hassle. Anything you want, right off ferry.' He hissed invitingly, the sound thickened with mucus. 'Anything you want. You know what I mean. Just ask for Harry Feng, and say Vic send you. Harry take care of you for sure. When – ah you come back?'

'I've no idea. No idea even if we're going yet.'

'Try come back on Saturday. This day they show snuff-movie on ferry, but hard for you see show. If Saturday you tell Harry Feng. He fix it for you.'

The hotel had a leaflet advertising Weh's attractions, suggesting that in our present circumstances a short side-trip to the island might not be a bad thing. It spoke in eccentric English of Weh's weird beauty, and of the 'wild pigs running at you with firing eyes out of the darkness'. It claimed the snorkelling was the best off the coast of North Sumatra, and reading this it occurred to us that, as an enthusiast for water-sports, even if he had never tried snorkelling, this experience might help to steady Andy's nerves in preparation for the more strenuous part of the trip, yet to come.

By good fortune a ferry to the island was leaving next day, and at midday we drove down to port, squeezed the car into the last empty space and set out on the 1½-hour crossing to the small island port of Sabang. The passengers were quite clearly returning islanders, laden with enormous bundles and fighting cocks crammed into wicker cages, all of them in a state of emotional turmoil induced by the adventure of travel against the torpid background of island life. The moment the gangplank was let down a desperate, almost frantic rush ensued and a struggle up and down companion-ways and through narrow passages to reach and secure a seat in the first- or second-class saloons – both of them identical in the stark amenities offered. From the moment the anchor was raised until the ship tied up on the quay of Sabang, video programmes would be shown on the television in both saloons, and the struggle – irrespective of the ticket purchased – was to wedge oneself firmly in position out of reach of ticket collectors in the first class, where the most lurid videos were shown.

We found ourselves, quite unintentionally, among the first-class travellers encumbered by vast bundles of rabbits and poultry. All the more popular videos were based upon Kung Fu themes, and the one we were condemned to watch was the attack of outer-space invaders upon what at first glance might have seemed defenceless women. The leader of the invaders, although hampered by robes of the kind worn by a mandarin of the distant past, was an amazing acrobat who could leap into the air and somersault before delivering terrible kicks, sometimes on the vulnerable parts of pretty women. These were also into kung fu and picked up less effective space invaders and tossed them about in all directions. Fairly simple and repetitive action seemed to go on for a very long time, but those engaged in it came unscathed through their prolonged punishment. The motives of the invaders were sexual rather than predatory. Unable to carry out a rape by physical means the leading invader had recourse to chloroform, but his victim, recovering her senses at the last moment, was still able to knock him out. What surprised in these scenes of depravity and lust, these disordered garments and limbs, these lascivious gropings and frustrated thrustings of the buttocks, was that they should have been represented despite severe Islamic prohibitions. Could it be that anything went on a ship?

As was to be expected, Andy was revolted by the entertainment. Much to our surprise, having listened to his criticisms based on technical objections, he informed us that he had been granted certificates of proficiency in peucali silat, and ilmo kebasinan, both versions of the martial arts practised in Indonesia. Did he ever put them to use? we asked him. 'Never,' he replied. 'I am saying no to violence. Martial arts only for improve inner serenity and spirituality of conduct. If space invaders to be shown coming to this earth, better is understanding discussion with earth people.' We all agreed. 'This thing is not funny for me,' he said. 'When we come back, I am sitting on deck.'

There was nothing – certainly at first sight – of the stereotype of the island paradise about Weh. Sabang was a small port, busy in its unmechanised fashion with carpenters making doors, mechanics degutting ancient cars, and work going on in the harbour itself to scrape away the ulcers of rust and repaint a dry-docked ship. Middle-aged people here remembered a time when Sabang had been a free port with a casino, said earlier still to have been busier than Singapore, but in recent years the Muslims fundamentalists had tightened their grip and the population was in steady decline. It would take another ten years, the owner of the losmen where we stayed thought, before Sabang went out of business as a working town. In a way, he thought that might be a good thing, because the tourists would come.

Something extremely perceptible in the atmosphere separated Weh from the Sumatra mainland, where outside the towns practically everyone grew rice or had some connection with its production. Ingrained, inherited occupations produce their own psychology, their own kind of man. No rice farmer would ever voluntarily switch to other forms of agriculture, or adapt himself with any enthusiasm, say to forestry or a sea-going life. In Weh, for numerous generations people had depended upon cloves, and we still saw cloves everywhere, laid out to dry. Provided the market holds, growing crops of this kind is devoid of strain. Long periods of the producer's existence can be devoted to contemplative satisfactions. The clove grower can sit back feeling little but pleasant expectation throughout the long months in which the cloves grow and then dry. He has little conception of urgency, and what he lacks by way of ambition he recovers in confidence and calm.

This may be the secret of the pleasant people of Weh. No tourists came here to startle them by unfamiliar behaviour, and there was therefore no trace of what might be described as mainland xenophobia. No sooner had Andy set foot ashore than his worries were at an end. It was impossible to imagine enemies in these narrow lanes where men spent so much of their time in chairs at their doors waiting for friends to pass, or to hail strangers like ourselves and ask them where they had come from, and where they they were going, and why.

An example of islander tolerance and generosity arose immediately in our contact with the owner of a losmen to which we were directed in search of rooms. These were quite acceptable but the access to the building was so narrow that we would have had difficulty in parking the car. The place which we finally settled on was run by a most genial Chinese from Hong Kong. He welcomed us with vanilla tea, gave us a fan apiece and said. 'You are English, so tomorrow there will be cakes and jam for breakfast.' This man had a marked sense of humour. The washroom contained an enormous tank instead of a bath. 'Careful with this,' he said. 'If in danger of drowning ring bell.'

An embarrassing matter now arose. Since it was agreed that Andy was to snorkel we asked where masks and flips were to be hired only to be directed to the previously investigated losmen-owner whose rooms we had felt obliged to turn down. Tails between legs we had to return to him. No-one could have been more charming. The equipment was too small for us so he went all over Sabang in his determination to fit us up. This he was able to do.

Well Beach Number Three, as it is called in Indonesian, was accepted to be the best place to snorkel and it was also a place of social consequence, particularly among the young. We went there on Sunday afternoon when ritual visits were paid to it from all parts of the island. When we arrived boys and girls were on the beach parading stiffly in their holiday clothes. One boy promptly detached himself from a group and walked towards us, lingered for a moment when he was quite close, then returned to the others, to whom he clearly reported what he had been able to discover. This was the signal for one after another of the young paraders to leave the others to approach us, stop, and mumble a few words of polite, broken English. In one case a whole group arrived for the inspection. They seated themselves in a row, heads slightly turned away to avoid the discourtesy of staring into our eyes, then got up and departed. By this time we had schooled ourselves in several phrases suitable for use on such occasions, but for Andy the words were too few. 'In this country place you must say more. They go because you do not speak to them. These things are easy to say. They will be happy.'

The leaflet had described Weh as weirdly beautiful, and on our way to Well Beach Number Three it had seemed a little unearthly in parts. At some time in pre-history it had started as an upthrust of small volcanoes from the bed of the sea. What remained of them were no more than tumuli of ancient lava, a surrealistic addition to a setting of scrub forest, maniacally distorted trees and the black girdle of the coastline, visible at all its points from a high place.

The beach offers inducements of a more comprehensive kind: rocks to be climbed, a glowing multicoloured sea, and the well itself at the back of the beach, dribbling the purest of water eternally down immaculate sand. The memory of old animistic enchantments and the presence of a benign water spirit still attracted respectful attention from weekend visitors. People came here to drink the water or to wash their clothes in it in the hope of gathering a little of its magic influence. While we were there someone was occupied in this way in the tented enclosure, and the scented soapsuds in the water trickling from beneath the canvas had attracted a number of black butterflies with extraordinary pleated wings. As we watched these a young woman wrapped in a wet sarong came out and stood looking from side to side, but quite clearly keeping us under inspection. Since we were still in the early stages of our studies of Indonesian protocol it was hard to to decide whether or not she resented our presence, but as we were about to make a cautious retreat she suddenly faced us directly. Very slowly and carefully she enunciated the words I suspected she had been working on. 'Now will you go for a swim?' She smiled. It was her contribution to the demonstration of island good manners.

We changed in a shack at the end of the beach. This called itself a restaurant. Part of the ritual of the Sunday visit was to sit on its verandah a few minutes and look out in silent admiration over the sea. The visitors came and went all the time but nobody ordered food while we were there. A bill of fare, listing a number of dishes, was nailed to the wall, but on this day nothing was available but tinned sardines and vanilla-flavoured tea. The shack, Andy discovered, was also the official meeting place of the village council, and a number of notices relating to its activities were displayed on a board. All these, as was to be expected, were in Indonesian, but among them a single announcement in English came to the aid of the Anglo-Saxon who found his way here. *Alcoholic beverages are hard to find in Sabang. But in event of real thirst consult with staff of hotel where you are staying.*

The time had come for Andy's introduction to sub-aquatic pleasures. We fixed his mask for him, pulled on our own, and waded into the water. We were the only swimmers. People came here to stand alone or in groups to derive benefit from looking at the sea, but I was beginning to suspect that only the occasional foreigner entered the water. This may have contributed to the fact that there were more fish and a greater variety of them here than I had seen anywhere, even in such remote Pacific islands as Raiatea where hardly anyone lived, and for that reason the fish went largely undisturbed. It would have called for many hours of exploration of the coral heads and the innumerable shallow caves to catalogue the varieties present in this small bay. Watching terrestrial animals, even in the most plentifully stocked reserve, may offer a wide range of pleasures but rarely exceptional surprise. If there are colours, with the exception of some exotic birds, they will have been chosen by nature to blend defensively with those of the drab backgrounds of forest or plain – sober, and therefore unassertive.

The world of the coral reef had nothing to conceal. Or could it be that these wildly self-advertising colours proclaimed inedibility? Fish filled every crevice of the field of vision with impossible combinations of purple, lemon, chocolate, violet, scarlet and black. How could it be that such colour clashes, such violent contrasts, were acceptable in a fish although certainly in nothing on land? Some of the fish were strikingly marked, scribbled upon with symbols, Arabic dots and diacritic signs, hieroglyphs, and black sprawling graffiti on brilliant walls. These were fish that changed colours, as if at the touch of a switch, puffed themselves up, deflated themselves, fish like Disneyland toys, clownish fish, and transparent fish – visually a matter of guesswork, apart from a floating eye linked to a digestive tract.

They moved slowly, indifferent to us, sweeping in listless peregrination through clear aqueous space or the thousand particles of glittering small-fry into the coral thickets and out again. Why this extravagant discord of colours in the vast sameness of the coral, which, it was to be assumed, imposed an identical environment upon its myriad inhabitants?

Terra firma has its confident biological answers to such questions, but they are less easily provided by the sea. A few hundred yards out, on the brink of the deep water, the coral came to an abrupt end with a row of heads emblazoned with sea anenomes, thrust like final bouquets into the misted depths. Beyond this a few predators, small sharks and barracudas, hung in passive suspension, camouflaged to match the grey monochrome of the sea.

Iboih was right across the island where the east–west road suddenly broke into fragments. Before this happened it had curved round the bruised slopes of what remained of the volcano Guning Meradi, which in bad weather occasionally deposited landslides of tufa upon the cracked road-surfaces. Cyclopean black boulders, some of them the size of a house, are poised precariously on the slopes and a number of them have rolled down to the beach. It is this which makes the area memorable and a little fantastic, for in addition to innumerable orchids, these rocks have trees growing out of them – some very large. The oldest of the trees have succeeded in plunging their roots through the rock into the earth. A final stage in the process is reached when the tree swells up to envelop its host so that the rock is lifted, like an enormous goitrous swelling, clear of the ground. Dali would have been at home in Iboith.

There was no real village here, just a line of shacks yet, in this place where tourism had hardly issued from the womb, the tourists were awaited. A man with a watchful, calculating expression and a fawning smile learned in a big city had established himself in a café here. For those who had walked the many dusty miles from Sabang, bottled water was on sale at double normal prices. Several doubtful characters lurked in the vicinity.

'Put up car windows,' Andy said.

'Why, what's the problem?'

'They may drop packet of dope in car. The policemen will come and arrest us.'

On my return to Banda a second letter from Claudia on the subject of the Pasola awaited me.

It was altogether different from anything we expected. It turned out they hold three pasolas. They are the most important ceremonies in the Merapu religion, and they are based on harvests of sea-worms, called myale, at three different points on the south coast. Timing is uncertain. It can happen any time in February or March after a full moon. For one day only the tides bring in the annual crop (unappetising-looking

worms, about 9 ins long) which is ritually scooped up by hordes of
people on the beaches, and then the Pasola starts. Apart from being
jolly delicious, these worms have great significance as omens of the
coming harvest – depending on their quality and abundance. The
Pasola is to welcome them, and to entertain the sea spirits who have
helped with their arrival. A few nights ago the whole family we were
staying with rushed down to the beach to sniff at the sea breeze with
great excitement, and were able to tell with all certainty the worms were
on their way and due to arrive the day after next, which they did.

Apparently, at Wanokaka the worms turned up about a month earlier
than usual and the ratu priest called for the Pasola to take place, with
everybody ready assembled. Unfortunately the local governor, top
brass, and police were there to forbid the proceedings. It transpired
that a recent glossy brochure published by the Jakarta tourist board had
stated that this year's Pasola in Wanokaka would be on 26 March, and
various Jakarta notables and tour groups had arranged to come. It
seems that centuries-old tradition and the very significance of the
Pasola is to be sacrificed to tourism. Reminiscent of the government
tax-incentives to encourage Torajas to hold their celebrated funerals in
the peak tourist season.

We were lucky at Kodi, where there was a huge crowd but few
soldiers and police and the event went off in traditional fashion.
What happens is that thirty or forty mounted men armed with
javelins line up in semi-circles facing each other and, after an
exchange of taunts and insults, champions challenge each other to
single combat and ride out to do battle. The government has
forbidden the use of steel tips on the javelins so the the contestants
break off the ends, leaving jagged spikes of wood. No-one was killed
at the Kodi Pasola, although this sometimes happens, but a rider got
a javelin through his cheek. They have very strict rules against
cheating or throwing a javelin when an opponent's back is turned.
This happened while we were there with a wildly excited crowd
pouring into the field of battle, and the police blazing away with
their sub-machine guns – luckily for us into the air. The one
drawback to all this excitement was the ritual food we had to eat.
The ratu stood over us while we were forced to consume really
enormous piles of rice cooked in brackish water. This took up at
least a half-hour, and the Pasola had started before we had got it
down. The story is that Jakarta is thinking of having a Pasola every
month.

There was another note, too, from the friend who had sent me the cutting from the *Financial Times*: 'I gather you're in this part of the world now, so thought I'd send you the enclosed, published in *Tapol*.'

On 1st June a Dutch journalist published accounts of two mass murders in Aceh. One occured on 12th September 1990 on the road from Bireuën to Takingeun. A truck carrying 56 detainees from Rancong Prison, Lhokseumawe came to a halt. The detainees were shot with M16s, their bodies thrown down a ravine . . . in April a truck with 41 men and women drove to a point 30 kms from Takingeun. The victims alighted and were shot dead. Local people insist that the murders were the work of army murder-squads wearing civilian clothing. [NRC Handelsblad 1st June.]

A second cutting gave the views on such matters of Major-General Pramono, military commander of North Sumatra, as expressed in an interview with the Jakarta weekly *Tempo*:

I have told the people the important thing if you see GPK [the army term for Free Aceh Movement activist] you should kill him. There's no need to investigate. Just shoot him or knife him. People are forced to do this or that and if they don't want to they are shot or get their throats slit. So I have instructed people to carry weapons, machetes or whatever. If you see a GPK just kill him.

We discussed these new revelations concerning our immediate geographical surroundings. Suddenly our involvement in Aceh had changed. Until this moment we should always have remembered Lhokseumawe for a huge breakfast served in a splendid but vacant hotel, but now this image would be overshadowed by the news of its prison where so many final solutions were arranged. The thirty miles from Bireuën on the coast down to Takingeun and the peerless Lake Tawar had staged for us a succession of mountain and forest profiles that would endure in the memory. But now I understood that it was for its loneliness and therefore for the absence of prying eyes that it was chosen – for the concealment of those they preferred not to bury in a grave, but simply put away out of sight.

FOUR

THERE WAS A discussion before we set off about the policy to be followed
with Andy. Our short stay at Weh seemed enormously to have improved
him. He had given up locking himself in the car at night and occupied a
room in the losmen in which we stayed. Snorkelling, with its revelation of
sub-aquatic marvels, had give him something to talk about, and he spoke
of the possibility of training to become a diving instructor at Lake Toba as
soon as the tourist industry revived. We were all agreed that he suffered
while with us not only from fear, but from boredom. It was clear that given
the chance he was an active and energetic man, but so far there had been
little for him to do but sit in the back of the car, awaiting the time when his
services as a guide would be required, and this moment was about to
arrive.

We took advice from the manager of the Sultan Hotel where we stayed
while in Banda, who told us that so far as he knew buses still went to the
small towns at the northern end of the west road, but after that no-one
could say. Much of the road was under repair, and unrepaired stretches
before Tapaktuan were in extremely bad condition, and quite impassable
in rain. Bridge replacements in some areas had been suspended as result
of the troubles, necessitating detours through swampy terrain in which
anything but a powerful four-wheel-drive vehicle (which our Toyota was
not) could expect to get stuck. Against this, although the rains were only a
week or two away, the route was as dry now as it would ever be. This was
what we wanted to hear, and we threw our odds and ends into the car and
made a start.

Our first stop was the lively township of Lhoknga, which had something
about it, both in appearance and atmosphere, of Dodge city in the 1860s
as depicted in nostalgic old American movies of the western frontier. It
was Dodge city in all but the hitching posts, though with the addition, as
one turned a corner, of a spectacular but confusing vista of the sea.
Lhoknga was full of shops, advertising for the benefit of those who felt like
chancing the west coast road that this was the last place for 200 miles
where provisions of almost any kind could be obtained. The general store
to which we were taken to stock up was an Aladdin's cave of essential

supplies and domestic bric-a-brac run by a family in a mean street. These people had on display a greater variety of goods, from decorated enemas to masks worn by line-fishermen to deceive the fish, than I had seen in a shop of this kind anywhere in the world.

All round the main cavern ran twelve deep shelves upon which thousands of items were crammed, and passages led off in all directions to stock-rooms under neighbouring premises. Above all there were thirty varieties of washing powder upon the abundant use of which advertisers have been able to persuade Indonesian country folk that their prestige depends.

As so often happens in the case of successful shopkeepers, the people running this emporium were morose. The wife, who served me, although fat and sad was incredibly beautiful. We had to buy spare five-gallon cans to carry petrol and these were instantly produced. Gawaine and I had a small bet as to whether they could supply a funnel. The wife pointed to a notice in Indonesian on the cluttered counter which said: 'We have *everything*. If there is something you do not see here we will get it in five minutes', and a funnel was produced.

We inspected several tins of canned foods nestling among elastic knee-supports and electrical machines that delivered a therapeutic shock, and decided against them. The owner thought we would be unlikely to find much to eat before Tapaktuan and recommended a good square meal of *nasi goreng* at a restaurant he owned before we left. Instead we laid in a supply of biscuits and stale but excellent cake.

Fortunately enough, Andy was not present at this time: we had brought him cleaning materials, and he was outside polishing the car. A lot of rumours were flying about and a shopper practising his English on us had depressing news. The army had been in action in the vicinity, and only a few weeks earlier a truckful of their Acehnese prisoners had been taken to a lonely spot a few miles away down the road, and there massacred.

From Lhoknga on, the road fell into sudden decline. It had been built to serve a scattering of villages populated by small farmers whose problem even in recent years was to protect their flocks from nightly incursions of tigers from the forested mountains. Latterly the traffic using the road had broken it up. Potholes were many and deep, and resurfacing perfunctory. Nevertheless, from the point of view of a beautiful drive, nothing equalled it on our Indonesian journey. This was how the depths of the Amazon forest had been before the building of the desert-maker highways. The road twisted through the steep-sided foothills at the edge of the coastal plain. No-one had touched these trees because they could not get at them – growing as they did on precipitous slopes and in narrow ravines. There were not even any villages nearby from which the villagers could stream out daily to cut their firewood. This, then, was the showcase of a magnificent forest, of which so little remained, presenting its immensely tall trees with their pale, slender trunks, no two appearing to be the same. Orchids of many colours were suspended, as if in florists' baskets, from their branches – and sometimes, where decaying vegetable matter had made a substantial lodgement, a version of the arum lily unfolded its maculate and slightly sinister bloom. These trees were enswathed in extremely tall ferns, some reaching twenty feet high. We stopped and climbed down to the nearest tree to look at them. Small, bright, fussy birds – babblers, barbets, minivers, sun birds and bush robins – fidgeted among the leaves, popping into sight and back out again. We were at the very edge of a plain covered in brilliant grass with mountain streams threading through small lakes to the sea. Further on we came to an abandoned coconut plantation. A gale had smashed the tops off most of the palms but nobody lived here any longer to pick up the nuts that lay scattered by the hundred on the ground.

Stretches of the road had suffered near-demolition through the passage of large and extremely heavy vehicles, and wheels had left deep gouges where temporary surface repairs had been carried out. We shortly trundled over the first of numerous recently built iron bridges. None of these improvements was likely to have been planned for the benefit of local buses, and it was to be supposed that the road would be made negotiable in all weathers by log-transporters coming up from the South, which so far had been unable to reach Banda Aceh by this route.

Driving all day at hardly more than a walking speed, we had covered an extremely low mileage by the late afternoon. Sundown was to be expected shortly after six, and being unenthusiastic at a prospect of having to pick our way after nightfall among the many hazards likely to await us ahead, we decided to look for somewhere to stay the night in Calang, the only village the map showed in this area.

Once again, as had happened from time to time in the past, I felt a sensation of having come to the end of the world. The village was down by the water meadows; a row of what might at first sight have been deserted shacks. There was no-one to be seen. And then doors opened and people stood in their doorways, all smiling in a sleepy fashion as if just awakened from happy dreams. They fitted into their surroundings in an exemplary way, and my feeling was that they and their ancestors had been where they were for a very long time. We were directed to what passed as a losmen, which had two partitioned cubicles in its only room. Like the rest of the villagers, the man and woman who owned it were small. They had a son with a big head, and the village's fixed smile.

I found it hard to see what these people lived by, as there was no evident source of livelihood. Perhaps they fished, but there was no fishing gear in sight. There were a lot of intelligent-looking dogs about, who by our observation lived on each other's excrement. At the losmen they asked us if we wanted to eat and showed us the saturnine left-overs of a bat-stew, which Andy accepted. The rest of us decided to stick with the cake.

We went for a walk before sunset. Terns by the hundred were drifting over like flakes of white ash, on their way to roost on the cliffs. A clump of trees attracted us by their smell of camphor and, spotting flying foxes among the top branches, we wondered if this was the larder that had supplied Andy's stew. When we got back he was still at work endlessly polishing the car. We went in, listened to the BBC's World Service, and Gawaine and Robin settled under their power lamp for an hour or two of a continuing chess match before going to bed. All day we had rattled and bumped over clattering bridges, through the sticky vestiges of swamps, round chasms caused by road subsidences, and through ruts, a foot or more deep, left by the many vanished transporters. Now the void of night confronted us and demanded to be filled, and the chess pieces came out, to be assembled on the board in their previous positions. My companions seemed unable to exist without contest, and chess was called into service to offer its equivalent of the problems and hazards the road had supplied with such prodigality.

Next day we journeyed on roughly as before: mountains to the left, palm-fringed lagoons to the right, the incredible sight of orchids growing among rocks, a hopelessly broken road, so many bridges we had ceased to count them.

This was the part of the journey Gawaine and Robin had looked forward to, and revelled in. Two years previously they had paid $800 for a decayed Ford Maverick in a junk-yard in San Francisco, patched it together, and taken three months to drive to South America. Was this the worst road they had ever driven over? Probably not, they thought. Bits of Venezuela might have been worse. They had divided up the driving into fifty-kilometre stretches, assiduously checking on times and distances, while on the alert for rotted timbers in old bridges, concealed patches of swamp, and landslides that had always occurred just around a blind bend. Each in turn ploughed competitively ahead, by necessity largely oblivious to the drama of the landscape traversed. The bridges concealed the worst hazards. Few spanned flowing rivers, and all that did were safe. The bad risks arose from the new bridging programme which did its best to cope with flooded streams. Sections of these less important bridges had sometimes been dumped in a hurry off the transporters and left lying around, calling for a top-speed diversion from a road surface of fragmented boulders into a hollow with puddles among the grass, then a charge up the other bank. For these performances I awarded or deducted marks.

Untouched by such emergencies, Andy reclined in the back working with a cloth and cleaning fluid on the small, stubborn stains here and there on his denims. There had still been no occasion to use his services as a guide, for, shattered as the road was, there were no turnings, no possibility of losing the way. One either went ahead or turned back. A slight note of urgency had been added to this enterprise when Andy, who seemed well informed on the subject of weather, mentioned in the most casual way that there were differences in the climate of North Aceh and the South, which we should shortly be entering. In South Aceh the rains arrived earlier, and were now expected any day. Should we be caught in them he recommended us to take no chances, in view of the condition of this road, but to turn round and make for the dry North just as fast as we could.

It was hard to say what produced the antipathy we all felt for Meulaboh. It had lost all those things that hold a good village together, but had never quite turned itself into a town. Youths with nothing to do were kicking their heels and staring angrily into space on the street corners. Cars coming from the South that had made it as far as this, and would go no further, were driving round revving their engines to attract attention and stirring up the dust. Part of our feelings might have been due to anticlimax after two days spent in settings of exceptional charm. Weh, too, had spoiled us with its calm Buddhistic smile and its withdrawal from the hurly-burly of Acehnese politics and religion. The boys lining the main street watched us silently with empty faces. The car was coated with red dust, and as soon as we left it they moved in after studying the number plate, and began to write in the grime with their fingers. Andy avoided telling us what they had written, but his mood had immediately slumped. There was a feeling that we were in a war zone.

Only one losmen was open and although larger than the one at Calang, it was more wretched. Music and mosquitoes poured through the wide interstices in the losmen's boarding, and lizards sprinted backwards and forwards across the soap powder advertisements providing its decoration. Nevertheless we did our best to ingratiate ourselves with the owner in the hope of an escape from rice on this occasion. But this was not to be. The losmen's food was kept in a showcase screened by tattered curtains. We were taken to this by a boy with sore eyes who whisked the curtain aside to display a sad array of the kind to which we were becoming familiar. He picked up a succession of grey collops, turned them over one after another in his hand, and let them drop back, accepting rejections as a matter of course, and shaking his head in a despondent yet sympathetic manner.

The alternative was stale cake identical to the kind we had just finished, and served with a kind of pickle. This had just arrived when we noticed that an excited crowd had formed at the street door. It proved to be awaiting the losmen's evening television show – clearly the daily event that made life in Meulaboh just tolerable. Quite soon a crowd of perhaps one hundred had gathered, of which less than a half could be crammed into a small, dim area dominated by the 24-inch screen. The shutters closing the room off from the street were pulled back so that viewers who had come late and were left outside would at least catch a glimpse of the picture. This was almost a religious moment, as shown by the respectful silence, and the rapt, devotional expression on all faces. Someone switched on and there was an uproar of distorted music, the screen began to flicker with jumbled shapes and colours, then to our amazement we found ourselves watching an English cup-tie football match.

Next morning it was clear that Andy's morale had collapsed. He had kept close to our sides the night before during a barren exploration of the town. He had even waited unhappily just inside the door of a shack calling itself a night club and serving only a repellent pseudo-beer, tolerated by the religious authorities on the grounds of containing less than one degree of alcohol.

He had spent the night locked in the car under a blanket in the space between the front and rear seats, and now showed signs of terror, due, we could only suppose, to real or fancied hostility shown him in the village. He was even more concerned than us at the possibility of being trapped by the rains, and the woman who ran the losmen fetched her English-speaking brother to advise us on this matter. 'We are praying for them,' he said. 'Soon they must come.'

We left this place with relief, turning shortly away from the sea, and making for the mountains, but first we visited the important trans-migration settlement at Lame, of which we had already heard contra-dictory, although largely unfavourable, reports. There should have been some way of softening the shock of this place, a transitional period from the constant visual excitements of the west road to the infernal vistas of this settlement into which the traveller is projected without warning. Dismissal from Arcadia occupied no more than seconds. We turned a bend and there was Lame amid its theatrical devastation. This had been the rainforest in all its glory, and now it was a prairie of ashes, spiked all over with the blackened stumps of trees that had been burned or felled, in theory to provide land for the migrants. We had plunged suddenly into what must have been one of the early zones of settlement, illustrating all the errors of the first waves of transmigration, repeated throughout the outer islands of Indonesia.

Possibly the forest would have been cut down here in any case, but there was no doubt of the intention to settle landless peasants from Java and Bali, because there were small wooden houses all over the place, although none we could see from the road was occupied. This part of Lame had overprinted the ghost image of an outer suburb – the sweep of curving avenues, crescents, a central square, a shopping arcade – on a desert of tree stumps and charred wood. The buildings were all tiny cabins of identical shape, each with its minuscule front garden enclosed in raw breeze blocks. No garden was cultivated. In some cases huge tree stumps with abstract designs of fungus painted over the charred wood occupied half the garden space, sharing the rest with weeds pushing up through the cracked earth to unfold leathery leaves. This area of forest had not been 'clear-cut' and the loggers had taken only saleable timber, but for some inscrutable reason they had smashed the trees they had left, leaving a background to this ghost town suggesting a forest of ships' masts devasted by a terrible storm.

Settlers from over-populated Java had poured in here and into similar sites all over Indonesia in the greatest mass-movement of people in history. By the original scheme each transmigration family received a house standing in .25 hectares of land, along with two additional hectares of cleared land ready for cultivation. They were to receive aids of food, seed for planting and agricultural implements. Many promises were not kept and transmigrants by the thousand were dumped down on sites without infrastructural development, or even where no houses had been built. As in the case of Lame, the transmigrants were left with cinders, and ash, and forest soil damaged through loss of moisture and exposure to the sun, on which nothing would grow. From where we stood on the highest point of the development, no crops had been planted anywhere in sight, nor was a single human being to be seen. It was a repetition of what happened to such experiments tried previously in Brazil.

There were several miles of this Brazilian look-alike before the road suddenly splayed out, took on a more solid surface, and we shortly drove into a species of circus, enclosed by a number of recent buildings, some flanked by piles of constructional materials and clearly incomplete. A service station had no petrol for sale, and there were no mechanics about to deal with semi-degutted lorries in for repair. The population of a large village appeared to have been emptied into the small centre of what it was hoped would become a metropolis. A hundred yards or so away, the rows of the familiar standard cabins started, 18 foot by 12 foot with partitions. The aroma of baffled expectations and stagnation hung heavy on the air.

Tucked away in an obscure corner was something quite out of place in the heartlessness of this setting, a little café glistening with fresh paint, its protest against Lame on the brink of despair. We went in to find a smiling young Balinese couple, who had been in business here for three years. It may have been the smallest café anywhere, only able to contain four customers at a push, with the owner and his wife squeezed into three square feet of space behind the counter and three delectable children popping in and out of a hole in the wall. There was a picture from a magazine of a *legong* dancer, and a three-inch chaplet of flowers on our table in offering to the household spirit. Although I had never at this point visited Bali I was sure that the café in the backwoods of Sumatra enshrined the grace of that island unreached by the cataclysm of tourism.

We inspected what was on offer: chicken-noodle soup, and a pile of the most elaborately wrapped sweets. We took the soup and presented the children with a few sweets apiece, enormously repaid by their delight. The man had a few words of English and, helped out by Andy, we were able to listen to the story of their recent life. They had been in business here for three years and, hard as it must have been, he made it sound no more than the minor frustrations suffered by the hero of a side-plot in the *Ramayana*, certain of eventual triumph. Unaccountably, they had been separated from fellow Balinese with whom they had hoped to start the new life together, and dumped down in Sumatra with a mixed bag of Javanese, whose language they did not understand, and whose lifestyle was different in every respect. None of these people who had come from city backgrounds possessed agricultural skills, although they had been brought here to raise crops. Some went home, others found jobs on the palm oil plantations, or with the logging companies, as did he. After two years of it his left arm had been crushed by a falling tree, but he had saved enough to start up the café, and here he was.

In her splendid book *In the Rain Forests*, Catherine Caulfield tells of the predicaments of some of these early Balinese arrivals in Sumatra. She describes the adventures of a family whose choice was the village of Karangsari in Lampung Province, where they had asked to be sent because they had friends there. However glowing the description they had been given of this place, they found that it was a desolate fragment of what had once been one of the most celebrated and extraordinary of the game reserves of South-east Asia. Shortly before their arrival loggers had removed 250,000 acres out of 300,000 of the original forest, and the Suwendris found they had been allocated a patch of elephant grass on which nothing would grow until they spent six months burning and clearing it. Now, twenty years later, they have created a little corner of Bali. 'Today 566 families live in Karangsari . . . the houses have the same beautifully elaborate stone carvings, the same strictly ordered arrangement of domestic buildings and temples. Not only did the pioneers of Karangsari struggle to make this unfamiliar land productive, but they worked to make it home. Flowering shrubs surround every house, the roadsides are lined with hedges and dotted with trees.'

It is hard to keep up to date with the millions that have been shipped from Java and Bali to the outer islands. By the end of the first Five-Year Plan, back in 1984, nearly 4 millions had gone and there was euphoric talk in Indonesian government circles of moving some 65 millions in the next quarter of a century. Impetus has been maintained almost to the present time, when a slackening is perceptible. The existence of spontaneous migration in the reverse direction by failed transmigrants is now offically recognised and referred to as *reimigrasi*. Those making their way as best they can back to their native villages in Java and Bali have given discouraging or even horrific accounts of their experience in some of the island backwoods. The site may have had hardly more than a phantom identity, with houses unready, or not even built. Their reception by the local people might have been hostile. In remote areas wild animals could pose a problem; two sites in Lampung have repeatedly been attacked by wild elephants. Settlers have been murdered near Banda Aceh. They seem to receive no advance warning that their customs may differ dramatically from those of the societies with which they are compelled to associate. For this reason they may give extreme offence. Muslims from Java and elsewhere are killed by the Papuans of Irian Jaya for ritually washing their private parts or urinating in streams.

An additional cause for waning enthusiasm for the programme is the realisation that the supply of suitable sites is finite. All prime agricultural land has its owners. Even the areas left unclaimed through difficulty of access or low-grade fertility have largely been handed out, and when they are at an end, where is the living space to be found for the incoming multitudes?

Foreseeing this problem back in 1967, and in the hope of heading off troubles that were bound to arise, the government passed Basic Forestry Act no. 2823, stating: 'The rights of traditional communities [natives of the islands] may not be allowed to stand in the way of the establishment of Transmigration sites.' This meant that the forests by which so many of these people lived could now legally be cut down to provide living space for the newcomers. By an ironic twist, many of those threatened by this act were the very transmigrants it was supposed to protect, the first of whom, arriving in the 1950s, had managed to establish what are approvingly referred to as mature sites, in which the transmigrants – after years of pain and travail – have finally conquered all the setbacks of the alien environment and settled to a comfortably regulated life.

There are few of these, one being Palanpanggung, also in Lampung Province. These people had been advised to abandon all hopes of growing the crops they had been accustomed to raise in the old days and to turn themselves into coffee growers, which they did with considerable success. By 1988 they numbered more than 40,000, but in this year the government applied the Forestry Act to their case, according Palan-panggung 'protected forest' status, and then served the successful transmigrants with relocation orders. The younger members of the community, aged between twenty and thirty-five, would be sent to a new transmigration nucleus on the island of Riau, off the Malaysian coast (nothing was said of the fate of the rest), and no compensation would be paid.

By November 1988, no-one had been persuaded to comply with this order, so special police squads appeared on the scene and burned down 476 houses. Defending this course of action, the Lampung Governor, Poesjono Pranyoto, told a press conference that allowing the villagers to stay in the forest would be more inhumane than evicting them. It appeared that concessions had been granted to a plantation estate which was in a hurry to take possession, and in clashes with the armed forces a number of villagers were killed. Following this, another 2,000 houses went up in flames. This time Vice-Governor Sukki Hassan put the government point of view. When asked why he had ordered so many houses to be burned, he replied: 'Because it was cost effective.' The local authorities didn't have enough time or personnel to demolish the houses one by one, he said. The provincial government admits allowing the burning to go ahead because it was short of funds. (*Tempo*, Jakarta, 29 July 1989.)

The burnings were followed by a government notice: 'All persons found in this area of the forest are to be arrested and sentenced to one year in jail.'

Painstakingly, all Brazil's errors in the movement of populations from rural wastelands and city slums into the Amazon were copied in Indonesia, although on a much larger scale. It is obvious that in both cases those who were persuaded to leave their homes in the hope of a fresh start in a far-off place of which they knew nothing would have been the less skilled, the less energetic, the possessors of less ideas and initiative. The main and much publicised aim of transmigration was to relieve Java and Bali of the pressure of excess population. This has not happened. Perhaps because the more effective elements of the community have been given more breathing space, an increasing birth-rate in both islands has more than compensated for the number lost, and demographically speaking things are rather worse than at the start of the programme.

The secondary aim was to guarantee national unity by the spread of Javanese culture through the islands. This so far has not happened. In fact the resentment provoked by what are generally viewed as government-sponsored Javanese colonies tends to diminish whatever ingredient of Indonesian patriotism may have previously existed. However many transmigrants are sent to East Timor, nothing is more certain than that only a permanent presence of the army will prevent it from declaring its independence.

Once clear of the straggling remnants of Lame, the road collapsed. Inacessible and unspoiled Aceh was now at an end, and we turned into the foothills of the Gayo Height, where the loggers had only recently done their worst and made a mess of the landscape – before dropping everything, we suspected, and scurrying away at the approach of Free Aceh Movement separatists. All the signs were of a panic-stricken withdrawal. Demolished trees lay abandoned everywhere. Branches and ferns were scattered over the road itself, which had only recently been cleared of the trees that had fallen across it. The largest bulldozer I have ever seen lay on its side where it had fallen into a gully. Apart from this recent disruption and the additional hazards involved in avoiding or removing fallen branches, we had learned in Lame that there was little to be hoped for of this road for another hundred miles until we joined the main north–south highway at Sidikalang.

The Gayo people of these hills, and the villages where they had settled to enjoy life, came as a relief from the dismal hugger-mugger of the transmigration settlement. At the Lamainang market girls in blue and scarlet were bargaining excitedly for jungle fruit and several kinds of bats. A pet stall offered cockatoos, long-tailed mice and a small member of the tarsier family which surveyed the world with troubled eyes, as it climbed, baby attached to its underside, with gentle, sluggish movements up the pole on which it perched. Everyone's existence in Lamainang was enlivened by a clear mountain river squeezing through this small town, which drew a happy attendance of people out for a stroll with nothing to do. They stood on the bridge for a moment to look down into the water as people like to do the world over, then moved on clearly the better for it. We followed their example. Below us, the black gondola-shaped boats were lined up, with their owners making small unnecessary adjustments to them, or playing cards or chatting with their friends. Laughing, kite-flying children ran up and down the street: a thin old man, trousers rolled up, dabbed in a pool with a net; a woman brought her duck, carried under her arm, for its daily excursion on the river. This was life as it had once been in most of Aceh.

We were soon approaching the western boundary of the G. Leuser National Park, calculating that it could be hardly more than five miles away. The 8,000 square kilometres reserve is the largest in South-east Asia, and it has been claimed that the richness and variety of its wildlife are unequalled elsewhere on earth. These opinions may have been founded upon a situation which has brusquely changed. The reserve was once recorded as containing many species of monkey, the Malayan Sun Bear, mouse and barking deer, tigers galore, elephants, tapirs, hundreds of species of birds, and thousands of insects, including a whole catalogue of butterflies to be found nowhere else. Tracts of it were said to remain unexplored, and if so, would remain in their pristine condition until the logger invasion reached them.

The rumour that the park itself had already become a principal victim of the all-out attack on the forests of Sumatra seemed feasible when you considered the UN study which had revealed that, out of eighty-eight nations, rainforest clearance in Indonesia is exceeded in annual acreage only by that of Brazil.

During the next few miles our fears that a massive invasion had already occurred were strengthened by the appearance of side roads too new to be on the map, all leading inland in the direction of the park. They plunged straight into the low hills and the laterite soil laid bare on the road surfaces and the steep embankments cut through the hillsides had been sun-seared to that shade of vermilion which warned that nothing would grow on it again.

Barriers kept private vehicles out, and there were threatening notices in Indonesian warning off unapproved visitors. Nevertheless we passed through and continued on foot to a point where a road crested a hill, and offered a wide view of the surroundings. The forest had once covered these hills, but it had been clear-felled and then burned over. What was left here was a painted wilderness of sand, a billowing Sahara doodled over with patterns of ash.

Conquistadors of the kind who once went overseas in the hunt for gold ran the country, and as deeply in commerce as politics pursued their conquests at home. A single log of a rare dypterocarp fetches up to £2,000 in Japan. In Indonesia, timber is the gold of our day.

FIVE

DESPITE WHAT MUST have been in normal times the almost constant thunder of log transporters through their villages, the fishing communities of this zone exuded an immemorial tranquillity. Their names – Kutabuloh, Teungoh and Keu Deu Tantanoh – ended, as Andy pronounced them, on a soft aspirate, as if the last intake of breath before sleep. Nevertheless, committed to a calling in which time and tide waits for no man, an imperceptible but meticulous order of the day's activities was not to be avoided. There is a time to bait the fixed lines, a time to repair the nets, a time to salt and dry the catch, a time for post-dawn sleep. Special urgencies rule in the seasons of the shoals of fish, and those are timed, too. Fishermen the world over, apart from those drawn into an industry based upon big ports, lead self-sufficient, immutable lives, bound to the wheel of custom, and it was clear that this applied in Teungoh.

We arrived at the moment when some of the younger men were beaching a number of heavy canoes. This, everywhere, is a communal effort in which all spare man-power in the village is called into action. The primitive communism of fishermen is an unescapable fact of life. Nobody can own the sea, from which it follows that the property-owning qualifications of the fishermen are scant. In this case they would have amounted to little more than a house, a boat and tackle. Once again the world over, fishermen behave in roughly the same way. What little money they have, they squander. They are addicted to gambling; inclined to throw their money away. The gods they worship in secret are not those of the peasants settled upon their hard-won and closely guarded plots, located in this case only a few hundred yards away. After a big catch the fishermen buy new clothes for all their womenfolk. No fisherman ever became rich. They leave nothing to their descendants when they go.

The stilted houses on the shore at Teungoh spoke of these propensities. They were neat, orderly and uncluttered compared with the cheerful squalor of the peasant hutments built along the edge of a black ditch at the furthest point of the village from the sea. There a shop sold bicycle tyres, biscuits, powdered milk and paper kites, and besides such necessities plastic and china ornaments, including smirking Disney animals, put on display in peasant houses as symbols of wealth. The fisherfolk would have none of this. There was nothing in the sparse dwellings, with their carefully tonsured thatch and split-bamboo walls that served no purpose – pots and pans, a sack of rice, pets, fishing gear, a coffer to hold festival clothing – the tools of existence, and no more.

A man of standing suddenly appeared among the group, and the others drew away. The headman, as we took him to be, was in his late forties; eyes creased from scanning far horizons, a patrician expression that rejected the promptings of chicanery, a conclusive and instantly fading smile following all his pronouncements. With a sweeping gesture he invited me into his house, and since he spoke only the Acehnese dialect, Andy was called upon to do his best with a translation. It was a tricky business, for difficulties arose not only from differences of language, but of minds. 'They are speaking always like words of a song,' Andy said.

The man spoke of the Acehnese fisherman's life. The calling, he said, was a hereditary one, and nobody could be accepted into it without being born into a fishing clan. In the village of Beuloh, marriage partners were sought only among the sons and daughters of other villages. It was fortunate – he laughed – that weddings did not happen too often, because they were expensive affairs that could land the family in debt for up to a year. Funerals, too, were expensive, involving the burning of boats, which the government had now banned as being backward and contrary to the national culture. In the household the woman handled all the financial business, but in no circumstances was allowed to enter a boat, and could be divorced if she did so. The village was as close to being self-sufficient as any village could be. They even possessed a part-time cobbler who made the shoes, and a dozen men working together could build a house in ten days. To be able to take the measure of the outside world, however, every man was obliged to visit the town of Tapaktuan, forty miles away. In this way curiosity was cured, and it was an experience, the headman said, with another of his short decisive laughs, that few wished to repeat.

According to the headman, matters of health were the only aspects of their existence calling for the intervention of an outsider. A healer travelled up and down the coast, despite governmental prohibition, to look after their physical well-being, and a dentist from Medan turned up every few months to take care of their teeth. The headman said this man was so good at his job that, having removed a few teeth, where necessary for cosmetic reasons, he would cement in the artificial replacements, leaving the patient 'looking like a politician'.

For this genial conversation we sat together along the edge of a platform in the village's largest room, which, the headman told us, was used as a council chamber by the notables when affairs of importance had to be discussed. At this point most of the platform space was taken up by a woman weaving on a loom. When we showed interest in the design, the headman waved us away with a gesture of impatience. A pointless whim, he said. Something to use up time. Custom did not permit a woman to wear a garment she had woven for herself. It would have to be given away. While these discussions went on, beautiful, grave-faced, silent children wandered in and out. Occasionally averting its eyes, a child would risk a quick, shy fingering on my clothing. Strong on protocol, as usual, Andy told us that custom did not allow the fishermen to smile in the presence of a guest.

Supplies and communications were the fishermen's current problem. They themselves lived on the less prestigious varieties of fish, but lobsters and crayfish, much in demand in the town were picked up by the bus and taken in to Tapaktuan. Now, as a result of the emergency, the buses had ceased to come. One had been attacked, or so it was said, the headman didn't know where or when, and some said the driver had been shot. Rumours were flying about. Everyone said something different. Here in the village they had begun to run out of the little luxuries of life, sugar for example, and betel nut. Life could be hard in a place like this when kerosene was in short supply, but they had found a way round the problem by burning fish oil.

I risked a question. 'Do you ever see anything of the freedom fighters?'

It was a subject which embarrassed Andy and I noticed that in translation he preferred the official government title for protesters of all kinds: 'security disturbance gangs'.

The headman thought about this, eyes narrowed. For the first time I noticed the small worry beads he fiddled with in the fingers of the right hand. 'We live here by the sea,' he said, 'sometimes the wind troubles us, no more than that.'

'They're not in these parts?'

'They are in the hills. I hear stories and I forget them as soon as I can. If they have friends here, I cannot say. Now I have told you everything I know.'

There was nothing in any of the books about Tapaktuan, yet a tiny circle on the map showed that what until recently must have been a fishing village like Beuloh and the rest had enlarged into a sizeable town. This was confirmed on its outskirts by the presence of a police station sited in a spacious rose garden outside which motorists were being stopped for contributions to a police charity.

In situations such as this Andy was invaluable. The complexities of Indonesian protocol had been extended to road-users, with a code of correct conduct applicable not only to other drivers but pedestrians. Possibly from motives of prestige, many villages went in for unnecessarily complicated road systems, and in these cases we depended on Andy to enquire the way. At first whoever sat next to the window had wound it down to allow him to call to the nearest pedestrian, but Andy assured us that in Indonesia this was discourteous. It was correct to stop the car, get out and approach the passer-by, introduce oneself, say a few words about the journey, and only then put the necessary questions. Any encounter with the police was a more delicate matter, and there were rules for dealing with this, too. In this event you slowed to less than a walking pace but kept moving unless actually stopped. If it was a request for money, you listened, smiled, nodded, and if you dared produced an excuse. In this case Andy said, 'My friends are foreigners. They are going to change money and will return.' The policeman seemed unhappy, but there was no order to stop, so Gawaine accelerated briskly away.

After the harmonious, undemanding presence of the fishing villages, Tapaktuan came almost as a shock. Lake Toba, fifty miles away across the mountains, was currently the greatest tourist lodestar in Sumatra. It was comfortably outside the borders of Aceh, the climate was splendid, the views in all directions magnificent, and cheap domestic labour was available for the many rich citizens of Medan who had built themselves villas by the lake. Andy, having worked with his water-sports firm on the lake, was surprised to find that most of them soon got tired of life there, and of the Batak people who were their neighbours, who resented the presence of city folk. About four years earlier work had started on shortening and improving the rudimentary road linking Toba with the coast, provoking a stampede of Toba-resident capitalists down to Tapaktuan to put their money into land, and be first with a holiday home before this place, too, was spoilt. It was a process that was well advanced. Lulabah, Teungoh and Tantanoh, under the constraints of poverty, were beautiful. Tapaktuan, now rich, was on its way to ugliness and there was a smell of corruption about it. Coming into the town we looked down on rows of brash new villas, set among freshly planted palms in a wasteland of fresh concrete. The villas had high walls topped with glass, and in each case the view through decorative iron gates was of a garden with a summer house made of painted concrete logs. There were many guard dogs about on leads, and when we stopped so Andy could jump out to ask for a hotel, an elegant lady passed dragging a woolly Alsatian of the kind much fancied in Indonesia, whose efforts to lift his leg she frustrated with

whisks of a palm frond carried for that purpose. Although devoid of
traffic, Tapaktuan had a one-way system that sent us all round the town in
our search for the hotel to which we had been directed. It was full of
notices warning of motoring offences, and requests not to park, and a
squad car prowled in this emptiness, in the direction of which we nodded
and smiled with what affability we could muster.

That evening, after our long, unvarying intake of rice, bananas and stale
cake, we dined with relief at The Select. The manager told us it was a
special evening. A personality from Berastagi was celebrating his
birthday. It was also a karaoke evening and he hoped we would join in.
The town, he told us, was dry, but in announcing this he succeeded in
conferring a privilege, for with a narrowing of one eye and a flickering of
the eyelids he indicated that this would not apply in our case, and we were
led through a curtain into an inner room in which the writ of Islam did not
run.

Most of the tables were already taken, and Indonesian protocol lay
heavy on the air. Following Andy's instructions we exchanged greetings
with each table in turn. These were the people from Toba, engaged in
ceremonial conversation and tittering very faintly at ceremonial jokes.
Our surroundings could have been the corner of a furniture showroom in
a London department store, and there was a tendency to the ornate. This
was the temple of artifice. What was to be done in a situation where
orchids are as common as weeds? The flowers on the table were artificial,
yet so subtly contrived that even fingering these plastic petals it was hard
to be convinced of their unreality. An unusual-looking palm had been
placed in a tub, and even its living model's tiny defects of leaf and stem
had been copied with bewildering fidelity. The room was still festooned,
remarkably enough in a Muslim country, with decorations for a
Christmas long-since past, featuring gold-sprayed cupids and plastic
holly. Behind the curtains the well-heeled old timers from Toba had
joined in the choruses of 'Bright Eyes' and 'Down Mexico Way', and now
the celebrations for the important guest started with party-poppers and
Happy Birthday To You.

'Ep-pi bir-deh di-ya Koentjaraningrat,
Ep-pi bir-deh to you.'

Through the window we looked down on a nightscape of sand and sea.
In these latitudes the coming of darkness never quite drops a shutter over
details revealed by the day. There may have been a moon somewhere, for
the sky was the colour of pewter, and the slow, black waves could be seen
moving up the beach, each in turn tossing down a little phosphorescence
into the hollow it was about to fill. Rocks were embedded in the sand like

pre-historic reptiles, and while we watched we realised that excited juvenile noises came from boys about to hunt land-crabs by torchlight. We had watched them that afternoon before they had been called away, and their game broken up, for a meal perhaps, or for prayers. A promising hole would be enclosed by a circle of sticks or stones some twenty foot in diameter and the boys would retreat, fall in behind a line, and wait until the crab had scrambled across this before giving chase. In a variation of this game, one of the boys released a crab, deemed for this purpose to be his property. If judged to have lost him points by a poor performance in the chase, he would tear one or two legs off and throw it into the sea.

The patrons of The Select were outstandingly gregarious. In between the slow appearance of courses they got up and wandered from table to table practising the art of Indonesian small-talk. Some of them had brought with them paper hats. The men bent over the women's hands and presented them with stunning forgeries of blooms, artfully concealed until this moment. A woman came up to us who might have been brought here at the end of an immensely protracted Sumatran wedding ceremony, for her face was stark white with powder, and her eyelids blackened with eye-shadow. She held out a pink-cheeked male doll to be admired. 'Name is Charlie,' she said. She was followed by a man in a pin-stripe suit and cravat. 'Good evening, gentlemen. How you are liking this country? I am collector of taxes. This Maria. I am Karim. Please meeting. And you are from England? I am familiar. Manchester United, Buckingham Castle, Trafalgar Road. Seeing you again soon. Bye-bye.'

T-shirts would normally have been excluded from an establishment of this class but at this point a youngster belonging to one of the select families drifted into sight wearing one. 'Fantasy', it said, 'is O.K.' And this about summed it up.

Among Tapaktuan's minor corruptions was the hotel. The losmen, reported as 'simple and pleasant' and which would have suited us well, was closed. Of the two hotels, the one recommended in the book, which was also the cheaper, was down by the sea front. We went there, and although there were no signs of life about the place, we were informed that it was full. The clerk picked up the phone, and made a call to the more expensive hotel, where with a congratulatory smile he informed us he had been able to reserve the only two rooms left in town. They were 'executive' rooms we were told on arrival (everything in Tapaktuan was executive, or exclusive: 'expensive but with every comfort and convenience'). A mania for folksy imitation was responsible for bed-lamps disguised as spotted red toadstools, but these would not switch on, and nothing really worked. It was hard to believe that we were not the only guests. We discovered that both hotels had the same owner.

The town's principal mosque was a hundred yards along the road and at 6.30 the loudspeakers fixed to the base of its colossal aluminium dome called the faithful to prayer in a voice which extinguished all the other sounds of the town. This was followed by Koranic readings which might have lasted a half hour. That at an end, all the television sets in Tapaktuan went into action, with the daily instalment of 'Puff the Magic Dragon'.

We found Andy down in the square, where in the absence of newspapers people went to pick up and sift through the latest rumours. One glance at his face and the sag of his moustache was enough to realise that the news was bad. 'Road closed,' he said.

'You're joking.'

But Andy's jokes were of a different sort. 'Many trucks in crash,' he said. Steel girders all over the place. For three days no can go to Berastagi. What can do?'

'We wait,' I said. 'Put up with it and wait. When they clean the mess up we go. Where did this happen?'

'Kalakepen,' he said. 'Big smash up. Trucks are in river.'

'Cheer up,' Gawaine said. 'We can always turn round and go back.'

Considering that possibility, Andy's deep tan seemed to have lightened. A group of women were ready with disturbing details of what had happened. 'They say we must stay here many days,' Andy said.

'How do they know? I'll go and talk to the police.'

We drove down to the road-block outside the town, where a policeman who looked in his teens lounged and spat. Andy spoke to him. 'Bridge over Simpang-kiri river at Kalakepen gone,' he says. 'Is that in Aceh?' I asked. If it were, this might have accounted for whatever had happened, I thought. The policeman said it was.

We decided to discuss the setback over a beer in The Select's curtained room. Looking around for Andy he seemed to have slipped away. Gawaine and Robin went in search of him, and there was something about their manner on returning that made me guess what was coming.

'Andy's on his way.' Gawaine said.

'Sorry, I don't follow.'

'He's pulling out. Off to Medan.'

'With the road closed?'

'Don't ask me what's happened. They're letting a bus through, so it's all rubbish about the bridge being down.'

'Where is he now?'

'At the bus station.'

We drove round to the bus station where Andy was waiting for me, and doing his best to raise a smile. 'What's it all about?' I asked.

'Last night I telephone my wife. She worries for me.'

'I know she does,' I said. 'I appreciate your problem. If the bus is going now, there's no reason why we shouldn't. We'll be out of Aceh in a couple of hours and your troubles will be over. All you have to worry about is the rain, and the forecast is OK.'

'They say they no let your car go.'

'Come and ask him with me.'

The policemen had been changed. This was an older man with an expression of professional severity.

Andy asked him in the ingratiating manner it is safer to employ with the Indonesian police if we could safely go to Berastagi. Using one of the five forms of the negative which complicate the Indonesian language, he replied, 'belun', meaning 'not yet'.

We thanked him and backed away. 'Well that clearly means tomorrow, doesn't it?' I said to Andy.

'Can mean tomorrow, or maybe one month. Can mean anything you want.'

'So you're absolutely set on going?'

'My wife worry and I must go to her.'

We walked with him to the bus where two other hopeful travellers had already taken their seats and the driver was at the wheel. Our leave-taking was an affectionate one, and we were sorry to see him go. He had been dogged by fear almost from from the first moment of our meeting, but on the whole had managed to keep it in the background, and had made himself useful and pleasant in every way he could. In his unobtrusive way he had managed to impart information about the way his people looked at human relationships that I suspected many foreigners who lived or worked in the country may not wholly have understood.

Always descend from car, smile and ask for excuse before requiring directions of road.

Say always taxi man, 'Where you learn drive so well?'

Not to drink lady's health in glass from bucket of soap powder.

For waiter you must be saying, 'Food delicious.' If not delicious saying, 'Sorry for cook too busy today.'

In crowd with ladies best keep arms folded.

With us he had never had the opportunity to prove his worth as a guide except through the labyrinths of oriental protocol, where he would have been hard to beat.

There was an afternoon to be used up. We had plans for the exploration of what sounded like untouched rainforest that actually came tumbling over the mountainside down to, and within sight of, the town. On further consideration it was decided to devote a full day to this the next day, planning instead to spend an hour or two in the old fishing village, so far overlooked.

Even in an uninteresting town like Tapaktuan that happens, at least, to be on the coast, it is always pleasant to spend time in the port area, to enjoy the shape and colour of the boats, and the animation of the maritime scene. Tapaktuan possessed no port, but miraculously the old fishing village, unchanged probably for a thousand years, had so far not only been spared but ignored. It was at the end of a few hundred yards of beach, full of shallow lagoons and savagely coloured rocks, standing on great slabs of sandstone which descended like stepping stones to the water. The fishermen had built their houses of dark ferruginous wood, under deep blond thatches, and they were in the shade of wide-spreading firs through which the breeze never ceased to stir. A great assortment of feluccas and catamarans had been lined up in short order on the beach, and around them were heaped up the nets, fishing pots, windlasses, anchors and the rest of the cheerful paraphernalia of the sea. So far the fishermen remained in possession of the most desirable site for many miles, but it was impossible that this should long continue to be the case, and slowly the town was moving its frontier of white cubes and high, glass-topped walls towards this maritime Arcadia.

In the meanwhile the fishermen's village remained solidly rooted in the past, and I was interested by the survival here of a pre-historic pre-culinary process which I had previously believed to be confined to Burma, and in particular Mergui, famous for its 'Bombay Duck', which is considered the best in the East. In Mergui the whole of the town's extensive seafront is closely covered, in season, with small fish which are split, salted and laid out to dry. Their exposure is not only to the sun, but to numerous dogs which pass up and down their rows, marking their territory in the usual way. In Tapaktuan the limestone shelves replaced the Mergui seafront, but the process was identical. In The Select they did not call it Bombay Duck, but it was much in demand, and there were cries of *enak* (delicious) from diners who had ordered it. No-one within earshot remarked that the cook had been busy.

The next morning, conveniently alerted by the mosque, we were up at dawn, then down to the road-block, where after a glance at our passports the policeman waved us through. 'Road bad,' he said. 'You go, OK, but if trouble no-one come for you.'

We expected it to be bad, but not that it would be the worst any of us could remember ever travelling over. Someone had told us that they were repairing and widening it at the rate of thirty kilometres a year, but every year the problems got worse. People who popped down to their holiday villas once in a while could never be sure how long their weekends might last.

The first few miles out of Tapaktuan inspired us with false confidence. It wasn't so bad after all. We were skirting the foothills where the cataclysmic rain to come would drain quickly down to a wide marshy plain, with the sea in the distance, so there were no dubious bridges to negotiate and no wide holes in the road surface to be filled in. The mountain slopes above the road had been logged, and with the loss of the sponge effect of the root-system there could be sudden floods where the road dropped to marsh level. We should be well away by then. At least the road surface was better than it had been before Tapaktuan. We suspected that the trouble had been no more than a few girders gone out of control, and felt hopeful that this had been cleared up.

Although still in Aceh we were coming to the end of it, and the feeling was of the slackening of tension and an end of a war-time atmosphere. Fifty miles back much of the countryside was deserted, and we drove all day hardly passing a car. Here, so far as we could see, things were back to normal. There was some traffic and many more people about, some of whom actually waved.

The traditional villages we were passing through were exceptionally picturesque in a slatternly fashion. They seemed in microcosm to illustrate an Asian pattern where fertile soil stimulates uncontrollable population growth. They were built in and along the small, swift-flowing mountain streams, which were chocolate in colour from the silt in suspension, and which over the years and centuries had enriched the peasants' fields. Possibly from custom, no paint was used on any of these places. Buildings were of raw wood under layered roofs of palm thatch or, where the owner could afford it, corrugated iron. People packed the road and streamed like ants in and out of their doors. Domestic gear of all kinds was piled up outside houses into which nothing more could be crammed and there was a sensational amount of litter. Here was the problem at its source, for which a solution had been sought in transmigration, but when the authorities decided to move out surplus humanity from such villages as this it could only be a matter of years before an inborn urge to increase and multiply put things back to square one.

There were transmigrants here, too, living in a kind of ribbon development along a lengthy stretch of the road, in conditions that might have discouraged the production of too many children. Settlements were bare, stark, hot, and above all regimented. The established villages had long since taken possession of those choice situations where there was water in plenty, fertile soil, and the shade of ancient, carefully conserved trees. The transmigrants, in their cleared area, had no shade; sometimes they may have had piped water, but we had heard of many condemned to a daily trek to the nearest river. Above all it was hard not to believe that they suffered from boredom in such surroundings. The vastness of the undertaking in which they were the pawns, coupled with the planners' lack of vision, had constructed vistas of unimaginable monotony, of endless austere little grey cabins set up in straight lines with nothing to refresh the eye. The planning authorities may have equated standardisation with progress, efficiency and manageable subservience, but the onlooker, and probably the homesick migrant, longs for the generous muddle of the average village. A passion for tidiness on the transmigration site itself is sometimes bolstered by notices urging the occupants to keep streets and houses clear of litter. Yet this concern for the immediate environment goes with indifference to the hellish wasteland in which the project is so often located.

Somewhere along this stretch we found ourselves crashing and bucketing over what we assumed to be the bad road of which we had been warned. For a moment we were mystified at shocks that suggested a major earthquake was taking place under us. The explanation was that the road was cratered with deep potholes camouflaged with a filling of dust. For the boys this was no more than another opportunity for testing driving skills, and spells behind the wheel were rationed and timed. Apart from the driver the problem was to avoid cracking heads on the roof, and this could only be done by hanging on to the bases of the seats.

This was the area of the Simpang-kiri river, and a wide and glowing plain, edged with a glittering tinsel of sea. It was here that the bridge was rumoured to be down. This was not so. In fact the road followed the river for some way and crossed and recrossed it over new steel bridges. The work on these had not been finished in all cases, involving some detours with the chance of getting stuck in the mud. For my part the slow going and delays added greatly to the interest of the journey, and many of the rare and spectacular birds I saw were familiar only from ornithological books. Mostly these were waders: stolidly contemplative painted storks –

one in every pool – cranes mincing along the edge of streams, a white ibis, a purple moorhen, a scarlet minivet, a yellow oriole, a blue roller, and that great speciality of Indonesia, a green pigeon almost as large as a goose, pecking at seeds at the edge of the water. Two hundred yards away a fishing eagle planed down to rip ineffectively with its talons at the surface of a pond, then settled for a moment in an heraldic pose before launching itself on the air and flapping away. We wound down the windows and listened to the melancholic outcry of all the small birds of the marsh. There were the sounds of the mudflats of estuarial England, and half the small ducking, dodging, scampering water-birds in sight we shared with Sumatra.

Turning inland soon after this we realised that the moment of truth had arrived for suddenly we were driving over a switchback with exceedingly deep troughs holding sand and dust in their bottoms. This called for full throttle in bottom gear up the slopes, with the Toyota's rear swinging like a pendulum as the wheels lost their grip, spun, took hold again, and we finally slithered, churning sand, foot by foot, over the top. This must have been the area where the steel girders had come adrift and it was hard to imagine how they could have been retrieved, for we passed two transporters that had dug themselves into the troughs, and another that, having slewed sideways while breasting an incline, had ploughed off the road. The ticklish problem now arose of lightening the loads. As a gesture of international friendship we stopped and offered to do whatever we could to help the drivers in their predicament. In reality the Toyota lacked the power to be of any use at all, but the drivers showed themselves delighted at our concern. They were the most courteous and genial men we had met on the journey.

Our target for that day was Berastagi, and the vote was unanimous that we should stay on the outskirts in the Bukit Kubu Hotel. This had possibly been the hardest day's driving that any of us had done in our lives, and between us we were suffering from a list of minor ailments: abrasions and bruises inflicted by the road, infected mosquito bites, queasiness of the stomach, a touch of asthma, and general fatigue. The hotel had been described in the guidebook in terms that suggested it was a good place in which to rest up for a couple of days. Too often in the past fortnight in the matter of food we had had to fall back on *nasi goreng, mie goreng*, or stale cake. The restaurant at Bukit Kubu was praised, and the feeling was that in a hotel of this category enclosed in its own substantial grounds we would also enjoy the luxury of silence after so many nights of the babel of Indonesian small towns. The *Indonesian Handbook* said: 'You'll feel like a Dutch colonialist in the gracious Bukit Kubu . . . this is one of the most faithfully preserved colonial-style hotels in Indonesia with complete and original Dutch furnishings, and a fire at night in the lounge . . . one can hire horses and hope they don't throw you off.'

And so it turned out to be, for it was as near a reproduction of Holland under a tropical sun as it could have been possible to devise in that fateful year, 1939, when it was built. With power about to fall from the Dutch grasp, this must have been among the last batch of the optimistic small enterprises in the colonies. It was a solid bourgeois mansion set on a hilltop in a great spread of lawns with cunningly spaced European specimen trees, and a wide, undulating landscape behind it that had nothing about it of the orient. Such a vista would have attracted great admiration in the Low Countries, where there are few prospects that include hills. In the rear of the hotel the view had been left to itself and was largely monopolised by the shape of a volcano, its glowing flanks coppered in the last of the light, and detached a little from the earth by the gathering mist. A private road, illuminated as if for a fiesta, curved up the hill to the entrance, reached by skirting a park for 100 cars, all its spaces empty. Despite a suspicion that there were few guests, there were staff in plenty: a rush of bellboys to unload baggage, a head-waiter listing the fearful contents of a welcoming Bukit Kubu cocktail, maids in national costume polishing and picking things up, a man who wanted to know if he could book us horses for the morning.

Treading softly over thick pile carpets we were taken on a tour of bedrooms, some of them enormous. The Bukit set out with some success to create a Victorian atmosphere. The furniture was dark, ornately carved, and with that slight ghostliness imparted by innumerable coats of wax. Heavy brass fittings on doors and windows provided a measure of pomp. The bathrooms housed ancient geysers bearing warning notices, and a tug on what looked like a cathedral bell-rope released a Niagara in miniature from the cistern.

Although we could not discover that, ourselves apart, anyone was actually staying in the hotel, prosperous-looking Indonesians dropped in from time to time for a silent ritual in the lounge, as if seeking benefit from an aftermath of past greatness in its atmosphere. A row of deep and comfortable armchairs looked on to the fireplace, and the visitor seating himself in one of these faced a message in letters beaten in a large brass plate. This said *Elke Gast Brengt Vreugde-An* (Every guest brings happiness) and it was a testimony to the irrepressible mateyness of the largely vanished Dutch.

A Dutchman had come in while we were there and lowered himself into a chair, glancing up at the happiness notice before turning away quickly in our direction to begin an eager conversation. He introduced himself as Peter Manders, a bridge-building engineer, a big man with an earnest expression and dressed in local Sumatran style in a jacket buttoned high at the neck, which if anything – as such items of oriental regalia worn by a foreigner often do – emphasised a nordic appearance. He lived in a villa down the hill, but popped up here from time to time for a change of faces, and a chat with anybody he happened to know. At this point he made some mention of being bored.

'Not enough for you to do here?' I asked.

'No,' he said. 'Not that. With life I am never bored, but the job I am doing is too tedious. I am here to look after bridges but they look after themselves. Nothing goes wrong with them until they collapse. Then I must order a new bridge that is all. The hope has been to save money by cutting quality of standards, but the bridge falls down and money is lost. I am expensively paid to watch the happening of a process over which I have no control. This is bad for my professional conscience.'

We were interrupted by an assortment of maids on their morning round, who scrambled round the room to empty ashtrays, pick up the petals that had drifted in through the window from a flowering tree, and impart a rapid and perfunctory polish to all the numerous brass objects in sight. Manders nodded approvingly. 'Karo girls,' he said. 'They put out offerings to the spirit of domestic work.' He laughed and for a moment was unrecognisable.

'So what do you do to amuse yourself?'

'Oh, I climb the volcanoes. There are two of them, Sibayak and Sinabung. You saw Sibayak on your way up here.'

There was a pause. I waited to be told what else he did, but after a moment I understood that he had nothing to add.

'You mean you've climbed them more than once?'

He laughed again, and I sensed that he was glad to have been asked the question. 'Oh yes,' he said, 'so many times.'

'Wonderful exercise I should imagine.'

'I have worked out a system. I climb Sibayak, then I maybe leave it a week and climb Sinabung. After that it's Sibayak again. I think maybe twenty climbs apiece.'

'And the two of them keep you happy?'

'They keep me happy because it's never twice the same. Sometimes I climb by a different route, or a different time of the day, or in different weather. Always the volcanoes' moods are changing, and I also respond to them. Sibayak is female, Sinabung male. This is the Chinese yin and yang. I have a great collection of photographs. Many hundreds.'

'All of the volcanoes?'

'All. There will be an exhibition for them in Amsterdam when I return. Maybe in London, too.'

'I look forward to seeing it,' I assured him.

Life burgeoned in all its forms in indulgent surroundings. The gardens abounded with rampaging hot-house plants, with rampant climbers, weed-stranglers that garrotted plant invaders with bony vegetal fingers, daturas wrinkled like aged skin at the end of the day, sinister floral traps with insects dissolving in laryngitic throats. We picked our way through day-old chicks scampering everywhere. In the hotel's famous lounge spoilt cats with violet eyes and only half a tail waited by each chair for the invitation to leap into a lap. Sparrows popped in and out of the eaves, but otherwise, repelled by the nine-hole golf course, and by a logged-over section of forest, birds in general were nowhere to be seen.

Once against we discovered that breakfasts in Indonesia are often of staggering proportions. At the Bukit it started with six eggs apiece, followed by steak, optional curries of various kinds, then toast and jam. Mounds of butter were shaped like volcanoes. 'Why no guests?' I asked the head-waiter. He shrugged. 'This is North Sumatra.'

'But it isn't Aceh.'

'We are a very short distance from Aceh.'

He suggested a paradise cocktail to start the day. He turned out to be an efficient, energetic and enthusiastic man driven almost to the edge of despair by the atrophy that, as a result of the emergency, had affected all the services he controlled.

'May I ask if you have any special plans for your stay?' he asked.

'We shall be out today. Touring the neighbourhood,' I told him.

'Should you wish to eat in the hotel when you return a meal can be served at any hour of the day or night.'

There were other hopefuls in the vicinity, including a spruce and zestful young man collecting funds for a Protestant fundamentalist sect. He had chosen the golf course as his pitch, for it was occasionally in use by persons not staying at the hotel. Gawaine and Robin were playing a round while I looked on, and he headed us off at one of the putting greens. He was extremely insistent. 'I want to visit you in your hotel,' he said. 'When will you be possible?'

'At this stage I couldn't say. When we've finished our game we shall be going out.'

'This is important for me and, I think, important for you. Please to give room number.'

'What is it you want to say? You may as well say it now.'

'We are doing God's work with backward people. For this we are needing all generosity you can give. But I want to talk with you. Long talking is necessary to tell how you can become helpers for God's purpose. What time do you eating? Here it is half-eight. So I will come at seven tonight?'

Robin emptied his pocket and handed over the few hundred rupiahs he was carrying. The man took them and laughed out loud in furious derision. He was the first rude Indonesian we had encountered on this journey.

Waiting his turn behind the disgruntled evangelist, who clearly still refused to accept defeat, had been the man in charge of the horses. He now came forward with an expectant mime. By this time the boys had exhausted almost the full potential of the Bukit's range of attractions in swimming, tennis, squash and golf, and now they looked to the experience of a jungle ride referred to in the hotel's brochure. But since the man spoke no English, we could learn nothing whatever of the details.

Indonesian is the supreme example of a language proving that on the whole grammar is unimportant, and that human communication can be maintained without conjugation of verbs, past or future tenses, case endings, genders, definite and indefinite articles, and the rest. This is Malay brought up to date, which in its original form planters were compelled by their contracts to learn in one month. All the foreigner has to do, is to pick up as many words as possible, string them together, and bring the meaning into clearer focus, when required, by adjustment of the context. Two or three hundred words coped with rudimentary conversations. By this time we could master the routines of polite small-talk, ask and give directions, order food, express pleasure or dissatisfaction. Not a single word we could muster between us had any bearing on horse-riding. We were obliged to agree with nods of the head to what the man unintelligably asked of us, and to send him away with appropriate gestures to fetch the horses. I then questioned Gawaine and Robin as to their equestrian skills, to be told that these had been provided solely by tired Mexican hacks on the beach at Acapulco. 'Did you gallop?' 'Well, not really. The fellow with them gave them a whack on the backside when we started off, and they galloped a bit, but only a few yards.'

'They were worn out,' I said. 'The trouble is these won't be.'

The man was away longer than we had expected, and after a while one of the porters came out of the hotel and crossed a corner of the golf course, making in our direction. 'Good afternoon,' he said. 'You waiting for horses?'

'Yes. Will they be long?'

'Not long. Very soon. This is not waiting-place. I take you now for waiting-place. Please you come with me.'

We walked together, crossing the course to reach a hotel road leading to a pavilion and a children's play area with coloured light bulbs and speakers suspended between poles, toy motor-cars – in all cases short of a wheel – and a large Mickey Mouse shoved in a corner on its back. 'This waiting-place,' the porter said.

'Where are the horses kept?' I asked. 'At the hotel?'

'Not at hotel. Horses at farm. Now they are coming.' He gestured at a bench. 'You please taking seats.'

Gawaine sat down and instantly the speakers burst into life and we were overwhelmed by glutinous Indonesian rock.

Silence was something for which payment was demanded in the East. The cheaper the losmen the more insistent and ear-splitting the noise. On this score the Bukit had been very good, for until now the only music had been the distant grumble of television from the servants' quarters somewhere in the depths of the building. The lady in Jakarta reached a powerful, warbling crescendo, and I rammed my fingers in my ears.

The porter's concern took the form of an embarrassed smile. 'You no like?'

'Can you switch it off?'

What he had to say was swept away in an immense caterwauling, but I caught that most characteristic of Indonesian Bahasa words, *belun*, with which absolute negatives are usually avoided. 'What he's trying to say is that it can't be switched off from here,' Gawaine said. 'I suppose we can put up with it for a minute or two – in any case, here come the horses.' I followed his glance and saw the horses coming towards us round the shoulder of an artificial hill at the edge of the course, making a composition of striking simplicity in their setting. For a moment they were silhouetted against the volcano: the two small horses, one prancing and tossing its head, the man who was trying to control them. The volcano, overlooking the small-scale grandeur of the Bukit's topiary and lawns, was in some way unexpected and extraordinary, cast from metal in a mould rather than earth and marked with the spoiled colours of an ancient incandescence under its thin chaplet of cloud.

I looked back from the volcano and the horses to the porter with his unchanged grin, which had something about it that reminded me of the ingratiating foolishness carved on the face of the Mickey Mouse lying on its back. The horses were coming close. 'They don't look very big, do they?' Robin said.

'No,' I said, 'but that shouldn't foster a false sense of security. They probably haven't been exercised for weeks. They'll take it out on you.'

The porter seemed to have followed the gist of our discussion. 'Horses good, very quiet,' he said. The speakers were yowling and bellowing and he tried a joke. 'Horses are liking this music,' he said.

'They're all right,' Robin said. The groom held their heads while he and Gawaine patted their necks confidently. They had rough coats the colour of coconut matting, and when flies settled on their flanks they slashed at them with long tails, and they responded to the patting by showing the whites of their eyes.

The groom and the porter held the horses' heads while the boys got on. 'How do they compare with the ones in Acapulco?'

'Quieter if anything,' Gawaine thought. Apart from the fact that they were half the size, the main difference was the stirrups. Mexican stirrups were iron boxes shaped like shoes. 'Don't put your feet too far into these,' I said. 'Otherwise you might get dragged if you're thrown.'

At this point another man had appeared, as if from nowhere. 'This guide,' the porter said. 'You want guide for jungle?' They did not.

In theory the forest began a hundred yards away. A path led up a slope into woodland where a board had been nailed on a tree trunk bearing the word jungle and an arrow pointing to the left. The switch in environment was sudden and dramatic. Where we stood a hibiscus hedge did its best to screen utilitarian buildings, but immediately beyond the turn in the path the lower part of a giant forest tree was entirely concealed by its aerial roots.

'How do we get these going?' Gawaine asked.

I told them to kick with their heels, and they moved off in an unhurried fashion up the path. Despite having been waved away the guide went trudging in the rear. The boys found the pace too slow and urged the horses on with cries of encouragement and more jabbing with their heels. They turned the corner of the path into the trees, and with that the voices died away almost immediately, and silence fell.

A long time seemed to pass. The porter and the groom had followed the guide in the direction of the forest. The Indonesian rock, previously bland, had been replaced with the Righteous Brothers' 'Unchained Melody', and I went up to the hotel, got them to switch off, declined a cocktail, and came back. I was just in time to see Gawaine and Robin on foot, on the path coming down from the forest. They were both red in the face, somewhat dishevelled, and talking excitedly. There were signs of blood on them.

'What happened?'

'They threw us.'

'How far did you get?'

'No distance. Mine only wanted to go sideways, and when I tried to straighten him up he threw me over his head. Robin landed up in a clump of bamboo.'

'So where are the horses?'

'The groom caught them and took them away. We chased them all over the place. They play a game with you. They wait for you to come up, then they take off again.

'Who won this time?'

'Robin. He stayed on longer than I did.'

BERASTAGI WAS JUST down the road, and as we drove in it came as a surprise to see travellers in plenty, instantly identifiable by their money belts suspended like marsupial pouches over the lower area of their stomachs. On the whole the travellers were unconcerned with politics, and the ugly sounds reaching Bukit Kubu from just over the border in Aceh were inaudible in the self-absorbed tourist world of Berastagi itself. Berastagi, in the Karo Highlands, could have been anywhere. Here was a main street, with travel agency, bank, Modesty Souvenir Shop, Superfast Filling Station, three Chinese restaurants with nightly karaoke, and a tiny hole of a place in a back street with dog stew bubbling in a cauldron. It was ritual food for the Karos, normally consumed by them only on great occasions, although here it attracted the attention of the occasional foreigner prepared to go to almost any length in search of exotic experience.

There was a joint letter from Claudia and Rod awaiting me, which I was lucky to collect because it had taken only half the normal time to arrive. It was from Siberut, which had been the final and supreme goal of Claudia's journeyings. This island not quite the size of Bali, off the west coast of Sumatra, was outstanding at many levels of interest, so much so that in 1981 the whole island was declared a 'Man and the Biosphere Reserve'. Despite such international interest and the Presidential Decree of 1992 declaring that its future would be safeguarded, Siberut had suffered outrageous exploitation. Intensive logging continues even at night; its indigenous people have been forbidden to practise their religion, and deprived of their means of existence by compulsory relocation to coastal areas which cannot provide a livelihood. Relief organisations are harassed by the police, and although Claudia and her friend were able to visit parts of the island normally out of bounds, they did so with extreme difficulty and probably at some risk.

The people here on the coast who have lost their plantations inland have to get their food from the Menang traders – either *beras* (low grade rice), *supermie* (instant noodles) or tins of sardines at vastly inflated prices. The money for this is any *gaheru* they may have saved, or *copra*. Gaheru is a fungus causing a fragrant resin to grow in the heart of a local tree (now rare). The traders buy this at a very low price. It finally ends up in the Middle East as frankincense at thousands of pounds a kilo, and the islanders are persuaded to spend the money on cigarettes, radios, electric torches, T-shirts, etc. The plan is to hook them on 'modern' things, but where will they turn when their savings are gone?

The trip inland to Pokukul was our first experience of trekking in Siberut, which is an island made totally of mud. To make the walking easier on very muddy climbs, descents or crossing ravines or rivers, there are notched logs along the path. These might be very useful for the Mentawaians with their splayed-out, huge, flat feet, but for whities it's a complete nightmare. The health situation is appalling. There is cholera in the region every year, the worst period being in 1975. The spread is probably increased by their method of mourning which is to stroke and kiss the dead one.

When we reached the Sakkudei and gave them some coloured wool, they put skeins and skeins round their waists, wore it as armbands and in their hair. Some of the men wear their hair down to their bottoms, but that's an imprisonable offence if they're caught. The old religion of the Sakkudei people is fascinating, and a very little persists today in the more remote areas, which is where we've come. Basically animism (that everything from trees, rocks, rivers to the weather are imbued with their own spirits) and worship of the ancestral spirits result in a cultural adaptation of the people to the life of the rainforest in an almost perfect harmony, preventing over-exploitation of local resources. Hunting is an important social occasion for the men, the prey usually being monkeys and deer. A complex act of rituals must be performed prior to the event. A ceremony is performed where the *Dukun* (shaman) conjures up the spirit of the monkey and apologises to it for its imminent death, pointing out that the clan is obliged to eat, and also trying to persuade the monkey spirit that coming to live in the *uma* (big clan house) is a great idea and it is a really nice place.

Felling of forest trees, too, is strongly tabooed, as trees are believed to be homes for spirits of the deceased, as well as having spirits of their own. Thus when a tree needs to be felled to make a *sampan* or maybe a village clearing, a ceremony must first be performed to apologise to the resident spirits.

The Italian Catholic pastors here have a very liberal attitude towards Sakkudei traditional culture. We trekked a day through the mud to Liman to attend a ceremony in the newly erected church. Everyone stood outside with palms to listen to the pastor then filed into the church. Then the dukuns took over, slaughtering a few pigs and wringing the necks of the chickens. The two oldest dukuns were gorgeous long-haired old men, one of them with the most captivating smile. We'd met him on the trek and he said we could stay in his house, where his little adopted daughter used my feet as a pillow. He had been wearing a splendid bark loincloth the first time we met, but for the church festival the kids made the dukuns change into shorts, and in two cases dirty Adidas towels. The dancing was the most amazing I've ever seen anywhere. In addition to the professionals, all the most important figures, e.g. school teacher, *kepala desa*, pastor, etc., were expected to do their bit with a song or a dance number. At the last minute we found that we had to perform something typically British too. After a good deal of blank-minded panic, I came up with Morris dancing. For this we decorated ourselves with leaves, borrowed horse bells from some children, and made a bamboo stick each. We made real fools of ourselves prancing about on stage – but people seemed to get quite into it.

I wonder if any of the tribal life we've experienced in the outer islands still exists in East Timor, after all they've gone through. From all one hears I very much doubt it. Anyway we shall soon see for ourselves and I'm living in hopes. It won't be long now. See you in Jakarta.

Clear of Berastagi the pulse of life in North Sumatra quickens. The village streets fill up, smiles return; the mixture is one of bustle, yet extraordinary tranquillity. There are animals everywhere – cats, dogs, chickens, goats – indifferent to the congested traffic in a narrow road, and it comes almost as a revelation to see a lorry driver pull up, climb down from his perch and gently shoo a hen and her chicks from his path before grinding into action once again. Whence comes this tenderness for animals? These lorry drivers and villagers were in the main Karos, many of them only converted to Christianity or Islam at the time of the emergency in 1965, when to be an 'atheist' in many areas was to run the risk of inclusion in the general slaughter.

Nevertheless, many who had survived through prudent conversion remained animist under the skin. Remembering the Indian animists of the Amazon, too, and their villages full of tame parrots and of small jungle animals that wandered about and through their houses fearlessly, it seemed to me that the difference lay in the tribals' acceptance of the animal's soul, rejected by monotheist belief. The Karos, too, were great pet people, and in most villages there were tarsiers on offer, perched on a pole – often with a baby in arms – watching the world through their wide, deep eyes, mirroring all the human emotions. Passers-by stopped to admire them and pop slivers of cheese into their mouths. Despite solidarity with the animals, the villagers were carnivorous, and there were always stalls with plentiful bats for sale. They hung head-down in rows, absolutely inert apart from sensitive claws, constantly in languid movement, like the fingers of a tired pianist over the keys of a piano. I would have imagined that the Sakkudei of Siberut, too, ate bats, and assumed that if so these would have been included in the ritual apologies made to animals that went into the pot.

Within the bounds of its 13,677 islands Indonesia contains a greater variety of tribal peoples than any other political entity in the world. There are many hundreds of communities such as the Karos, possessing their own language, the separate culture developed over thousands of years, their own customs and their own beliefs. All are now referred to in government pronouncements as *suku suku terasing* (isolated and alien peoples) and it is the announced intention to destroy this isolation and to turn isolated and alien islanders into the equivalent of Javanese peasants or industrial workers.

The PKMT, the office created to deal with the problem of tribal peoples, has listed among its numerous objectives the imposition of 'religion' based upon one 'Almighty God', the development of tribal ability to produce works of culture and art 'in tune with the values of Indonesian society', and the settling of isolated communities in an area within government administration and with 'permanent orderly sources of income'. They are therefore to be stripped of their religion, made available as a low-paid workforce wherever labour is in demand and, in the case of certain tribes having a reputation as creative artists, forced into the production of banalities for the commercial market.

The tribal peoples of Indonesia are almost without exception extremely receptive to visiting foreigners, who may even find their unvarying hospitality bordering on the excessive. Outstandingly, the Karos welcome the presence of sympathetic outsiders on the occasion of any of their numerous ceremonies. More than fifty of these are listed, the most interesting – and in a way moving – being the washing of the bones of their ancestors. This, from the governmental viewpoint, fails on several counts. In the first place it is unacceptable because it shows regard for the ancestral spirits, thereby demonstrating animistic traits that are to be eliminated. The ceremony will have been presided over by a traditional healer, now outlawed, and in the way of all such ancient religious ceremonies, it will not have been fitted into our calendar, but remains like Easter in the West: a movable feast dependent upon the phases of the moon.

A problem now presents itself. Indonesia derives a huge and expanding revenue from tourism, the hope even being that, a few years from now, when the income at present provided by its logging industry comes to an end, tourism will have been sufficiently developed to plug the wide hole in the national resources. Tourists are attracted to Indonesia because it has remained 'colourful' in the way their own countries have long since ceased to be. It can provide ceremonies by the hundred like the traditional bone-washing of the Karos, performed under the compulsion of belief. These are largely what have drawn tourists to Indonesia, and these they will flock to see. In their stead the government proposes to create a lifeless folklore which visitors will instinctively avoid. Neither will tourists wish to see tribes such as the Dayaks of Borneo, whose long-houses were burned down prior to their relocation in settlements of one-family dwellings of corrugated iron and planks.

Bukit Lawang is a splendidly located village on the banks of a turbulent little oriental imitation of the Wye which has given its name to the nearby Bohorok Orang-utan Rehabilitation Centre. The information provided by the centre's leaflet, stating that it is principally visited by foreigners, is wildly out of date. We arrived at the worst time, a weekend, finding ourselves at the entrance to the village in a traffic-jam of cars overflowing with exuberant locals – mostly from Medan, with the noise of car radios and cassette recorders coming from all directions – and then had difficulty in finding anywhere to park. For a moment we were tempted to call the expedition off, although second thoughts were unexpectedly rewarded, for somehow an environment of potentially grandiose solitude was able to cope with the invasion, to stifle the outcry and conceal or disperse the litter. It turned out that Bukit Lawang is also a centre of the sport of 'tubing'. Tubers float twelve kilometres on inflated car inner-tubes in vigorous motion through the last of the Bohorok's shallow cataracts down to the edge of the great eastern plain of Sumatra. But in the end these, too, go, returning the tubes to the many hirers, or taking them with them.

The orang-utan station was now run by the Indonesian government although it had been initiated by the Frankfurt Zoological Society, and a Germanic respect for time, which may even have been passed on to the great apes, was discernible in its publications. The visitor hoping to see the orang-utans in the morning must arrive strictly at 07.00 at the location, and if in the afternoon, he must be present at 14.30 sharp, since the time established is the time to feed (the free) animals. Leaflets put out by Indonesian guest houses make good reading for their wildly beautiful and often evasive English, but the Germans called a spade a spade. There is nothing about the reasonable need for caution in your approach to a wild orang-utan. 'They are capable', the old German leaflets tell you flatly, 'of cracking your bones.'

The function of the centre is to take over orang-utans which have been kept in captivity and then released by their original owners, or confiscated by the State, and to organise their resumption of freedom in the wild.

This is shown as a complicated business indeed. After arrival a long period of quarantine follows, in which the orang-utans are kept under medical supervision in cages or a limited area surrounding their cages. A further interval of training follows in which an animal, deprived of the ability to fend for itself in the wild, is acclimatised to the forest existence. It is both extraordinary and sad that the life of these highly intelligent animals has been so deformed in captivity that they have to be retaught all the natural occupations such as climbing, making a sleeping nest, travelling in such a way as to keep clear of the ground, and – most difficult of all hurdles – discovering edible vegetation in the wild.

The fact is that with the awakening of eleventh-hour concern for the loss of so many species, and the increasing threat to those that remain, the ripples of alarm have finally touched these remote shores, and suddenly there are popular excursions from Sumatran towns to Bukit Lawang to see up to twelve animals out of the several hundred believed to have survived.

Thus, by the greatest of good fortune, orang-utans have become a major tourist attraction, so much so that a number of agreeable guest houses such as the Wisma Leuser Sibayak, at which we stayed, have been built along the banks of the river. It is possible to forecast a time when this delectable village will have expanded into a modest town dedicated to the needs of people who come to watch monkeys.

Mild theatricalities have been built into the routine of the visit in order to foster a sense of adventure. Foreign visitors are directed to an office where they show their passports, which are solemnly studied and details entered into a register before a pass is issued. The official's manner is congratulatory as he hands this over, mentioning that only fifty passes are granted each day. There follows a pleasant walk upstream along the river, then a crossing over to the further bank by a boat on a rope. This, the boatman's gestures and expression suggest, calls for skill and caution. Landing is followed by a further small charade when visitors report to the park rangers in another office, where permits are minutely inspected before being put in a safe place until the return to the boat. Such precautions reflect measures instituted to baffle the efforts of armed poachers, said to employ helicopters to snatch the orang-utans from the treetops. These, it is believed, are sold for huge sums of money through middlemen to zoos – amazingly enough until recently in most cases behind the former Iron Curtain.

From this point, a short but exceedingly steep climb leads up to a jungle post in a clearing among tall trees, where a platform has been built, and where the orang-utans show up on time to the minute. Their arrival overhead through the treetops is sudden, but above all silent. At one moment the trees are empty; the next the animals are there with hardly the flutter of a branch, and not a twig broken. One by one the heavy, rubbery bodies drop down to the platform but there is no sound of concussion, for in this instant they demonstrate their difference from the humans they so much resemble by the flexibility and the smoothness of all their movements. A ranger waits with a blue plastic pail of milk, into which he dips a blue plastic mug and hands it to the nearest animal, who takes it delicately by the handle, drinks without haste or gulping and hands it back. As we noticed subsequently, he and his friends use only their right hands, and the ranger tells us that, although ambidextrous, the orang-utans, who are acutely observant, have picked this up from watching the rangers although they still use both arms to throw sticks with considerable accuracy. He thinks that they also like the blue plastic mugs – a colour with some religious associations in Islam, of which he, too, is particularly fond.

During the past seventeen years of re-introducing orang-utans to their natural habitat, a total of 170 released from captivity were brought to the station. Of these 120 were successfully returned to the forest, while 35 died in the process of rehabilitation. At the time of our visit 15 remained in the care of the station, of which 7 turned up on the morning we were there.

Conduct on the feeding platform seems ruled by some inscrutable simian protocol that calms and subdues the tremendous athleticism demonstrated in the trees. In this instance five adults – one a female with a baby clinging to her neck – gathered in a sedate contemplative group, with what might have been a pretence of taking no notice of an impudent foot-long youngster playing sly pranks in their rear. A latecomer appeared suddenly, carried through the leaves as if by currents of air before twisting headlong like the most accomplished of yoga exponents, to drop spongily on to the stage. For some reason he was ignored by the early arrivals, but on making a move towards the bunch of bananas supplied with the milk, one of the group of five simply waved him away.

The offered diet of milk and bananas is by intention monotonous, in order to stimulate the orang-utans to search for more appetising food in the forest. It was taken as a hopeful sign that none of the animals seemed particularly hungry. Several did not eat at all, and the ranger explained that they were just there 'socially'.

These orang-utans were on the verge of a totally natural existence. Once again I noticed how radically different is the behaviour of such animals from that of those, for example, denaturalised by associates in the vicinity of Hindu temples, or of course of those shut up in zoos. I find it hard to forget the spectacle of the luckless gorilla Guy, favourite inmate for many years of the London Zoo, hunched psychologically *in extremis* shortly before death was to terminate the long incarceration in his concrete cell.

Zoos drive many animals mad, inspiring suicidal frenzy or delivering them to the cataplexy of ultimate despair. The reflective manner and the calm of these orang-utans reminded me of the only occasion when I had had the opportunity to study monkeys at close quarters in the wild, when they, too, had seemed to me to exhibit reactions emphasising the similarities with human beings.

I was in Mali, in north-west Africa, in the only hotel in a remote area, frequented exclusively, as it turned out, by big-game hunters. Its owner, Monsieur de Willfahrt, explained to me that the hotel was very expensive but that everything was thrown in. 'You may shoot an elephant, or a bison,' he said. 'Both, if you like, but as you are inexperienced I would be inclined to recommend the bison.'

'I'm not a sportsman, Monsieur de Willfahrt,' I said.

'In that case what would you like to do?'

'Go for a walk.'

'I'll send someone to look after you.'

'A quiet walk in the country by myself.'

'Very well then, but our regulations compel me to ask you to take a gun,' de Willfahrt said.

I took the complicated hunting gun, which I knew I would never be able to use effectively, and de Willfahrt went with me to the door. 'If you see an elephant or a bison,' he said, 'it might be better to drop the gun and run for your life. You can climb a tree but remember that the bison will remain some hours in the hope you will come down. There are one or two hyenas about. The method is to lie down and remain perfectly still until the animal comes to investigate – then you can easily shoot it.'

I thanked him and walked out into a lightly wooded savannah. It was the height of the dry season, with the ground crackling underfoot. The small, grey shining leaves in the trees looked as though they had been stamped out of tin. A movement screened by some spiny bushes caught my eye and, finding a gap in them, I ventured cautiously into an open space, followed by a bird, alarmed at the intrusion, that made a noise like a creaking gate hinge at ten-second intervals. In this space I found a congregation of thirty or so chimpanzees, who had gathered there, as it seemed to me, to communicate with one another in an area like a monkey forum set aside for this purpose. I stood, keeping as still as I could on the perimeter of this scene, knee-deep in tough savannah grass. The monkey's meeting place had been flattened and smoothed by their feet – it was to be supposed over a long period of time. The chimpanzees curled their lips in an expressive manner, and sometimes they gestured with their arms, but no sound came from them. Little groups had formed circles, heads close together, as if in earnest discussion. Others strolled in twos and threes, in one case an animal had flung an arm over its friend's shoulder. Sometimes a promenader would break away from his companion to spend a moment with another acquaintance before continuing the walk.

There was almost an eerie mimicry of human behaviour in what was going on here, and all the more extraordinary since not a head was turned in my direction although it was certain that these animals, always on the alert against stalking predators, knew that I was there. In all the years of sporadic animal- and bird-watching in foreign parts, this was the strangest of my experiences.

For children born in the village, Bukit Lawang was a paradise offering a legacy of childhood pleasures that must have helped set them on the high road to a successful adult life. For any child a river made this place. It poured in a clear, mild turbulence from the foothills of the National Reservation, thrashing its sparkling suds against the carved and polished limestone of the boulders lodged in its bed and its bank. In all probability the village had been deliberately established on a fairly sharp bend in its course; here water had been trapped to form an aqueous haven separate from the mainstream. This plunged over a drop of a few feet into lively but shallow rapids, manageable by all but the youngest swimmers, and it was this stretch of the river which provided pleasure and excitement of a kind which clearly never dulled. There seemed to be no time during the day when there were less than a dozen or so accomplished water babies in view. Were there ever any accidents? I asked. The answer was no, never. The children swam as soon as they walked. When the rains started the headman would order swimming for children to stop, and that would be that.

The Economic Guest House had built an open-air restaurant, elevated in such a way as to offer an excellent view of these aquatic activities, and a vantage point for the survey of village life in general. In the tourist season this was largely associated with the preparation of food saturated with spices of many kinds, few of which were to be found in other parts of the world. These tasks were accomplished by the women, who worked slowly but with intense concentration and a finicky regard for detail. Where there was butchering to be done, this was left to the menfolk. Families were huge and the children were everywhere, being treated with extreme tolerance. Bukit Lawang's practice of the Muslim faith seemed fairly easy-going and less than exclusive. The river was under the supervision of a benevolent water spirit, and frequent dips in it were considered useful in the treatment of asthma and conditions of the skin. Smartly dressed visitors from as far away as Medan would come here to draw up a chair on the river's bank and sit for hours on end, sometimes strumming a guitar as they absorbed curative influences and, if they were ladies, cuffing away dragonflies attracted by the fragrant unguents on their skin.

Several groups of foreign backpackers had taken much of the accommodation in the village. It was a situation adding to a longstanding confusion among the Sumatrans, to whom all Europeans, apart from extreme physical differences in the matter of size, looked roughly the same. It astonished them that this standardised collection of large pinkish people should speak a variety of languages, and it frustrated the ones who had painstakingly acquired a smattering of English to discover that only about one in ten of the visitors they tried to practise on had any idea of what they were talking about.

The staff at the Economic Guest House studied the racial assortment changing almost by the day, and assigned them recognisable characteristics. The Germans, said a waiter with whom I discussed this matter, were on the whole identifiable because they shouted at the top of their voice. It was likely to evidence high good humour rather than rage, and they were larger, pinker and had louder voices than the rest. All Belgians had been branded as a result of a single rash act, it seemed, when one of them, on being served unsatisfactory food, had simply thrown it over the restaurant's handrail into the river. The Swiss made a note of the sequence in which orders for a meal were taken, complaining bitterly if any one was served out of turn. French diners, the waiter said, played silly tricks. He described an incident where one had left the table to go to what he entitled in the prim Indonesian way 'the little chamber', and the man's chair was replaced by one with a broken leg, causing him to sprawl on the floor when he came back.

Thus incurable misapprehension developed and was perpetuated. Every day in season the waiter had one or more incomprehensible foreigner to deal with and to be added to his list of stereotypes. His beliefs were damaging him and it was adding to the corruption of tourism that had already invaded the culture of Bukit Lawang. This man had come to dislike foreigners. The antipathy, I believed, concerned fear, and surliness sometimes showed through obligatory smiles.

Mr Pencastu, who had been in the States learning his trade before coming back to start the guest house, called in at our bungalow to say he was getting married. The years in the United States had made him stand out among his fellow countrymen. The villagers as a whole tended to let life flow over them; Pencastu moved in a buzz of energy. He snapped his fingers, waved to attract attention, and shouted back when the Germans shouted at him. I noticed that staff members who drifted into his magnetic field straightened up and seemed to break into jerky action. He was amazingly frank about his private affairs. 'A slight problem,' he said. 'Eighteen months ago I shacked up with the lady in question, and we just had our first child. Now I have to put myself right with the village and a bunch of nice old guys who run the religous side. The plan is to throw a party for them tomorrow when the knot is tied. Next day we'll have a get-together for the whole village. I sure hope you'll come along.'

'Thanks,' I said. 'We'll be there.'

'This place is goddam quiet,' Pencastu said. 'The idea of a party here is to bring in a couple of fellows with guitars. The women go off together and maybe dance around a bit and the men eat goat's meat with rice. I aim to do better than this, so we're getting some guys down from Medan to set up a discotheque. They're using one of those new Yamaha amplifiers.'

'With independent tone-control?' Gawaine wanted to know.

'No, they just blast it out. The volume is terrific. The people in the next village down the river will be able to sit in their houses and listen to it, and if they want they can come here and dance. We're putting on Springsteen's latest album. You heard "Born to Run"?'

It was agreed that it all sounded great.

'We kick off with a buffet supper. After that there's a firework display. You heard of spring-bombs? We got a few of them from the Chinese. They really tear the place apart. Then comes the discotheque, which we hope will go on most of the night.' He glanced up at the whiteish noon sky. 'Some talk of rain,' he said. 'We gotta hope it holds off.'

'I heard something in the village about trance dancers?' I said.

'Right,' he said. 'We'll be having those, too. And I can assure you they're good ones. Those guys chew glass. They give you the day you're going to die. You want to try the experiment; they make you believe you're a frog and they have you hopping around all over the place.'

The prospects sounded good. Despite his exposure to the scepticisms of the West, Mr Pencastu showed himself as deeply impressed by the powers of what he called the magical men. They were tribals living in the remote forests of the Leuser Reservation, and they had no contact with village people except through such alarming performances. 'They stick skewers through their cheeks and no blood comes out. You want to try that? I guess you don't. Let me tell you, you're not going to believe what these guys can do.'

Dawn on Pencastu's great day promised well. The sun, fanning down from a hilltop, lifted the mist from the trees like a flying carpet. The earliest of those who had come to meditate were already in their chairs staring into the arcs of water curved over the polished rocks. Someone was tapping ancient temple music – a sad little tune of five notes – on a gamelan out of sight. The scents of charcoal smoke, and of the braised flesh of chilies, were wafted from the centre of the village where a start had already been made upon the day's innumerable chores.

Every single villager over the age of seven had been conscripted into Pencastu's labour battalions, and once again undercover Sumatran protocol showed through – this time in the division of the work. Piles of coconuts had been dumped in the spaces between the houses. These were spit exactly in half by experts with the machete, then turned over to young women of no special standing, who were allowed to do no more than grind the flesh. This, as with boiled rice, was delivered to members of the semi-skilled workers in their early middle years who measured and mixed in a number of spices. At the head of the operation were the matriarchs in command of the giant woks, of which the village appeared to possess about a dozen, who added meat from various piles before ladling the final concoction into the sizzling oil. When the cooking time was up (big old-fashioned alarm clocks were used), the food was transferred to large shallow dishes, and then covered with a layer of chilies, to await reheating for the meal.

At the back of the restaurant, next to the serving hatch, three days had been occupied by the erection of a fine, barbaric construction known as the wedding hut. In this three-sided room, lavishly decorated with sheets of gift-wrapping, ribbons, plastic flowers and plaited thatch, the bride and bridegroom would shortly take their seats side-by-side on gilt, mirror-glass-inlaid thrones to receive the congratulations delivered one by one, and often in the form of a short speech, by several hundred guests. The carpenters were still knocking nails into the wooden structure when one of them drew attention to the unusual behaviour of several dragonflies. These had come zigzagging in from the outside, then settled, and having folded their wings appeared to be attempting to camouflage themselves against the strongly coloured plaited straw decoration.

This was taken by the aged wiseacres, who credited such insects with the possession of infallible sensitivities, as a promise of rain to come. They linked the omen with the report by a line-fisherman that the fish had moved out of the rapids where they normally lay in ambush for their prey, into deep pools devoid of shrimps but safe from bad weather.

We had planned our congratulatory visit to the wedding hut for the late afternoon, in the belief that by then the queue of well-wishers would have shortened or even come to an end. Now, with half the residents and visitors snatching restorative naps before the entertainments of the evening began, a single sound dominated all others in the thickening silence. This was the deep, unearthly purr of the yard-across principal gong of the village gamelan, struck at measured intervals by a seven-year-old boy, whom I had already seen in action. He would strike the gong, count to five, then stifle the flood of vibrations with a touch of his hand. This tiger's breathing resonance represented the voice of a watchful demon, and its warning to any intruder pervaded the village.

There was some delay when we finally presented ourselves at the hut. A curtain had been drawn across its front, but was swept back for a full view of the happy couple, embowered in roses, and reminding me of painted wooden dolls in a shrine. They sat bolt upright, a foot apart, hands on knees, absolutely motionless, unblinking. Pencastu wore a grey, pin-striped suit with a cravat, diamond tie-pin and pinkish gloves. His bride had been tightly wound in nuptial silks so as to suppress excessive evidence of femininity. A tiny face carved from chalk was supported on the slender pedestal of a neck encased in brocade. As we came in a servant dived past us to snatch up and empty a bowl placed on the floor to catch insects and the occasional gecko incinerated by an electrical device fixed to the ceiling. We advanced to take each limp hand in turn and mutter a brief minimum of appropriate phrases learned for the occasion in Indonesian. As custom required, Pencastu's gaze was directed elsewhere so that our eyes should not meet. A layer of powder pulsating slightly at the corners of his mouth suggested a furtive smile. 'I have a stiff neck,' he whispered. It was all he said.

He had chosen a local feast day for the wedding, and those who had come here to take a curative dip or simply to meditate in congenial surroundings had settled in rows along the river bank – a few in classic yoga poses on the ground, but the majority in folding chairs brought in their cars. Some had guitars on which they strummed in an amateur fashion. They played chess, smeared insect repellent on exposed skin, and took flash-assisted photographs of each other in the declining light filtered through a screening of riverside trees.

Sunset was proclaimed by the tremendous detonation of the spring-bombs in the darkening sky overhead and the yowling that followed among the terrified village dogs. With that the guests got into line for the buffet supper. Most of the foreigners at the guest house had assumed that the interminable preparation of the food that had gone on throughout the day would now culminate in an exotic banquet. Pencastu, released from his throne, had other plans for them. To those in the line-up who voiced surprise at the Big Macs and Kentucky Fried Chicken rushed down from Medan, he explained that the traditional foods they had seen sizzling in the woks over charcoal fires were to be distributed among local households, whose culture although showing signs of some progress still remained at a primitive level.

'You'll be joining us in the Kentucky Fried Chicken, Mr Pencastu?' I asked.

'I sure will. I was hoping some of the heads of households would have showed up too, but they haven't. They're nice guys, but I guess they haven't lived. We're going to try to persuade some of them to dance with their wives later on, but that may not happen either.'

'So you're not a traditionalist?'

'No, sir. That I'm not. I go along with the State philosophy. Part of our responsibility is to educate these people. Take a short walk with them into the future.'

'How about the old-style wedding? Does that fit in?'

'It's part of the deal. "I get a cramp in the ass sitting on a throne all day," I say. "So you gotta do something for me, by which I mean dance once in a while in a civilised style." '

Pencastu had made a start with the discotheque while the foreigners were still picking among the bones of the chicken. The intelligent choice for the heads of households was Country and Western. He had rushed away to bully, and finally persuade, three couples dressed in the style of the last century to climb the restaurant steps and present themselves at the back of the dancing area. Holding each other by the finger tips, with Pencastu running from one couple to the next pouring out instructions, they executed a few shuffling steps before being allowed to escape. He came back, sighing. 'I guess that's enough for one day,' he said. With that,

Country and Western was at an end, and now it was time for the new Springsteen album; the rock thundered, and the foreigners took to the floor. It was a scene of unpremeditated poetry, for spotlights had turned the river below into milk coursing through alabaster banks, and the dancers wore haloes of moths. They had been invaded by innumerable lean dogs, drawn to this spot by the many Kentucky bones awaiting disposal. No-one appeared to have noticed their presence, for it appeared that these long-distance travellers had already acquired the beginnings of oriental indifference.

There was a telephone call with bad news from the Weather Centre in Medan. Rain was on its way, and was to be expected in Bukit Lawang within the hour. But it came sooner. The rockets were sent up, but too late, and their tails were twisted off, and the scintillating explosion at the top of their climb reduced to a few random sparks chased through grey festooning of rain. For the half hour that followed we were prisoners of water and silence, then the flood passed, and Pencastu was with us under a scarlet umbrella. 'Someone let the dogs up to the restaurant,' he said, 'and they went over the place. The mountain men just got here.'

They were standing at the bottom of the steps in water-sodden capes, with a little blood from chewed glass – offered in evidence of serious intentions – trickling down into their thin Mongolian beards. One carried a black cockerel with red wattles and comb. Pencastu said he was going to bite its head off and sew it back but the rain had fouled everything up. 'Something went wrong with the magic. They say if we can fix up some sort of a sacrifice, maybe a couple of hens, they can stick skewers through their cheeks. I might find myself in trouble if I allowed that. The sacrifice, I mean. I'm a little worried as it is. Some of the guys up there are smoking joints.'

A small group of villagers had gathered with water past their ankles, but now they began to wander away, holding mats over their heads. 'Is there anything they can do without a sacrifice?' I asked.

'They can make people believe they're frogs,' Pencastu said. 'If you want they can read your mind. It's not much of a scene. If you cut a cock's head off and sew it on again, that's something else, otherwise it's a disappointment. Hell, this could be falling apart.'

The rain had slackened off. An outburst of cheering overhead greeted 'Out of time' as the music thundered into action again, and there were loud groans as it petered out. The loud crackling indicated that someone was fiddling with the wiring. Rain had diluted the blood on the magical men's chins. They chewed disconsolately and a fresh trickling appeared at the corners of their mouths. A big, wide-eyed American came tumbling down the steps. He threw away a half-smoked joint. 'Holy shit! What's going on?'

Pencastu explained. 'These are mountain men, Mr Boone. They're down here to amuse the party with their tricks, but the rain spoilt the act.'

'What can they do?' Boone asked.

'Read your mind, for example. Maybe tell you what you got in your pocket.'

'That all, for Chrissake?'

'They make people behave like they're frogs.'

'And how does a frog behave?'

'It hops about in the water. It croaks. If it can find any it eats flies.'

'And these people you see around here do that?'

'They sure do, Mr Boone. When our foreign visitors leave us this is a quiet place. It's anything for a laugh. It's a matter of prestige, too. If you can do the frog thing well, your standing goes up.'

'Do they know what they're doing?'

'I haven't tried it personally, but I don't think so.'

'Know what we call that? We call it hypnotism. You heard of hypnotism?'

'I've heard of hypnotism, Mr Boone, but I'm not sure you're right. These guys can cut a chicken's head off and put it back again, and it just gets up and runs about.

'You never saw anything like that, Mr Pencastu, because it's impossible. You just thought you did. That's what hypnotism is about. Many people are hypnotisable. I happen to be someone who isn't. I'd like to show you what I mean. Would you mind asking this guy what he has to do to get me hopping about like a frog.'

Pencastu spoke to the man, who was smiling shyly through the blood. 'He needs you to put out your tongue,' he said.

'Well, OK. I don't want that guy to touch me, that's all.'

'Don't worry Mr Boone, I seen this before, many times. He won't touch you. It's all in the etherial waves. You quite sure you want to mess with this thing?'

'Yeah, of course. I already told you. Hell, I've seen it before and I know how it works too. Tell him I'm sorry to spoil his act.'

'He's to go ahead, then?'

'Sure he's to go ahead.' The tip of Boone's tongue showed through his lips. 'That's fine,' Pencastu said. 'Now take a deep breath and hold it.' The magical man, who was much shorter than Boone, reached up and wagged a blood-smeared forefinger an inch or two from Boone's tongue.

'OK, what goes next?' Boone said. His voice seemed to have thickened.

'Nothing,' Pencastu said. 'That's it. He says to tell you you are a frog.'

'A frog, huh? Like you said.' He began to lower himself over a puddle. 'You want I should croak?'

'You must do what you feel, Mr Boone.'

Boone, who was splashing about in the puddle, produced a belch. The magical man bent down to watch him closely. His two assistants giggled in a nervous, shamefaced way. The thought occurred to me that, spurred on by the cannabis, Boone might be playing a trick on us, or that he had been enlisted by Pencastu as part of the act. 'Is this some sort of a joke?' I asked.

'This is no joke,' Pencastu said. 'If you fed Mr Boone flies right now, he would swallow them down. I just told the man no flies.'

'So what happens now?'

'He'll splash about a bit and then he'll snap out of it. Act like nothing ever happened. Best idea is to go along with him. Ask no questions. If the guy wants to forget it, well, OK.'

Boone dragged himself clear of the puddle and got to his feet. He took off his shirt and wrung it out. A few heavy drops of rain were falling again and he looked up at the sky. The chief magical man, looking a little worried now, spat out blood. The new set to Boone's jaw made him almost unrecognisable. That, and an intercepted side-glance in our direction, spoke of confusion.

There was a sudden clatter of running feet over the boards above us, loud and continuous laughter, then a muddle of shouting, waving figures appeared at the top of the steps.

'More customers for our friends here by the looks of it,' Pencastu said. 'The hash sure doesn't help. Give it another hour or two and they'll all want to be frogs.'

Oriental festivities of these days are designed to prohibit sleep, and peace – as so confidently predicted by Mr Pencastu – returned to Bukit Lawang only at dawn. It was time wasted to go to bed, and with the call to prayer in our ears we set out for Medan, reached in a couple of hours over empty roads.

Here we split up. Gawaine and Robin had decided to use up the last few weeks of their year of freedom in Vietnam in search of the ingredients of adventure that might help see them through the flatlands of computerised living that lay ahead.

I was delighted to be able to contact Claudia by phone in Jakarta and give her the flight number and time of my arrival next day.

EAST TIMOR

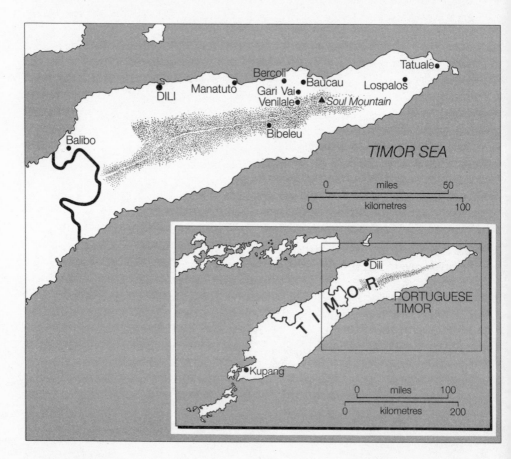

SEVEN

CLAUDIA AWAITED ME at the Jakarta airport, looking, to my relief, little the worse for peregrinations of the kind endured rather by Victorian masochists than the travellers of our day. There had been long gaps in our correspondence, and my suspicions at the time that they were through illness proved right. Inevitably both she and Rod had suffered from malaria in addition to a short list of tropical sicknesses, all exceedingly unpleasant. Such experiences serve only to harden travellers of her kind and I knew that I was in for an interlude of basic accommodation whenever this could be found, of spiders in the thatch and drowned geckos in the water tank, of spiced tea, boiled rice, the absence of bed-springs, and mosquitoes galore.

Her ambition now was to round off her Indonesian year by joining me on a visit to East Timor, which could only be reached via Bali. Our hope had been to make the connection the same day, but we were told at Jakarta this could not be done. We should have to make an overnight stop-off at Bali, said the man at the Garuda counter, and fly out by Merpati next day.

Having been discouraged by the reports of friends who had recently visited this once star attraction of the Indonesian archipelago, I should have been glad to miss this stop-off, but there was nothing for it. There had been six flights from Jakarta alone on the day we arrived, and at Denpasar airport ordeal was by seething crowds, among faces stamped with anxiety and surfeited with predicaments. Eventually we unscrambled our luggage from the carousel's jumble, then joined the long queue at the taxi office where fares had to be paid. There the news was that all hotels in Denpasar were full and the resort at Sanur offered the only hope of beds. Here, where we got in by the skin of our teeth, Claudia found none of the familiar discomforts that would have put her at her ease. It was agreed that we would look round for a derelict losmen next day, but as it turned out these had ceased to exist.

Sanur was a little worse than expected, the whole area having been exposed to the ravages of insensitive development. The situation was summed up by a car service-station two hundred yards down the road from our hotel. They had invested in a splendid gateway salvaged from the ruin of a demolished temple. Beyond the rich grotesqueries of its carving, men smeared all over with oil were hauling up an engine block with a pulley and chain. The hotel had struggled to hold back a little of the past. Wonderful old jungle trees had survived in the garden, thrusting steep-walled flanges supporting their massive trunks deep into surrounding flower beds, and when aware of newly planted saplings in their vicinity, lassoing them with aerial roots in an attempt to choke them, or pelting them with oily, malodorous seeds. Groups of staring youths lounged in the street where vandals had been at a majestic banyan. Notches had been cut all over its wood, 'to remind people of things', we were told.

We were at the Merpati office as soon as it opened next morning in the hope of picking up tickets for that day's flight to East Timor.

Our reception seemed strangely cool – almost to the point of hostility. This in itself seemed extraordinary in Indonesia where the level of politeness maintained in such everyday transactions is very high.

'When do you wish to go?'

'Today if possible.'

He studied us in silence for a moment. By this time East Timor had been open to outsiders for over a year, but few people as we had heard had wished to take advantage of the new freedom, and our enquiry may have been unexpected. He went to the back of the office, spoke into a phone and returned. 'There are no seats,' he said.

The news came as no surprise. 'Are there seats tomorrow?' I asked.

'No,' he said. He shook his head in an emphatic manner. 'Tomorrow the plane is full.'

'Can you put us on the waiting list?'

'The waiting list is full.'

'In that case would it be possible to find out when seats will be available?'

There were signs of impatience. He had been fiddling with a button, which he dropped on the counter and picked up again. A tiny muscle had begun to tug at the corner of his eye. He went back to the phone for a longer conversation than the first, then returned. 'There are seats in eight days,' he said.

'On the fourteenth?'

I was suspicious about the non-availability of seats to an island offering no attractions to the tourist, but there was nothing to do but settle for what was offered. I decided to discuss the situation with the tourist agent in the Bali Beach Hotel, who wrote down our details, went away to make enquiries and came back with the same story as the Merpati man had produced.

The hotel was full of joyous Australian boys who amused themselves by trying to proposition the stony-faced waitresses. The only Indonesian guest introduced himself as Victor Malik, picture editor of a Jakarta magazine. His predicament was similar to our own, for he had been on his way to a rajah's funeral in Sulawesi at which an enormous number of buffaloes were to be sacrificed, only to learn on arrival in Bali that no seat had been booked for him on the Sulawesi plane. Mr Malik took no more pleasure in Sanur than we did. A few moments before he had invited us to join him, the waitress, he said, had been rude to him. He had been served warm beer and, on making the mildest of complaints, the waitress had uttered an insulting epithet in the guttural, low-caste Balinese language, which, as it happened, Malik understood. Describing the incident, the smooth round face crumpled, and he blinked, as if on the verge of tears. 'I am very polite to persons in menial positions,' Malik said. 'It is the first time that one has been rude to me.'

'They're under a lot of pressure here,' I said.

'There is no excuse. I am a polite man. Why should such a person treat me like a dog?'

The waitress came with the replacement beer, and slapped away on her sandals, head averted. A whistle followed her from one of the tables. I had noted the angularity of her features, and the thin, compressed lips. None of the staff of this hotel, nor the youths lounging in the street outside, showed any signs of the demure amiability attributed to the race as depicted.

Malik sipped his beer, and calmed down. 'So what will you do while you are waiting?'

'Is there anywhere we should see?' I asked.

He laughed at the idea of it. 'My friends, you have come too late.' An idea struck him. 'Every morning at Jimbaran the fishing fleet comes from Java. You will think you are at the theatre. Here they don't fish any more so the Javanese people bring them the fish. This is not real. This is from the *Mahabharata*. To see the Javanese fleet – ah! But now they say the Javanese people will stop. Also, if you are in time I don't know, because the people at Jimbaran have sold all the land round the port and the ships cannot come.' His enthusiasm revived. 'How long will you be here? Please find out if the fishing fleet is still coming. I would like to come with you to see this sight if you will let me know.'

Claudia took a more hopeful view of Bali than I. In the previous year she had stayed some weeks in the houses of village people at the far-western tip of the island, and here, beyond the reach of the tourist invasion, she believed there had been little change. Perhaps Jimbaran, reached by a side road on the neck of the Bukit Badung peninsula, had also managed to escape. This I doubted but early next morning we picked up a taxi and set forth in hope.

We were lucky in having found a taxi owned by a driver who not only spoke English, but had taught it in a secondary school. Alec Sueba knew all about Jimbaran, the Javanese fishing fleet and the micro-climate of the port area which made it possible for the ships to discharge their cargoes on the beach whatever the weather. Included in this excursion was a side-trip down the road skirting Benoa bay while awaiting, according to Sueba's weather calculations, the arrival of the Javanese across the peninsula. All the coastal villages reached by this road had sold out to the water-sports industry, beached their fine, rakish ships and left them to rot, fitted all their children out with motor-cycle helmets, dismantled their shrines and rebuilt their houses with breeze-blocks and encircled them with high walls.

We went back to Jimbaran to make sure that we did not miss the great moment of the arrival of the ships. It turned out not to be a port as described, but a beach free of surf and mysteriously protected from winds in its curve of the bay. Five miles away across the isthmus at Benoa we had seen the wind blowing the tops off the waves. Viewed from above, Jimbaran appeared to be lapped by a lake of milk. You could even see the currents showing in the water as delicate blue threads like the veins in a young child's hand, although southwards along the coastline there were breakers under the Bukit Badung cliffs.

Jimbaran village was built in dry woodland and honey-scented scrub at the back of the beach and was quite devoid of water supply. The villagers depended upon rain to grow their sparse crops, and life there, Sueba said, had reached a low ebb after two years when it had hardly rained at all, and now they earned a few rupiah selling firewood, and one or two ill-nourished, long-snouted pigs. To add to their misfortune they had been adopted, said Sueba, by parasitic squirrels, who lived by what they could steal of the fish as soon as it was landed, and pugnacious and thieving crows that lined their nests with what trinkets they could find in the peasants' hovels. 'Surely they could get rid of them,' I said, and Sueba explained why they couldn't. 'They're Buddhists,' he said. 'They must tolerate all forms of life.' It was these people's ruin, he said, that was at the back of the loss of Jimbaran and the banishment from it of the Java fleet that would put an end to the daily pageant. The land here, he told us, had been owned in tiny parcels by numerous families. For some years the developers had been at work on them, prising loose their grip until in the end the last family had given in. All the rest of the isthmus land was now staked out for hotels, and the calm haven of the ships from Java was to be designated a water recreation park.

We went back to the shore again where at this moment the awaited ships, well separated and line-abreast, were squeezing through over the horizon between the whiteness of sky and sea. For a short time they remained ghostly – almost transparent – before the brilliant colours came through the ivory mist.

A crowd of some hundreds lined the beach, standing in entranced ranks to watch the approach of the seven ships. Nobody moved, the silence – as if for a religious occasion – was absolute. The beach was overhung with great leaves and the fluttering shadows of large bird-kites with operable flapping wings flown by the village boys. The boys sometimes made them swoop menacingly low over the heads of the crowd, but no-one paid any attention, Distantly, sails were furled, and the boats came in slowly and in what looked like strict order – the scarlet flagship with carved prow rearing almost to the height of the masts in the centre, the others spaced on each side at intervals of about fifty yards. Each ship was painted a different colour: Venetian red, emerald, lemon, ultramarine, gamboge, maroon. They were afire with burnished brass, and the glitter and glint of the tools of the sea put out on display. Brand new and meticulously woven baskets holding the catch had been stacked on the decks. Both the fishermen lined up in the boats, and those who waited on the beach to wade into the water and carry the catch ashore, wore ceremonial turbans. The anchors went down, and with that the scene came to life. A moment before, we could hear the crows chattering and the insects ticking away in the bushes; now there was a great human bustling noise. The turban-wearing unloaders waded in pairs to the boats, picked up the baskets slung from poles, and carried them to the shore. As soon as they were on the beach they put down their baskets and bowed to the sea. First the ceremonial baskets, and then the crates holding the less important catch, were brought up the beach, and a miscellany of unsaleable fish discarded everywhere. Children and old people were waiting for these, and when they had taken whatever they fancied it was the turn of the squirrels that came, dodging cautiously, then sprinting down the sand to snatch up what was left.

Rich volcanic soil was the wealth of Bali, and the successful distribution of this wealth created an equable and interesting society providing an enormous range of satisfactions for the whole population. In almost every village where two or three crops of rice a year can be grown there are a great number of pleasurable ways of occupying spare time. Hardly a week passes without a temple festival, a wedding, or a spectacular cremation to be attended in the vicinity. Balinese life is a web of social obligation, most of it enjoyable, and theatrical entertainments, largely confined to cities in the West, are a regular ingredient here of the rural life. The people of Jimbaran have been debarred by barren earth and their consequent penury from these organised pleasures. This scene provided a sort of ready-made substitute, and they watched with enthralled, even reverent attention all the details of what elsewhere would have been seen as a market operation, but here had been transformed into a performance. This was a daily involvement with the drama of life as played in the outside world, and an hour or two's release from the boredom of mere existence.

'What's going to happen to these people?' I asked.

'They may go to become transmigrants,' Sueba said.

'Would this be a good thing for them?'

He thought it would. What had they to hope for? Here in Bali peasants like this at the end of their tether would hang on to their patch of land whatever the misery they lived in. Now they would be forced to pack up and go. It was the best thing that could happen to them.

'And you think that whatever they find in Kalimantan or Irian Jaya is going to be better?'

'In such places they will quickly find work. Here there is no work and no money. There, they will be paid wages. They will fill their children's stomachs.'

There was a café on a headland overlooking Nusa Dua which was just about to become an eight-hotel complex (the biggest in Bali), and here we stopped to drink tea and discuss such matters.

Sueba expressed his views with such unusual frankness by Indonesian standards that I wondered whether he believed polite evasions were unnecessary because we were foreigners. He was pro-government, slightly reactionary. Besides producing cash incomes, he said, transmigration expanded the individuals' horizons. People wrote glowing letters home. He added with a touch of cynicism that they were obliged to do that. Opportunities were better, he thought, in the outer islands. Two policemen friends had volunteered for service in the carnage of East Timor, and had encountered no problem in imposing the national will in that unruly island. He was now on a subject carefully avoided by most of his fellow countrymen, but Sueba plunged ahead. A drawback, as one of his friends had explained, about doing one's bit in the police rather than the army was that the police were not housed in secure barracks, but billeted in villages where it was to be assumed that the whole population was hostile. The nice man next door who smiled and bowed every time you met, and presented you with a pot of stew made from a partridge he had snared, could be a bloodthirsty terrorist, capable of crawling through your bedroom window at night and slicing your head off as you slept. Soldiers were safe in their camps, with their enemies miles away in the mountains, and when they got the order to attack they went up there and killed them. After that they could relax again.

'And what about the nice man with the partridge stew next door?'

'Ah, the civilian suspects,' Sueba said. Two children playing nearby had come up and planted themselves in front of us. He told them in a kindly way that it was rude to stare, then gave them a wrapped-up cube of sugar apiece that had come with the tea. 'Well, in this case,' he said, 'the civilian suspects had to go. Too many of our people were dying. I think if we had been policemen, you or I would do the same.'

It was in course of these discussions that an idea began to take shape. All the Indonesians I had so far met avoided comment on anything that might be said even vaguely to touch on politics. Topics were invariably bland, and this may have been the case even among themselves. Not only politics but all controversial matters were left out of conversations, just as my little booklet on Indonesian protocol said they should be. In the company of young people one talked about celebrities, music, fashions, holidays, films, sport. The older people with families were obsessed with their children, and seemed invariably to be photographers who spent time looking at each other's snaps. My protocol book emphasised that Indonesians of all ages liked to give play to their sense of humour and much enjoyed jokes – the cornier the better. The ones I met did not seem to be greatly impressed by what was going on in the world. Most of the newspapers were very provincial indeed.

With Sueba it was evident from the first moment that these limitations did not apply. Being a taxi driver in a place like Sanur, he probably spent most of his waking day in the company of foreigners, which had clearly taken effect. He would have noticed that foreigners came out with what they felt like saying, and Sueba did this too. In any case he had nothing to lose. The foreigners were isolated from the Indonesians. They were here today and gone tomorrow. When he had told us about police killings in East Timor I was staggered and I was quite sure that he would never have taken an Indonesian fare into his confidence in such a way.

What had occurred to me was that this extraordinary frankness might provide the opportunity to learn something of the facts of the great Indonesian blood-letting of 1965–6, described by the CIA as one of the greatest mass-killings of this century, with a cost in human lives comparable to the slaughters of Pol Pot, yet so promptly and efficiently hushed up that few foreigners – even those who have visited Bali – have ever heard of it, and in Bali the subject remains taboo. Although the exact number of victims will never be known, the total number throughout the islands may have exceeded one million, and it is supposed that in Bali up to 100,000 were done away with. This holocaust was provoked by the refusal of President Sukarno – himself an ardent empire-builder – to fall into line with US strategy in the Cold War, and his eccentric determination to remain on good terms both with the USSR and China. This was at a time when the United States was dangerously embroiled in the Vietnam war, and from the evidence it is likely that the CIA masterminded his dismissal and replacement by General Suharto, of whose wholehearted collaboration there could be no doubt. There followed the great witch-hunt through the island for communists, atheists and such non-political minorities as the Chinese, who on the whole were successful in business and therefore generally disliked.

As I had suspected, Sueba had not the slightest objection to telling us about the massacre. Where was he at the time? Teaching at the school in his old village. I asked him if he would consider taking us to his village, and he said, 'Why not? Whenever you're ready.' Next morning he called for us at the hotel, and we set off.

Desa Pusang was down one of many narrow side roads feeding into the countryside from the main north–south highway from Denpasar to Kubutambahan. Leaving the main road we seemed to slip back instantly into the past century. There was no traffic, no dust; there were lots of holes in the road, and it was very quiet. The village was full of pinkish light reflected from many ornamental brick surfaces. It was scented with the water gurgling and gushing everywhere in ditches and conduits down the steeply inclined street to an overbrimming central tank guarded by gambolling stone lions. We saw courtyards full of images and doves, an ancient diaphanous man leading a vast white ox by the ear, another at a plough followed by ducks, paddies like slivers of mirror-glass, a corner of the grey skirt of the distant volcano of Batur. People had gathered socially down by the tank and we noted instantly that family resemblances between one another were very great. Fighting cocks in their cages had been left here, where they would be stimulated, Sueba said, by what was going on around them.

'These people are ruled by an all-powerful village council, the banjar,' Sueba told us. 'It keeps them in the old ways – nothing can be done unless it says, "OK. Go ahead." Only a single family has been allowed television and the number of neighbours who can watch the programme is strictly controlled. The government ordered them to open a factory, but it makes nothing but concrete shrines.'

The old man with the ox had caught up with us and the ox had decided to go no further. The old man was pleading with it and the bystanders were laughing.

'They have a strange belief,' Sueba said, 'they believe they have already reached perfection, so it is pointless to attempt improvement. All old men die at the age of sixty-five. It is the custom, so they refuse to go on longer. Only one thing has changed since I was a boy. In those days people died of cholera. Now they die of cancer.'

A child tried to force a handful of flowering weeds between the ox's lips, and the animal shook it away. This caused more laughter, and the child burst into tears and was comforted by a passing woman.

'They're so gentle, aren't they?' Claudia said.

'Yes, but they killed each other,' Sueba told her.

'It's hard to believe.'

'They were forced to. If it's another man's death or your own, even a gentle person will choose. The government told them the communists would take their religion away. That made it easier to kill them, but really they had no choice.'

Sueba led the way to the square, which was small and intimate in the Balinese way, with the banjar building and the fateful *kulkul* hanging in its tower, the ancient Founder's Temple and other buildings devoted to religious cults.

'I was in school when the kelian who is head of the banjar sent someone to beat on the kulkul to call the men to the square,' Sueba said. 'Knowing what was to happen, I felt myself begin to tremble all over. I sent the children home, closed the school, and followed the other men out into the square where we saw the soldiers and the Javanese men they brought with them waiting for us.'

'So it didn't come as a surprise?'

'No-one was surprised. We knew that the soldiers had gone to other villages to kill the communists.'

'And you thought the same thing would happen here.'

'Everybody had ceased to think. All we felt was fear. The fear was so great that all work had stopped in the fields, and the animals had been left to stray.'

'I can't imagine communists in a place like this,' I said.

'They had no real idea what communism was. All our people loved President Sukarno, and a lot of them thought he was a communist. There were some Christians who thought that the initials PKI really stood for Partai Kristen Indonesia – the Indonesian Christian Party – so they joined. These are simple people.'

'Why didn't they try to get away?'

'It was useless. In Bali there is no hiding place. If a man tries to escape he is certain to be caught, and that will be taken as proof he is a communist. The only thing is to stay and hope the priest will say this man is going to the temple every day.'

'So what happened?'

'The kelian ordered all the women and children to stay in their houses, then a Javanese man who was with the officer read names from a list.'

'Of communists?'

'And atheists. People who were not certified in the banjar as members of any religion. The kelian called out these people and the Javanese men who were with the soldiers roped them in lines. The officer said to the villagers, "These are your enemies. I call upon you to fight for your religion." He told us to put cigarettes in their mouths because they could not use their hands, but when we did this the cigarettes fell out again because they were too afraid. The officer was angry because nobody wanted to have anything to do with killing these men. He asked the kelian for lists of members of the Hindu or Buddhist religions. These were exempt because they must not take life. I was on the list as a Buddhist. All the other village men were given pangahs or clubs and told to kill the communists.'

'And they were prepared to kill the people they had grown up with?'

'They knew that otherwise they must die themselves.'

'So they killed them.'

'Yes, they did that. It was very difficult for them because village people are not practised to kill. One man fainted and a man from Java killed him with a club. Some old men were too weak even to kill a man tied in ropes, so the men from Java came to help them. One of these old men went home and never took food again. He starved to death.'

So this was the end product of the secret accords between Jakarta and Washington. Things had not been going so well as hoped in the war to contain communism. Those ancient adversaries, China and Vietnam, had been suspected of drifting together, and a precautionary blood-letting among those who had opposed the new president Suharto in East Java, Bali and the poverty-stricken outer islands of Indonesia might not be a bad thing. But it had to be discreet. The army officer ordered a severed head to be placed in the middle of Desa Pusang's square and left there for one day, with the warning that if it were removed the village would be burned down. In the meanwhile the bodies of the communists were to be hidden in the houses, and at night weighed down with stones and thrown into rivers or the Danan Batur lake. In no circumstances were they to be cremated or buried.

The story of the hauntings that followed attracted more attention in the foreign press than the great massacre itself.

'When did the hauntings start?' I asked Sueba.

'They started immediately. The day after the killings and as soon as the head had been taken away from the square, the ghosts came to the village.'

'Did you actually see them?'

'No, they were invisible, but they were everywhere. Wherever I went there was always a ghost at my back, in the house, the washing place, the fields. The ghosts were waiting for the ceremonies to be made, but the government said that it would cause too much anger and the ceremonies must be delayed ten years.'

'Which must have made things worse.'

'People suffered from depression, loss of memory, inexplicable fear, failure of virility, even speech. No girl in these villages could marry while the family was in mourning, and mourning also lasts ten years. The families of those whose bodies were never found could not go to the temple until the ceremonies were performed. Some families threw themselves into the Batur volcano.

'So when did all this come to an end?' I asked him.

'On New Year's Day nineteen seventy-six,' he said. 'On that day the Ngerupuk ceremony asking the ghosts to depart was performed by licence of the government. Next came the Nyepi, when all activity is stopped. Everyone must stay in the same place in his house without moving, speaking or eating, only meditating continually for one whole day. After that, when night comes, Ogoh-Ogoh, figure of the evil spirit, is carried round all the streets and presented to every house, and then burned. Next day of this year the greatest sacrifice of animals ever known took place on the island. They were buried by the thousand in the villages and thrown into Lake Batur and the sea. After that we made a feast of reconciliation. To pay for the animals and the ceremonies many families sold their lands, lost all their possessions and went bankrupt.'

'And having done all this,' I asked, 'did you get rid of the ghosts?'

'No,' he said. 'Now there are few left to trouble us, but some are still there whispering into the ears at night, "When will my ashes be in the cemetery of the Temple of the Dead?" '

EIGHT

BACK IN SANUR we made final preparations for East Timor, having little idea of what awaited us on arrival. I knew that police scrutiny was likely to be intense, and a further complication was introduced by a strong and active military presence. A friend who had recently visited the island spoke of the near-impossibility of travel except by short-distance village bus, and then under surveillance. Accommodation outside the capital, Díli, was reported as virtually impossible to find.

Our journey aroused mixed feelings and some re-examination of its scope and aims. We had both been deeply concerned by accounts of the sufferings of the ordinary people of this ex-Portuguese colony. Their long-entertained hopes of self-determination when colonial rule came to an end were crushed by the Indonesian invasion of 1975. Was there any place among the pleasant commonplaces of travel for a description of what we could contrive to see of the state of an island and its people, one third of whom had been massacred during sixteen years of occupation? We believed that there was. Few acts in the violent history of recent years can have exceeded the ferocity of the Indonesian attack, launched two days after a meeting in Jakarta between Suharto and President Ford, in the company of Henry Kissinger – dubbed by the State Department at the time as 'the big wink'. Earlier in the week the Australian Prime Minister Gough Whitlam, also closely concerned in what was about to happen, was asked what he proposed to do should the invasion take place? To this his answer was 'absolutely nothing'. An international coincidence of interests was thus proclaimed, and the stage set for the takeover whatever the costs might be.

The Indonesian invasion of East Timor had long been anticipated. In April 1975 an Australian friend, Jill Jolliffe, arrived in Díli as a freelance journalist to cover operations expected to be timed for the autumn of that year. The character of such an invasion was to be foreseen by the cynicism as well as brutality of some preliminary surprise attacks launched from across the frontier against villages in East Timor. Fortunately for her, Jill declined the invitation of a party of two British, two Australians and one New Zealand journalist to film the fighting in the vicinity of Balibo, where they took over an empty house, painted an Australian flag on the front and set up their cameras. Their murder by Indonesian parachutists an hour or two later was to inspire a ghoulish charade. The journalists were stripped, redressed in Portuguese uniforms and propped up behind machine guns with cartridge cases scattered all round. The first official account of the episode was that they had been combatants; this was followed by a version describing them as Australian communists impelled to join in the war. Later they were to become bona fide journalists once again, who had simply perished in the heavy cross-fire. Inexplicably their bodies were thrown into a blazing building and in this burned to ashes which were duly handed over to their embassies in Jakarta. Neither the British nor Australian governments showed interest in pursuing investigations into these deaths.

With this curtain-raiser Indonesia left no doubt in any mind as to the character of the war about to be unleashed. In the first week in December warnings went out from Jakarta giving all foreigners notice to leave the country within five days. Compliance was immediate and complete, the only person refusing evacuation being Reuters' correspondent, Roger East, who, shaking his colleagues by the hand, announced his intention of seeing the thing through.

On 8 December Indonesian paratroopers, trained in the ethics of total war, dropped from the skies in Díli. Roger East alone remained to tell the world of the carnage that followed. But nothing more was heard of him for several years until a refugee from East Timor who turned up in Lisbon reported having seen him dragged, spitting at his captors at the end of a rope, to the sea-front where the Indonesians were settling accounts with methodical efficiency with all those, including the whole of the town's Chinese population, who had given cause for offence. Such public executions, which went on for a number of days, were formal in style and invested with a macabre theatricality.

At 2 p.m. 59 men, both Chinese and Timorese, were brought on to the wharf . . . These men were shot one by one, with the crowd, believed amounting to 500, being ordered to count. The victims were ordered to stand on the edge of the pier facing the sea, so that when they were shot their bodies fell into the water. Indonesian soldiers stood by and fired at the bodies in the water in the event that there was any sign of life.

Earlier in the day, at 9 a.m., a smaller group, many of them women with their children, had been executed in a similar way. An eye-witness testified: 'The Indonesians tore the crying children from their mothers and passed them back to the crowd. The women were then shot one by one, with the onlookers being ordered by the Indonesians to count.'

This was the holocaust into which the imprudent Roger East disappeared. It was claimed that by the time the town's occupation was complete, 80 per cent of its male population, along with many women and children, had met violent deaths.

The plane for East Timor was small and austere, and although this flight had been said to be constantly overbooked there were a number of vacant seats. There was something about the passengers that it was carrying, too, that struck us as different from the assortment of holiday makers and businessmen normally encountered on such internal flights. Indonesian travellers are notably sociable and show eagerness to engage the stranger in the next seat in politely trivial conversation. This time we found ourselves in a plane-load of loners. Where there were empty seats, papers were in some cases spread over them by a youngish, well dressed man who worked on them assiduously through the flight. No foreigners had joined this trip. The only women passengers were three nuns, bent over what we supposed to be breviaries. There were no children. Already, with East Timor two hours away, something of its spirit, we felt, had touched us.

I had been given a copy of notes made by a friend who had undertaken this journey three months earlier in the year. He had stayed in the capital of Díli at the Hotel Turismo, to which all foreigners were directed, and it was an experience he had not particularly enjoyed.

For most of the time I was not aware of being under personal surveillance except when I was in the Hotel Turismo. I assumed that my possessions would be searched at some point. They were searched, in fact, on the third day, while I was travelling to Atambua. As far as I know only one document was taken . . . It was confirmed to me on my last morning that my room had been searched by the army . . . This was one of the occasions when the danger that accompanies any dissident activity became apparent . . . it was suggested that a film might have been taken.

I did not meet Carlos, who is reputed to be the hotel's chief spy, until the night before I left. He looked the picture of a snout – dark glasses, very curious and accommodating – I wonder if there is not a more important and more subtle figure as well . . . It is possible that I was followed more effectively, taken in hand all day by a man who was on the same bus as I was to Ermera. I caused him to hitch through the rain and walk back . . . He never let me out of his sight.

By all accounts, few people would have wished to choose the Turismo for a holiday break. Francois Luizet of *Le Figaro* arrived at Díli in 1989, shortly after East Timor had been nominally re-opened to the outside world, and seems to have been startled by his welcome: ' "Bom dia." My hello to the reception at the Hotel Turismo brings conversation to a halt. Silence. No sound except the whining of the air conditioner and the cries of caged parrots. A dwarf rushes towards me and says, "No-one speaks Portuguese any more." He's trembling. They all seem terrorized, paralysed. "Listen," the dwarf whispers, "there are spies everywhere. I can't talk. I might get a bullet in the head." The forces of occupation are explicit. "Don't talk to foreigners, or expect trouble." '

The US Ambassador's stay a year later was also less than a success. He was there to enquire about a number of arrests following the Pope's visit a month or two before. Once again there was trouble with students. They were there to call for UN intervention in East Timor and occupied a balcony from which a number were thrown by the police into the patio below, some being seriously injured with the possiblity of two hushed-up deaths.

I handed the notes to Claudia. 'There's something for you here about the town,' I told her. She settled to read the marked passages.

When I first walked round Díli I was struck by its dilapidated, untended appearance. I was a little shocked by my reaction. What had I expected? If I picture Díli now, I see images of neglect and poverty overlaid by rows of white government offices and barracks busy with young men in camouflage ... It was Díli's public spaces that are neglected. The pavements are full of holes. The draincovers have gone. The seafront is entirely undeveloped. Horses and goats browse the grass outside the Bishop's residence up to the edge of the unswept beach littered with tin cans and garbage, where landing craft from the invasion still rust in the water. Pigs trot up and down the road in front of the new cathedral. Cows graze next to a barracks.

Claudia handed the paper back. 'Good photography?' she wanted to know.

'Possibly. In a way. Of course they might object.'

Many months of travel in Indonesia had turned Claudia into a good mixer, and when I glanced up from my book shortly after this it came as no surprise to see her sitting with the nuns engaged in a spirited discussion. We were out of touch for the rest of the flight, and by the time we reached Díli it was quite clear that they were all bosom friends. It turned out that two of the nuns were among those running an orphanage in the mountains in the east of the island for children whose parents had been killed in the invasion and its aftermath. They had been to Bali to meet the third who had travelled from Rome to join the orphanage. Two of the nuns were Italian and the third was a Filipina, and two things struck me about this trio. One was how tiny they were and the other their incessant bubbling high spirits.

Landing at Díli airport, we found that there were no taxis in sight. All the waiting cars were there to collect the serious men we had travelled with, and we had posted ourselves somewhat disconsolately by our baggage when our three nuns sprinted into sight. A truck carrying yet more Salesian sisters had arrived to pick them up and, putting aside all our protests, they pounced on our bags and hauled them off to be loaded up with their own. By chance they were bound for the intimidating Turismo, where a room had been booked for the nun from Rome. The others were to pass the night at the Bishop's residence next door, and the following morning the party would leave for the orphanage in the mountains. They urged us to visit them there, and as much as we should have been glad to accept this offer on the spot, East Timor seemed hardly the place where such spontaneous visits were to be lightly contemplated.

The Turismo was yet another confirmation of my view that in travels of the more outlandish kind reality rarely corresponds to previous images formed in the mind. At first glance it could almost have been a somewhat run-down English country house in a large garden that had been kept under control but no more. A few wilted blooms showed on the bushes at the pathside leading to the door. The people at the reception seemed pleasantly ordinary. There was no sign of the probable spy with eye-shades encountered by my friend, nor did appearances suggest the hotel's involvement in sinister events. Otherwise it was seedy in a way it was bound to be, located as it was in the midst of a warlike situation that had continued for so many years. The decorative local woods incorporated in much of its structure had seen no polish for a decade and a half, and the carpet covering the wide staircase had long since been ripped away to reveal cracks which harboured the occasional spider. The stairs led to our rooms on a gallery overlooking the patio in Portuguese style, onto which the students were reported to have been thrown. The rooms were clean but dark and the air-conditioning grumbling softly did little to influence the stuffiness. Crossing the floor provoked a crackling from the loose floor tiles underfoot. The nun from Rome, deposited here, had instantly vanished to be seen no more that day, and although one or two depressed-looking individuals mooched glumly about the place, there was nothing to suggest that any of these were hotel guests.

We seated ourselves in the large but empty restaurant, and now the urgent question posed itself – which language was it to be? My Portuguese, learned twenty-two years before, in readiness for an expedition to Brazil, was ragged indeed, but the result of a three-month crash-course in Indonesian Bahasa was worse. My friend's notes had suggested that the choice of Portuguese might give rise to a suspicion of an unwelcome partisanship, and this seems to have been the *Figaro* man's experience. Nevertheless the waiter, an obvious Timorese, looked pleasant enough. I took the risk and believed that I detected faint indications of pleasure and surprise. The service was rapid, the fish excellent and the waiter's guarded geniality unflagging.

Later, a walk along the seafront followed where a row of beached craft had ploughed ashore sixteen years before. Some of them had become homes, in one case with a superstructure drooping ragged thatch over the rust. This, profiled against the hard, white tropical sea, in some way displayed a brand of desolation that no terrestrial building, however shattered, could have matched. Scattered for a couple of hundred yards along the beach, there was something in this delicate pattern of destruction recalling the work of some tribal blacksmith, of iron beaten and twisted into a decoration. Here, where the crowd assembled in clean shirts and well-brushed hair, and the smartly turned-out officer raised his stick like a conductor's baton to time the falling of bodies toppled into the water, a memorial will someday be raised. Now there is nothing, incredibly enough, but an 'Integration Monument' and an unused miniature children's park. The setting is Australoid: thin, wiry grass over earth polished by erosion, trees with leaves like arrow points, offering little shade. The children of families who had colonised the invasion hulks scrape in the sand along the shore for molluscs and chase through the underbrush on dry land after huge edible crickets. These people have the curly hair of some aboriginal island-strain, and they watched us as we passed with wide, incredulous eyes. It was a scene, said Claudia, that cried out loud for photography, and it was decided to return with her camera an hour or so before sunset, when the light would be at its best.

A problem now arose. Díli was a place of truly amazing old taxis. We spotted one which was not merely the result of obvious cannibalism but was composed roughly of two halves of different makes miraculously welded together. With island travel in view, I spoke to one of the drivers, once again unintentionally currying favour with my bad Portuguese, learning from him that he was not permitted to leave the capital, and that it was difficult to do so other than by bus. In the various trips into the countryside made by my friend he had always done this returning to Díli every night. He had been furnished with the addresses of various Portuguese priests in country towns, and so was I, but the impression that I got from his notes was that he was constantly aware of proving an embarrassment to them. His conversation with one of them he described as 'banal', and in reality, when every movement this good man made was certain to have been watched, and every visitor to him seen as a potential suspect, it was hard to see how such discussions could have been otherwise. The procedure to be observed by the traveller leaving Díli was to inform the Turismo of his destination, and when he arrived at this he was under obligation to report his presence to the local police. It had been suggested that we might be able to see two priests based in Díli itself, or seek a meeting with Bishop Belo, head of the Catholic Church in East Timor, but it was evident that even in the capital, where foreigners still remained conspicuous in the extreme, such visits might be unwelcome.

Even by the end of the first day, the feeling grew that a stay in Díli might not only be unprofitable, but uncomfortable. Shortly before dusk, as arranged, we set out on our photographic expedition, which from Claudia's point of view was highly successful, through the dramatic enhancement of the invasion's aftermath by an exceptionally splendid sunset in its rear. Having dealt with that we continued our walk towards the wharf, noting with the onset of night how rare and distant the town's lights appeared to be. Claudia said, 'I think we're being followed.' I glanced over my shoulder and said, 'I think you're right.' A moment before we had been walking in a vast seashore emptiness, and now, fifteen yards back, a dark figure trailed us on soft-soled shoes. 'He must have sprung up out of the ground,' I said. 'Maybe he was hiding in one of the boats.'

'What do we do about it?' Claudia wanted to know.

'Stop and wait for him,' I said. 'He'll have to pass.'

And this, without slowing down, he did. A few yards further on he crossed the road and disappeared among some darkening trees.

We turned back towards the hotel, showing the only light in this part of the town. 'Is this going to happen to us every time we go out?' she asked.

By 6.45, with the implacable fall of night, we found ourselves virtually confined to the Turismo's dim interiors, its silence, and the exhausted tropical odours breathed in from its garden. The weak strip-lighting made reading impossible. The patio area was full of mosquitoes, and those that had found their way into the bedrooms could only be defeated by lightning up a Moon Tiger – said to be bad for the health. It was an environment that fostered an unhopeful frame of mind, best countered by giving in and going early to bed.

Everyone is awake – gratefully – at dawn in such places, in preparation for whatever the day has in store. In this case there was a lively commotion round the hotel's entrance, where the two nuns who had spent the night in the Bishop's house had arrived, escorted by various friends from his household, to collect the sister from Italy. The truck stood at the gate and her baggage was being loaded on – an operation that produced the maximum of scuttling activity among all concerned. Watching this from the supine background of the lobby – these taut, purposeful, starched little figures – I was suddenly aware of an inexcusable personal inertia. At that moment, Paola, in charge, coping with everything, signing papers at the reception, checking that nothing had been overlooked, spotted and hailed us with a flood of cheerful Italian, alternating with a translation into English. 'So you want to change your minds, eh? You coming with us? You want me to, I tell these people you come along with us to Venilale.'

'But can we? I mean, would they allow it?'

'Sure they would. I tell them you stay with us. We sign papers for you. It is OK.'

Claudia and I exchanged cheerful glances. 'We'd like to do that very much,' I said.

We went up to get our bags. One thing was worrying Claudia – the state of her travel-stained clothing that had seen so many miles of mountains, jungles and swamps. She went off for five minutes and reappeared wearing a long white dress brought along for such an occasion, which had been crushed away for many months in the bottom of her rucksack. At one point a biro had leaked in a pocket, leaving a stain that could be lightened but never quite removed. The dress was patterned with innumerable creases, yet Sister Paola viewed it with admiration. 'Va benissimo,' she said. 'Tomorrow we iron. Is very good.'

With huge relief we threw our bags into the back of the truck and settled ourselves with the newly arrived Maria Letitzia and the East Timor veteran Sister Olive from the Philippines. It now turned out Maria Letitzia was not from Rome, but Naples, where I had had the good fortune to spend a war year, and had picked up some Italian with a marked Neapolitan accent. She was amazed and delighted to listen once again to the familiar sing-song in Díli of all places.

In the morning Díli was different, reduced to a false normality of boxy, half-finished new buildings, a non-functional traffic light, roadside mechanics patching fresh rubber on to worn-out car tyres, and a new store with a garish façade. Sister Olive, laughing, translated the notice: *Grand Opening Tomorrow*, but blinds of dust shone in the slanting sun all over the window, and it was clear that the grand opening remained far away. This was a city still grievously sick, although it was hard in these prosaic settings to believe in a commonplace of mass-murder committed to numbers.

We rattled past a church with a black line of elderly people facing it on their knees in the street. There were women in widow's weeds, and one old man seemed swathed in a shroud. They were rocking backwards and forwards, with a bell bucketing overhead, and a soldier in camouflage watching and leaning on his gun. At the very moment of our passing something went on inside the church that set off a quavering outcry. Sister Olive smiled affectionately. 'The worship of the common people of East Timor is very theatrical,' she said.

'Devout Christians,' I said.

She shook her head, smile undiminished. 'This is something I believed when I came here. Nothing could be further from the truth. They keep the Commandments, they pray, they attend mass, fast, give alms when they have anything to give, but their Christianity is skin deep. Underneath, they are animists. They worship a cockerel. There is a village where we are going where they worship a kind of worm.'

Didn't this come as a great disappointment? Claudia wanted to know.

For a moment I thought Sister Olive would burst into laughter. 'Not at all. These people are godly in a truly religious sense. We have learned to co-exist with their animism. Next week there is a church festival in Venilale, and if you are with us you will see the shaman performing the cockerel dance in front of Bishop Belo.'

'Incredible.'

'He has ten boy assistants who dance with him. In the Tetum language they call them the Cockerel's Children. It's something you must see. After the dance they come to the church.' She was actually happy to be able to present us with this picture. After our previous experiences of missionaries at work among primitive peoples we were astonished.

'We see the shaman as a force for good,' Sister Olive said. 'Out in the country where we are there aren't any doctors. Only us and the shaman. We work together. If people feel happier with traditional medicine they go to him. We hand out malaria pills. We give the shaman Nivaquine for his malaria. It has to be done on the quiet so as not to hurt his pride. "Take two a week," we tell him. "Just for luck." '

There were forty miles of coast between Díli and Manatuto and all of it deserted. It was open, deforested country offering no hiding place for the defenders from the pounding of naval guns. Once there had been fishing villages along this beach but there was no sign of them now apart from the occasional timbers of a boat, half-digested by sand.

Turning inland where the road twisted up through the hills overlooking the sea, cultivation of any kind had long ceased and the scene had returned to an aloof primeval emptiness. Nothing grew but an imposing native eucalyptus with trunk and branches polished like ivory soaring up from the smooth, sun-cropped grass. They were widely separated in a landscape with the barren allure and infeasibility of a de Chirico, even a Dali: the ivory of the trees against the brown wash of the grass, a scrawl of beach strewn with the boats' blackened timbers, a grey, overheated sky. The 'Final Cleansing' was the Indonesian government's term for what they hoped were to be the terminal episodes of their war, and it seemed likely that this area had been cleansed.

After Manatuto came Baucau, one of the most disturbing places in the world. Baucau had been the administrative centre of the government forces deployed against the turbulent eastern end of the island, a dishevelled town full of barracks and interrogation centres with high, windowless walls and electrified fences. Baucau had been the end of the road for so many real and assumed supporters of Fretilin, the resistance movement. Distraught wives searching in other locations for vanished husbands and sons were often turned away with the macabre jest, 'He's gone to Baucau to finish his education,' and with that they understood that their quest was at an end. A manual captured by the Fretilin entitled 'Established Procedure for Interrogation of Prisoners' describes the everyday routines of this place and instils a note of caution.

Hopefully, interrogation accompanied by the use of violence will not take place except in certain circumstances when the person being interrogated is having difficulty in telling the truth ... If it proves necessary to use violence make sure there are no people around ... to see what is happening, so as not to arouse people's antipathy. Avoid taking photographs showing torture in progress (people being photographed at times when they are being subjected to electric current, when they have been stripped naked, etc.). It is better to make attractive photographs such as shots taken while eating together with the prisoner or shaking hands with those who have just come down from the bush. If necessary the interrogation should be repeated over and over again.

The most sinister of all hotels is a short distance away, at the entrance to the town; a fun-fair structure painted orange with chromium trimmings, which it is impossible to miss. It is the only hotel in the east of the island deemed suitable for the reception of foreigners, but as part of it is used as a detention centre to cope with any exceptional overflow of prisoners, there have been complaints of sleepless nights from the occasional journalist lodged there.

At this point the road branched through forested mountains to the south, and after a 25-mile easy climb, we drove into Venilale. Instantly we were in a different world. At an altitude perhaps of 3,000 feet the tropics had been excluded. This we instantly realised was a redoubt of Portugal enshrining the nostalgia of men whose fathers or grandfathers, if not they themselves, had come from some calm and melancholic village in Alentejo or Tras os Montes in search of a fortune to be accumulated in a comfortable way. Venilale, in a subtle fashion, had distanced itself from the East. It was prim, clean, pastel-shaded and devoid of noise. Old men in dark clothes were strolling quietly down the street, not to go anywhere but because it was the custom to make an appearance at that time of day. There were no cars to be seen but a man drove by in a black tumbril drawn by a sprightly horse. An authentic Portuguese house, with ceramic tiles and embellishments of carved wood, had survived whatever had happened to the town, and a man raised himself from the russet gloom of the verandah to lift his hat as we passed. One could almost imagine a tang of the Atlantic in the fresh mountain wind.

The low, breeze-block administration building of the orphanage was located in the centre of the town, and Sister Paola took us there and found us a room. A number of young Timorese girls were in the first stages of their midday meal when we arrived, and it came as a surprise that the nuns should have raised no objection to Portuguese songs sung between mouthfuls of pasta. These aspirants were almost painfully polite. One was detailed to bring us soft drinks, and having bowed to us on serving them she turned round to bow for a second time before leaving the room.

A Sister Marlene from the Philippines showed us the town and the orphanage. Much of Venilale was now open space. There was a brand-new church at the end of the town, and clustered nearby a group of original buildings in damaged condition. Principal among these was what appeared at a distance as a Roman ruin, but proved to be the Portuguese school, built in 1905 in classic style. This, imposingly sited on high ground, and reached by a monumental staircase, managed despite bomb damage to retain considerable dignity, and fostered a certain theatricality in its vicinity by people's habit of placing themselves on the steps in gloomy contemplation of their surroundings. At the moment of our arrival one elderly man was standing alone, one arm thrown across his left breast, lips moving soundlessly, and staring out over the valley. At our approach he bowed and I bowed in return. Behind us, a few steps further down, a boy, also alone, plucked desultory chords on his guitar.

The orphans were housed a few yards away in a species of barracks built on the edge of a steep drop into the valley. There were 200 of them, boys and girls in separate dormitories with bunk beds, the youngest a boy of two, and the oldest boys and girls of twelve. They were looked after by four Tetum women, said the sister, and many suffered from both tuberculosis and malaria, the tuberculosis patients being served their food on green plates.

We asked Sister Marlene if the large number of children in each woman's charge caused problems, to which she replied that the children gave no trouble at all. 'The children of the truly poor are very disciplined,' she said, adding to this the remarkable information that such is the sensitivity of a young child that even before the age of speech a baby brought up by a mother who has escaped to the forest senses the presence of danger and can be relied upon to emit not the slightest sound. Sister Marlene told us that they often managed to keep mothers with their very young children for a while, or it could be arranged for them to come on visits. She found it sad that in cases where a child had been brought into the orphanage, and the mother had given herself up, or perhaps been released from prison years later, the child could no longer understand the mother's (Tetum) language.

It was clear that whatever their feelings might have been for each other, a degree of collaboration existed between the military authorities and the Catholic Church in the matter of the orphanage, which, had it been seen as a disadvantage to the former, would have been instantly closed down. The fact is that the Indonesians saw all five religions acceptable to the State philosophy as potential allies in the struggle for stability. The 200 children thus placed under protection constituted only a drop in the oceanic misery of the tens of thousands left largely to fend for themseves. But for the Catholics it was a step in the right direction, and there was propaganda in it for both sides.

Alongside their children the orphanage gave shelter to two celebrities, whom the mothers clustered at the doorway of the girls' dormitory scurried away to fetch. The first to appear was Justina, wife of Xanana Gusmao, the Fretilin Resistance Commander who still held on in the mountains at the head of a force now reduced from an estimated 10,000 to a thousand or two elusive guerillas. Despite the years of violence, illness and fear, Justina, now in her late twenties, retained the kind of beauty that transcends racial differences. Even wrapped in a dingy dressing-gown she stood apart. She greeted us in incomprehensible Tetum and with a lively smile. Through our interpreter we asked after her health, and she said that she had been sick but was now better.

Most of the women who had taken refuge with their menfolk in the forest eventually contracted tuberculosis, and when Justina was found to be suffering from this, Xanana persuaded her to return to occupied territory with their child in the hope of finding medical treatment. At that time their sector was encircled by troops, and she was shot and hauled off to prison, where she gave birth to a child by her gaoler before her release. Now, by some arrangement the orphanage had been able to negotiate with the military, she was here with Xanana's three-year-old, and the gaoler's offspring – still a baby in arms.

Fashion and fad, in their way, have touched even such far-off places as this, with a craze for the adoption of Western first names. The isles of Indonesia were full of Victors and Henrys, and it was no surprise to find that Justina's friend, whom we next met, was Selina, another pretty young girl with a child. Part of the Military's policy seemed to be to try by hook or by crook to deprive the resistance fighters of the solace of their womenfolk, while leaving them encumbered with children who decreased their mobility. When a Fretilin unit was reported in an area it was normal for it to be attacked from the air with bombing round the clock. At the end of this softening-up a pause might be called in the attack to allow women wishing to do so to surrender. In this instance Selina found herself involved in a subterranean deal in which forty mothers would be allowed to 'come out', bringing with them one child apiece. By accident or design this plan fell apart, and Selina alone finally appeared, bringing with her fifteen children. The first reaction of the awaiting commander was to shoot the lot – in the context of this war a by no means extraordinary reaction – but for once a more discerning view prevailed, and there was no slaughter of innocents. The girl was 'abused' and imprisoned, but when seen to be in an advanced state of tuberculosis, released with her child into the care of the orphanage.

The orphanage kitchen was a cavern under the school ruin. Skeins of blue smoke clung to the brickwork among filaments of soot from the ceiling, and such was the visibility that it was hard to make out through the mist the details of the damage suffered by the further wall. Two Timorese cooks were at work in a scene from *Macbeth*, the first using a pole to stir the soup in a vast pot suspended over an open fire, the second brushing the crumbs of earth from some root vegetables before tossing them in the pot. The fire's reflection had coated both women's deeply lined faces in yellow sweat. They were barefoot with distorted crippled toes, and dressed in rusty black jerkins and sarongs. Bundles of vegetables waiting to go in the pot lay scattered among the assorted debris on the earthen floor. At the moment of our arrival two women woodcutters were hacking branches from this to be exchanged for soup.

'When I came here and saw this for the first time,' Sister Marlene said, 'I felt a moment of dismay. I was on the point of tears. Surely we can do better than this? I thought. We offered to clean the place out, put in some shelving where food could be kept, and fit them up with a decent stove. They wouldn't hear of it. It all had to be left just as it was. They had a ceremony years ago when they started the kitchen, so everything was taboo. What they call leluc. If we change anything round without asking, the cooks will walk out on us. And we have to remember that they are very good cooks.'

'So they'll go on keeping the vegetables on the floor.'

'Maybe they'll come to us of their own accord one day and ask for the place to be tidied up, but I can't really see it happening.'

The sister had to be back for vespers and we parted company at the top of the main, and only, street. By this time the evening *passeio* had started, with lone promenaders and small groups – well-spaced and keeping their distance – on their formal but leisurely way to the far end of the town and back, a matter of three-quarters of a mile, taking forty minutes to complete. This staid procession was disrupted in places by the invasion of numerous children, and some of these, spotting my daughter with her blonde hair and travel-stained dress, surrounded us with wonder and delight and then followed us in droves. A very thin, tall man, with sweeping white moustaches, spats and cane approached, hand out-stretched. It was clear by now that a smattering of Portuguese was the key to acceptance in Venilale. Apologising, I did my best with what I had, and bowing, he replied in English, 'It is enough, sir, that you do me the honour to address me in my own language.'

Everyone exchanged bows during the ceremony of the *passeio*, and although most of the citizens I had observed had emerged from small, recently built houses of a standardised design, certain airs and graces had not been wholly dispensed with by those who had known better times. Some bows, starting at the waist, were ingratiating and profound; others little more than a slight inclination of the head. Of old the *passeio* had served as a marriage market, with the eligible bachelors of the town lining up to follow hard on the heels of the ranks of giggling girls. Now the regulars were old: three elderly ladies dressed gauzily in what might have been re-made curtains, a man entitled *Primeiro Cavalheiro* who had enjoyed the right to be paid a half escudo for every horse shod in town, the *Capitao das Festas*, in charge of Venilale's once frequent celebrations, an eccentric old convert to the Tetum religion who carried a splendidly plumed cockerel, cradled like a child in his arms.

At the far end of the walk in the old days a café once existed called in Portuguese 'The Elegant Tea', where they served nothing but coffee, brandy and wine and played records of *fados* imported from Lisbon. In those days four guitarists accompanied the *passeio*, and there was still one – the boy we had seen on the school steps – who was described as temperamental, but came along when he felt in the mood.

NINE

AFTER THE INITIAL attack, and the almost unopposed occupation of Díli and the villages in its vicinity, the invasion's impetus had shown signs of flagging. Apart from the élite Green Berets and paratroopers, the invasion force was poorly trained and lacking in combat experience. Infantry battalions had been largely recruited from peasantry of the flatlands of Java, many of whom had never seen a mountain before and had to be guided like crocodiles of schoolchildren through the dense tropical forest. In these unfamiliar surroundings there were numerous unexpected casualties through 'friendly fire', and it was to be expected that sometimes paratroop drops would be made in the wrong place or on the heads of their own floot-slogging infantry.

Resistance to the occupation was in the hands of the Fretilin (Frente Revolucionaria de Timor L'Este), the leading political party at the time of the invasion, which withdrew with its small hastily put-together army to the mountains of the north. Here it was handicapped by the large number of civilians it had to take under its wing, and by the absence of air-cover.

At this time a talk of stalemate began to be heard. The situation was remedied after the Indonesians' successful approach to the British and US governments for the supply of specialised counter-insurgency aircraft, notably the British Aerospace Hawk, described in a press-release as 'ideally suited for use against ground forces in difficult terrain'. Up to this point Fretilin strategy had been based upon its control of the country's mountain areas. From this time on the army could stand back and wait for saturation bombing of the mountains, in which a large part of the population had taken refuge, to do its work. Venilale, and all other small towns tucked away inaccessibly in their highland redoubts, now found themselves in the front line of combat. Venilale was badly placed in an area dotted with prime targets for the planes. It was built on the shoulder of a hillside overlooking a wide plain backed by a huge volcanic shape, similar to that of Vesuvius although perhaps twice its size. This magnificent, awe-inspiring and solitary mountain, clothed in dense forests and riven with clefts and gorges, is Matebian – in Tetum, Soul Mountain – place of sanctuary since pre-history, and still revered by a largely animist population. Here history, reshaped as folklore, recalled the facts of conquest and enslavement by which a tradition had been established. In times of trouble villagers over an area widespread in all directions from the sheltering skirts of the mountain left their homes to take refuge there – in the belief that in the sandalwood forests they were invisible to their pursuers. There they were prepared to live for months, even years, upon the berries, the edible roots and leaves, the grubs and insects which the Soul Mountain provided in abundance.

Reports of killings in Díli and in the western towns had left their neighbours to the east aghast, and now, with the news that under cover of the planes the invaders were on the way, the traditional stampede to Matebian and the Bibileu mountain, a few miles to the south, began. Thus Venilale, Baucau, Lospalos and many mountain villages were virtually emptied. It was an abandonment viewed by the Indonesian military as a hostile act, and deserted villages went up in flames. At Matebian the first of a series of encirclements was put into practice, with a large number of civilians, including children, forced to march ahead of the troops closing in on the mountain. Meanwhile, in two months of 1978, 700–800 bombs a day were dropped by planes round the clock. For the most part those captured in such round-ups received short shrift.

On 23rd November 1978, about 500 people who had assembled at the foot of the mountain in the belief that they were surrendering were executed by Indonesian soldiers. Shortly afterwards, in Taipo, 300 people were killed in a similar way; elderly people were burnt alive in their houses, women and men tied together and shot, and children executed in front of their parents . . . 118 people killed on the southern slopes of Mount Matebian between 15 and 17 April.

An attack on the Bibileu, the second mountain sanctuary, followed, and here again the accounts are sketchy and the numbers of victims probably estimated. It is quite certain that panic in the neighbouring village of Kraras was so great that the sick and elderly were abandoned to their fate, and many died in the flames started by the planes. Most of those who reached the mountain were killed, too, on its slopes. The number given is 500. Perhaps it was less, but no doubt a large number of innocent people died. There are few signs of life in this countryside nowadays.

The Soul Mountain operation was seen by the Indonesian military as an almost complete success and the model for further undertakings of its kind on an amplified scale. The assault of Matebian fell short of the military ideal only through too few troops being available, as well as too few civilians to act as their shield. *Operasi Keamanan*, generally known as *nagar betis* – the 'fence of legs' – was to incorporate the experiences learned on the two mountains with a ten-fold increase in the numbers involved. It was an encirclement as before, but this time not of single mountains but vast areas of the country. Up to 80,000 males between the ages of eight and fifty are believed to have been enlisted for the fence of legs, which after much secret planning went into action in early 1981.

No warnings were given before the round-ups of civilians, and the multitudes snatched up suddenly from their homes had no time to collect food or clothing. The conscripts formed up in lines stretching across much of the island, and the great marches began that were to go on for three months. Special army detachments went ahead burning villages and crops. Behind them came the civilian lines and then the main body of the troops. 'The fence started in the extreme west of the country, went down south, then along the coast to the east, then up north and along the north coast to complete the circle.' Christiano Costa, a conscript with the fence who escaped from East Timor in 1987, described the scene on the plain of Aitana when the marching was over, with journey's end not only for the quarry but for many of their pursuers, overtaken by famine and disease.

'I was with the troops when they reached Aitana,' Costa said. 'When the attack was over and mopping-up operations were under way a week or two later, our team entered the area. It was a ghastly sight. There were a great many bodies, men, women, little children strewn everywhere, unburied, along the river banks, and on the mountain slopes. I would estimate about 10,000 people had been killed in the operation. There were so many decomposing bodies that the stench was unbearable and we couldn't stay in the area. The Indonesian soldiers showed no mercy to anyone.'

More effective from the invaders' viewpoint than the casualties inflicted in the Soul Mountain and 'fence of legs' operations was the crop-burning that accompanied them. It was a strategy that brought the Fretilin close to the point of extinction, but it also imposed near-starvation conditions on the civilian population from which it has never wholly recovered.

In the presence of evidently sympathetic foreigners in Venilale, anguish sometimes burst through the seams. We had been taken to inspect the mass graves at the back of the cemetery. In these not only bodies but fragments of bodies of those killed in the forests of the Soul Mountain had been smuggled back at night for interment according to the practices of the Timorese people. Although not debarred by the authorities, visits to the cemetery were regarded as imprudent, and a woman who slipped quietly away into the shadows at our approach was called back by our guide.

'Whom are you visiting?'

The woman was holding a small tin of the kind originally containing dried milk supplied by a relief organisation. 'One of my girls,' the woman said in Tetum. 'I was taking honey.'

'Were you on Matebian?'

'We were up there for a year. When the bombing started our men told us to go. The planes saw us – all of us women with the children running and trying to keep together – and a bomb landed in the middle of us. I had to climb over the bodies. Some of them were blown to pieces and they were all mixed up. I saved one girl and lost the other. I had to find some part of her to take back to bury, a hand or a bone, or even a piece of her dress with blood on it. There was nothing I could be sure of, so to be on the safe side I carried everything I could. Some of this might be her, I thought. It was all I could do. I come here whenever I can and leave honey for her and hope for the best. Sometimes people try to mark the place when they've lost somebody and they come back for weeks and months hoping to find something they can recognise and take home.'

Such scenes and such memories are the commonplace of the grimmest of all the small wars of this century. The invasion of East Timor coincided with the United States' withdrawal from Vietnam and may be seen as its signal to a Cold War ally for action counterbalancing the communists' temporary success. By strengthening its ties with an ultra right-wing regime, the United States gained the right of free passage through the deep sea of Lombok and Ombai Wetar Straits for its SSBN nuclear submarines directed against Soviet targets. Such was its enthusiasm for Indonesia's expansionist policy that at the time of the invason 90 per cent of the weaponry used was supplied by American firms. Military aid peaked at the time of the Matebian and 'fence of legs' operations, which, if deprived of invaluable US counter-insurgency aircraft, might not have been carried through to success.

American interests in the seizure of East Timor were strategic. Australia, which chipped in with token arms deliveries and some loud-voiced support for Indonesia in the counsels of the nations, pursued wholly economic ends. Vast oil reserves were known to exist under the sea-bed of the straits between Australia and East Timor, and although the area remained under the legal administration of Portugal, a secret agreement was reached by which this should be shared out between the occupying power and Australia.

In the first decade alone of this conflict the UN General Assembly passed some ten motions deploring 'Indonesia's military aggression' against East Timor, and called upon it to withdraw its armed forces. They had little hope indeed of provoking the energetic action unleashed recently in the case of Kuwait.

TEN

ANYONE WHO HAS been subjected in childhood to the religious fundamentalism of an old-style Welsh farming community is likely to flinch secretly when the word religion is spoken in his hearing. My own family were a generation or so removed from the life of sheep farmers on bracken-infested mountain slopes, but their attitudes had remained unchanged, along with the conviction that no more than a strict mechanical adherence to the forms of their religion was required for them eventually to gain reasonable seating at the right hand of Christ in his glory. To the younger generation their religious opinions were of slight importance. What was supremely burdensome was that they kept holy the Sabbath day, a long and withering process in which all forms of pleasure were scrupulously eradicated. Games were debarred and, other than the tinkling of hymns on the piano, music – even whistling – was ruled out. When, in the case of the elder children, intellectual escapism came under suspicion, bookcases were locked on Sunday and only the *Christian Herald* made available in the long and inert pause between chapel visits. Services were a stern affair. When the Reverend Davies called upon his congregation to love their neighbours he made the word love sound like hate. He preached to heartless and unimaginative people, but even at the age of nine, after several years of force-feeding with this libel on Christianity, I was old enough to be amazed to be compelled to listen to a sermon, acclaimed in the Tabernacle by a standing ovation, on 'the sin of forgiveness'.

It was a background that left me ill at ease with all the organised religions apart from Buddhism, which seemed to me to offer the mildest of the prescriptions for salvation, and to be certainly incapable of devising a system by which on one day a week it was difficult for a child to be happy. It was only many years later in South America that I encountered men of the cloth whom I was obliged to admire. I had gone to Brazil for a newspaper to investigate reports of genocide practised against the Indians of that country, who were disappearing at such a rate that it was confidently predicted that not a single one would be left by the year 2000. D'Arcy Ribeira, the great Brazilian sociologist, had calculated that one third of these catastrophic losses was attributable to the activities of fundamental American missionaries.

Much as I shied away from their theology, I found it impossible not to admire the self-sacrifice of the handful of Catholic fathers working in isolation among the impoverished and the dispossessed of such countries as Bolivia and Brazil. Indonesia was my second experience of Catholic missions in the field, but in this instance the magnitude and complexity of the problems they faced were much greater. There were mutterings in the high echelons of the faith demanding why the fortunes of the large Catholic minorities spread through the islands of Indonesia should be placed at risk over the defence of a handful in East Timor. The fundamentalists everywhere went along with governments, however abusive their form, and had even rewritten a biblical text in claim of God's approval of such subservience. Indonesian Catholics saw this as going too far but applied pressure on the Timorese Church through Bishop Belo to accept the country's de facto unification with Indonesia. This the Bishop resisted, but a score of priests and a half dozen nuns could do little more than refuse moral co-operation.

The nuns were too heavily occupied by their spiritual and mundane commitments to do anything but leave us to ourselves for most of the time. They were eager for us to stay, holding forth the promise of the interest and excitement of the forthcoming fiesta, to be celebrated in traditional Tetum style. We suspected that visitors from the West might have helped to alleviate feelings of isolation which they would certainly never have admitted to possessing. Their working day was a long one. Sister Marlene, wakened by her alarm clock at 4 am, was the first up and about, and shortly after this the emphatic sounds of prayer reached us through the wall from the next room where the twenty aspirants were already at their devotions. Four years were to pass, three to be spent in the Philippines, before they would become nuns – members of the Salesian order which largely concerns itself with the instruction of the young.

My only previous contact with women in holy orders had been in 1981 when I had met Sisters Joan and Maria from the American Mary Knoll order. They were doing what they could in the stricken Nicaraguan frontier town Ocotal, to alleviate suffering among the civilian population caused by incursions of the 'Contras', supported and armed by their own administration. I had arrived within days of the murder of two of their members from El Salvador who had been staying with them. They had been raped and killed, along with the two sisters who had gone to meet them, on their way back from the airport to the Salvadorian capital. To this tragic episode Joan and Maria made hardly more than passing reference. The Mary Knolls wore ordinary clothing, including in this case check blouses and baseball caps, and I remember thinking at this time that the absence of outward religious formality helped in so far as I was concerned in the establishment of a sympathetic understanding.

By contrast, in Indonesia, at the beginning of our friendship, there was something slightly daunting about the Salesian religious uniform, its archaic style hinting at a repudiation of the physical world. For the first moments in the striking presence of the 32-year-old Sister Marlene in her immaculate habit, I was touched by the memory of medieval austerities, of the visions and voices of such as Teresa of Avila. Within minutes I was to see her demonstrating a vigorous Portuguese folk-dance to a class of orphan girls, and the original impression faded out with an article by a journalist who had smuggled himself into East Timor at the time of the worst trouble, and depicted her struggling through the thickets of the Soul Mountain to the assistance of children under attack by the planes. Thereafter I was reminded less of Teresa of Avila and more of Villon's 'bonne Jeanne' (que les Anglois brûlèrent à Rouen).

The nuns and the aspirants worked endlessly at their allotted mundane and spiritual tasks. At their head Sister Paola Battagliola was a living miracle of efficiently applied effort in which every minute played its part. She had the tiny, triangular face of the witch-fairy known as 'a buffona who is stuffed with sweets and hung from a tree for the Epiphany in villages south of Naples. All domestic tasks including those of the kitchen lay within her domain, where no idle moment was tolerated.

The aspirants completed the hours of prayer, praise and catechism, then settled, rapt-faced, to bake bread, sew garments and scrub floors. Twice a day they sat at an impeccably set table – at which the correct distances between spoons and forks etc. might be checked with a ruler – for a demure but swift intake of Sister Paola's excellent pasta, after which they scurried away to wash up. Excitement simmered constantly behind faces like pious little masks.

By the greatest of good luck we had arrived within a few days of the celebration of a great event in the lives of the Catholic community. This was the ceremonial unification of what had previously been the territory of seven petty rajahs in the vicinity into one parish of the Church; a reform initiated by Bishop Carlos Belo. The Bishop had been the replacement sent by the Vatican in 1983 following its withdrawal of Monsignor Costa Lopes after pressure from Jakarta where he had been seen as too outspoken in his defence of human rights. Indonesian military circles spoke with satisfaction of his substitution by a young inexperienced

Timorese, chosen largely for the same reason as Ivan the Terrible was crowned Czar, because he was believed to possess the most amenable personality among possible choices.

Just as Ivan had, Carlos Belo disappointed, causing initial alarm by a pastoral in which he denounced military abuses. This was followed by a bombshell in 1989 in the form of a letter to the Secretary-General of the UN in which he called for the question of East Timor's independence to be dealt with by a referendum. This letter alone was enough to spark off a repression in which the Australian press spoke of mass arrests, tortures and the precautionary detention of up to 1,500 persons in advance of the visit by Pope John Paul later that year. The bishop himself received a number of letters threatening him with death.

The Pope's visit fell short of being a universally acclaimed success. To an outsider who has always assumed ironclad solidarity in the Catholic ranks it came as a surprise that such a Catholic publication as *Timor Link* could have entertained some doubts as to whether the visit was a good idea in the first place, since it was seen by many as a victory for the Indonesian military. Of the Pope's pronouncements the paper said 'in customary fashion his language was oblique if not ambiguous'. Much stress was laid upon the ritual of earth kissing, on this occasion omitted. 'Would you have liked to see the Pope kiss the ground at the airport?' *The Advocate*'s correspondent asked Bishop Belo, to receive the flat reply, 'Yes, that was my desire.'

Nothing distils more to perfection the spirit of this occasion than the carefully prepared homily the Pope was dissuaded from delivering in Latin, which only two or three of the high-ranking ecclesiastics of his entourage would have understood, before finally compromising with an English translation comprehensible possibly to one in a hundred of his audience. I learned from *Timor Link*, as a further surprise, that Bishop Belo had contemplated cancelling the visit, and was even more astonished that it should have been in his power to do so.

It is evident that Bishop Belo remains very much his own man, and that this is recognised and fully appreciated by the people of his diocese.

In the absence of a priest, Sister Paola was called upon to conduct a service in the village of Gari Vai, some twelve miles away, and took us there with her. The church was large, and rather splendid for so small a place, although devoid of the usual furniture. That there had been a heavy loss of life in the parish was evident by the presence of numerous women in the deepest mourning. We were struck by the singular fact that they remained outside the church during the service – motionless black-shrouded statuary dotted through the surrounding trees, or placed kneeling by the windows or the door. Could this, we wondered, have been a Catholic concession to Tetum custom, with the distancing from the community of those seen as carrying the contagion of death? As usual, there were few men about, but at a certain moment, when the service was about to start, a small group burst through the door, fell to their knees, following this by full-length prostration in almost Islamic style.

Our appearance in Gari Vai produced the familiar amazed reaction among its people, although in this small and remote place where Tetum culture would have been less diluted than in Venilale, feelings were better kept under control. Instead, after the service, we were courteously directed to a double bamboo seat where the majority of the population formed a semi-circle, several persons deep, with the small children in front, to contemplate us in absolute silence. After two or three minutes of this experience, cautious smiles began to break out in the back row, and then one or two of the older children pushed through to kiss our hands. When Sister Paola came for us they all clapped.

From Gari Vai we drove to Bercoli, where the situation was much the same. Here there was less pressure upon us due to frantic preparations for the arrival of Bishop Belo, who had agreed to eat a midday meal with the villagers on his way to Venilale. The headman at Bercoli was a government appointee, who saw the occasion as an opportunity for reconciliation and goodwill. Learning of the Bishop's intention to break his journey here, this man had sanctioned and provided the necessary material for a hall to be built for his reception. This, a bleak breeze-block construction among magnificent banyans, had been erected in exactly one week. Thereupon the headman had called for volunteers to clear the place up, and now the inevitable teenage boys were hacking away energetically with their machetes, cutting the village grass blade by blade.

In his book *Indonesia's Forgotten War*, John G. Taylor mentions that in three days in April 1989 alone, twenty persons were shot in Bercoli. It is thus understandable that, with a shortage of men, a guard of honour for the Bishop could only be provided by combing the area for suitable women. These were being trained in drumming and marching backwards, a ceremonial exercise normal in East Timor, where such escorts were not permitted to remove their eyes from the face of the dignitary thus honoured. They were a taut-faced, rather fierce-looking collection, very thin as usual, with two of them oustandingly pregnant. These had been placed at the end of the two files, where it was perhaps hoped that their condition would escape the Bishop's attention. Drilling them was a Timorese army veteran. Although of extremely dark complexion, his

European features proclaimed him a descendant of one of that small legion of indomitable men who conquered half the world, then un-complainingly carried out the order to mate with any native woman they could, to produce the sons necessary to defend the new possessions.

The headman, wearing trainers and denims, looked on with approval. Although Javanese, he was so westernised that his eyes seemed to be changing shape. Quite unconsciously, while we were chatting, he took a plastic credit card out of his pocket, gestured with it, and put it back. A Tetum collaborator stood at his back, ready to smile whenever the headman did. He carried a cockerel under his arm for which the headman showed he did not much care. 'The Bishop', said the headman, 'is coming on a white horse. He is descending from horse, then we carry him in chair into hall for reception, speeching and good lunch. We are much praising his visit.'

A group of grass cutters came by, hopping like frogs and slashing with their machetes, and he nodded happily, and said, 'Cheerio.' After that he took me to a pond by a stream at the back of the village where they grew spinach. Here some old ladies were scrubbing away at the leaves they had cut, which would feature in the Bishop's lunch. 'Is very good for blood,' the headman said.

It was close to midday when we got back to what had been the village's dark centre, now illuminated by a flush of light squeezed through the tight-shuttered curtains of the banyans' roots. The severe-faced Tetum women – thinking God knows what – still marched in reverse, banging on the kettledrums hanging from their necks, and here and there the black-draped shape of a mourner still crouched facing east.

Some trestle tables had arrived and were to be carried into the hall, and the headman dashed off to supervise their positioning. It was the moment for an onlooker to sidle up with information in broken Portuguese he could no longer suppress. 'There was a man from here went away to work. They said he was Fretilin and they shot him and sent him in a coffin back to his father. But here they say there must be no public burial. So they dug a grave and tipped the body in just as it was. I tell you this, because it is not right.'

The man bowed, backed away, and was lost to sight.

Lospalos, close to the eastern tip of the island, had not only been at the centre of desperate fighting between the Indonesian forces and the Fretilin, but remained a stronghold of the Church. There were four priests in the area; the senior who held the ministry in the town itself, although an Italian, being remarkably known as Father Ernie. It was for this father that Sister Paola had an urgent message. Since the post did not function in East Timor, this would have to be delivered by the driver of the orphanage truck, and when she suggested that we might like to go along with him we readily assented.

The road impressed with a sensation of desertion even more than the one from Díli to Venilale had done. For a number of miles, long barren stretches of it ran close to the sea, after which, the way barred by plateaux bearing some similarity to the mesas of Mexico, it twisted south through the wide plain of Fuiloro to Lospalos. Much of the emptiness through which it ran had become familiarly known as 'dead earth' because all those who had filled it were dead and gone, and human activity had come to an end; although nature had already begun a re-arrangement of the scene in its own way.

Down by the sea there had been villages, and faint rectangles drawn in charcoal marked where the houses had stood. The water's edge was encarnadined with coral and the sea had flung the black remnants of feluccas up onto the beach, where salt had eaten through their vitals. Fish traps embedded in coral detritus had grown fur like that of a reindeer's antlers, with the sea-lice fidgeting over it in search of prey. Among this ancient wreckage a single sea-going craft had been streamlined and reshaped over the stagnant years by gentle, marine decay. The land was dead but there was submarine life in plenty. The fishermen, our driver told us, had harvested a great variety of molluscs in these waters, and the available crop had steadily increased throughout a decade in which they had been left unmolested. And there they were to be seen, inky graffiti of clustered shells scrawled through the shallows, and among the coral heads, and the drifting shadows of the fish.

Life inland, responding to a check in one direction, was on the move in another. Regular cultivation of the soil had come to an end with benefit to spontaneous and unaided growth. Seen from a hill's summit, the dead earth was marked out with what might have been taken for the inscriptions or traceries of pre-historic man, or even space-invaders. Rice paddies had been cut here, tended, irrigated and fertilised for generations, and now what remained of them were meticulous geometrical shapes growing wildflowers to rejoice the heart of someone indifferent to husbandry. Flowers had sprung up everywhere in the vacated land: bright doodlings where ploughs had meandered through the rocks, and windborne seeds had since fallen on fresh earth. The road ran on the edge of a paddy crammed with self-sown gourds like misshapen phalluses, fenced as if against thieves by vast thistles that had sprung up in the path surrounding it. Here the temporary calm and servility of a man-made oasis had been obliterated and replaced by an incomprehensible exaggeration as new forms of life smothered those unable to adapt to change. The dazzling pallor on the earth had darkened the sky, and our surroundings seemed to vibrate to the tremendous, symphonic wheeze of the crickets. It was at this moment that a horseman trotted towards us through the purplish band laid along the horizon. He was the first human being we had seen that day outside a town. As he came closer we saw that he wore a poncho sewn with feathers and had a bandage across his forehead in a way that partially shaded his eyes. He reined up, bowed and gave us a smile undermined by appeal. Then he turned in his saddle, following us with his eyes and waving continuously and with a kind of desperation as the distance between us increased and we finally passed out of sight. Our encounter with this lone figure added new depths to the intense sensation of isolation conveyed by the dead earth itself.

We drove down the glittering snakeskin of a road cut through a quartz outcrop under the first of the mesas afloat in a saffron mist. We passed more cracked and riven paddies with their sinister flowers, and so on towards Lospalos. Somewhere in this last stretch, the forest made its sudden appearance as a dark and solid flux of vegetation so dense as it poured over the hilltops that at a few hundred yards the eyes could hardly separate the trees. All efforts, with the use of defoliants, to demolish this arboreal stronghold had failed, and whatever the tangle of interlacing branches concealed by way of deep ravines and secret caves remained largely uninvestigated. It was somewhere in this vicinity in 1990 that the Australian journalist Robert Domm had paid a hazardous visit to Xanana Gusmao.

Lospalos, principal town of the district of Lautem, seemed not so much to have been devastated by the long and supremely savage war that had raged around it, as to have been subjected to a depersonalisation. It was like a place within range of the normal lava flows of Etna or Vesuvius, where the habit of living for the moment is engrained, advance planning inappropriate, and undertakings conditional. Here, people lived not by choice but an accident of fate, among temporary structures of corrugated iron, and kept going somehow with a minimum of security and hope.

Not all the plastering by the latest in counter-insurgency aircraft had quite succeeded in driving the insurgents out of these mountains. A curfew that for years had kept the population indoors from dusk to dawn had only just been lifted. Even now a largely peasant people were allowed to cultivate their crops only in sanctioned areas. Such measures could only increase local detestation of military rule, and when the Indonesians came to the conclusion that secretly or otherwise they were up against the

whole population, they were probably right. Their suspicions drove them
to invent novel methods of terror. Persons seen as unenthusiastic in their
support might be called upon to demonstrate their loyalty by joining death
squads charged with the public execution of captured guerillas or major
suspects. For such occasions they would be issued with an assortment of
farm implements, cudgels and sticks with which to do their work.

We located Father Ernie in his office surrounded by clamorous
supplicants. He was the mercurial southerner of legend, eyes full of
amusement and outrage, spouting a defective mixture of Portuguese and
Tetum, hands put to work to fill the gaps when verbal communication
failed. Papers slid from his desk-top as he shoved a passage for himself
through the crowd. It was soon evident that the appeals for assistance
were in the realms of temporal rather than spiritual matters. A goat
representing a family's total capital had disappeared. A woman was there
to plead for malaria pills (the supply sent by international aid had been
stolen and gone into shops), a man dragged the Father away from us to
display testicles swollen from a soldier's kick. There was sympathy or
admonition despite all the necessity for caution, a guarded optimism, the
shadow of despair sculpted in a delicate play of the fingers and expressive
narrowings of the eyelids, tongue clickings, and backwards jerks of the
head.

'Don't they come to you for confession?' I asked. He tapped the side of
his nose in a gesture that seemed to unite us in secretly shared knowledge
of a worldly kind. 'The poorer you are, the less there is to confess,' he said.
'These people are very poor. They're given a few hundred metres of land
to live on. If they want more they're told they must pay taxes for roads.
"What roads they ask?" There aren't any. "Anyway, what do we want with
roads?"'

We gave the father the message from Sister Paola. It was about the girl
Selina who had tried to bring fifteen children out of the forest, and was
now in the orphanage. In the last days someone had gone there to tell her
to go to Lospalos to see her mother, who was dangerously ill. Selina
suspected a trick to get her away from the orphanage and then kidnap her,
so this was an appeal to the Father to make local enquiries into the case.
He went aside to read it, stuffed it into a pocket and said he'd look into it.
'I'm busy at the moment, but Father Palomo will show you round.'

The next thing was to find Father Palomo. We climbed into the
orphanage truck and went in search of him, only to be immersed instantly
in the empty silent countryside from which we had just emerged. Within
minutes we were the subjects of an extraordinary experience. On these
remote roads one saw few trucks of the kind in which we were travelling,

though there were frequent military vehicles and the occasional pickup. I could not remember sighting an ordinary saloon car since we left Díli, yet here – where to leave the one main road was to plunge into a journey without maps along a narrow, rutted track – was such a car containing five Japanese. Four were young men dressed in normal Western style; the fifth, a woman, white-faced with kohl-encircled eyes and enswathed in ectoplasmic veiling, could have been a leading lady in a Kabuki theatre play. With huge difficulty and at a loss both for words and pronunciation, the male spokesman managed to get across the information that they were members of a born-again Japanese Protestant sect, of which the woman was the sect's 'sacred mother', who had commanded them to bring her here to settle the problems of East Timor. Now they were lost, and at this point the spokesman's English collaped, becoming for us a meaningless gabble, from which a single comprehensible sentence emerged, 'We are talking at cross purposes.' This we suspected he had learned by heart to cope with such emergencies. Nevertheless it was true, and understanding was in no way advanced by Father Ernie's evident belief that a series of courtesies delivered in Italian might be of help. There was nothing for it but to lead the way back to Lospalos, where the Japanese were left to confer with the headman, who possessed the only detailed map. 'I do not know what is born again,' Father Ernie said, and I had to agree that I didn't either.

Father Palomo was then run to earth, and Father Ernie went off to look into the Selina affair and left us to him. He sprang out of the chair in which he had been slumped when we came in, reminding me at that moment of an athlete gathering strength between strenuous events. There was an aroma about him of guarded pessimism, but my friend who had commented in the notes given me on the enforced banality of meetings with priests in difficult circumstances would certainly have absolved the father of this charge. 'The army just moved in again,' he said.

'We didn't see anything.'

'You wouldn't. We heard they were coming, which means that everybody knew. They're chasing after the Fretilin in these mountains, which means the Fretilin pulled out yesterday or the day before.'

'Do they ever manage to catch up?'

'So far as I know, no. They cannot finish this war and the Fretilin certainly cannot. Hunger will be the winner. The Fretilins run out of food. They have to eat anything. Leaves, grass. The people would feed them but they cannot. They have nothing left to give away. This island is so weakened it's hard to see it ever recovering. Do you know how many died in the war?'

'They say one third of the population.'

'More,' he said. 'Much more. A half.'

'Is Xanana Gusmao still up there?'

'Who knows? It makes some people happy to believe he is. I think this man must be alive, because if they had killed him surely they would put the body on display to prove he was dead.

The father had heard nothing of the contact made with the guerilla leader by Robert Domm in September 1990, which was published in the Australian press. From that it had been clear that the Fretilin resistance remained active. As an army organised on conventional military lines it had been defeated by the encirclement and annihilation campaign of the Soul Mountain and the 'fence of legs', and its commanders killed on the spot, or taken prisoner and subsequently executed. Shortly before the invasion Jill Joliffe visited the command headquarters of those days, being much impressed by Nicolau Lobato, the leader of old, but far less so with Xanana Gusmao, then a shy boy hardly out of his teens who had been put in charge of propaganda and seemed to spend too much time playing with a camera.

A silence of nearly three years followed the collapse, then the news leaked out of clashes with guerillas in the Lospalos area, and it was from the Lospalos-Venilale-Baucau redoubt, with Gusmao now in command, that an attack was actually launched in 1980 on Díli itself. Domm spent sixteen hours in the guerilla camp 'at the top of a miniature Matterhorn', many of them talking to Gusmao. The leader still appears as shy, although thoughtful, articulate and intelligent. Domm was amazed at the efficiency with which his mission was organised. Although at first startled when a Fretilin bodyguard dipped a finger into a supposedly magical substance and drew a symbol on his chest and forehead rendering him invisible to the Indonesians, he later thought 'perhaps the tradition worked after all', for they passed through thousands of troops, on one occasion within metres of them, 'but they never saw me'. So involved were the people with the Fretilin, Domm says, that 'people in the army, intelligence, police, shops, hotels ... are all really resistance people, who are regularly providing intelligence to the guerillas in the mountains'.

Father Palomo took us to the village of Maupara where the working population had been relocated to a roadside settlement following the burning by the military of a number of houses abandoned in the village. Everything had gone wrong for the people moved to the new site. The curfew had lasted until two years before and land could only be cultivated in certain unsatisfactory areas where those at work could easily be kept under surveillance. These difficulties had coincided with a long period of drought. In Maupara it had not rained for four months before our visit, with the result that the river had dried up, leaving only scattered pools in its bed.

We called on an average couple submitted to this fate. Their garden of 25 × 25 metres was 2 kilometres from the 12 × 12 foot shack they had been given, but they had to walk 1 ½ kilometres in the opposite direction to collect water from one of the pools in the river. The total daily trudge to water their vegetables was therefore 7 kilometres, one half of it while laden with the filled cans. These were the dust-bowl peasants of America of the thirties, almost drugged by resignation. Father Palomo asked the man to open his shirt. He did so, displaying his muscles and bones, like an anatomical chart. This couple seemed almost indifferent to their predicament and incapable of self-pity. They spoke in a dispassionate mumble, eyes lowered, hands clasped over their breasts as if in prayer. The father listened attentively, nodded in agreement with whatever was said. 'As soon as the troubles are over they have been promised a hectare [2½ acres] of land,' he translated. 'And do they believe that?' I asked. He shrugged his shoulders. For the peasants there was a congratulatory smile, followed by a hug. 'Baik lagi' (it will be better later), he said. It was an expression that enshrined the flickering flame of hope among the poor of East Timor.

From the relocation area and its dismal prospects Father Palomo guided us up to the village centre to inspect some beautiful old traditional houses that had survived. They were built on exceptionally high stilts – we wondered why, since none of these eastern islands of the archipelago contained animal predators. The platform, in the case of the best specimen, was used as an open-walled room, supporting two more rooms built one above the other and the highest thatched steeple-roof I have ever seen. Access was by a narrow, spindly ladder through a square aperture in the bottom floor. At the moment of our approach a baby of about two was being urged by its mother, who stood by shrieking encouragement, to climb up. This it was extremely reluctant to do, accompanying its resistance by penetrating infantile screams so rarely heard from the normally docile and well-adjusted babies of the East.

The Indonesian government frowns upon such reminders of a torpid past as traditional houses – however charming their appearance and suited to the climate – on the grounds that they are unhygienic and backward and, in the case of the famous long-houses of Kalimantan, that they foster immorality. It has demolished them throughout the islands by the thousand. Rural Indonesia, according to the official hope, is to become a countryside of planned villages of small, single-family shacks, the inhabitants of which, ideally, will work for wages on local plantations or in mines. It is envisaged that only a few select examples of such peasant constructions as we were admiring here will be preserved (although not usually lived in) as tourist attractions. But, currently, there were no tourists in East Timor, nor were there likely to be in the immediate future. Why then had these houses escaped the fate of so many works of art in the same category?

An explanation was provided by an unusually well-dressed villager who now approached. The house, he told us, speaking reasonable English, belonged to his friend, a rajah, whose property had been respected because he had not wished to run away and hide in the forest as so many had.

'Were you here at the time of the army's arrival?' I asked.

'I am in this village all the time,' he said. 'When the soldiers came, I say to them you are our friends. You are welcome. I shake them by the hand. I bring tea for drink. So I live in my house and no-one touches me. I am making no problem for anyone. So it is OK for me to stay.'

We left the rajah's friend and drove back to Lospalos, where a small embarrassment arose. Sister Paola had given us cassava cakes for the journey, and we were determined to avoid imposing in any way upon the fathers, for in Lospalos food was reputed to be in even shorter supply than in Venilale. The story agreed upon was that, having brought rations with us, we wanted to drive on to Tatuale, the last village on the island's eastern tip, where there were archaeological remains and striking views over the land's end of East Timor. The excuse was waved aside. Father Ernie would have nothing of it. He insisted on our staying to lunch, adding that preparation of the meal was already under way. There was nothing for it but to give in.

My impression was that the spaghetti cooked with local herbs, and eaten in the bare kitchen of the house shared with two more priests, was a rare treat. Once again I found it impossible not to compare not only the personal lifestyle, but the character of the mission – even of the faith – with that of the post-war wave of fundamentalists in South America who had caused me so much dismay. Although without doctrinal affiliation, it had always seemed absurdly anomalous to me that the standard-bearers of Western religious expansion among the so-called 'backward peoples' should display an affection for materialism so diverse from the self-denying lifestyle of the founder of their faith and so arrogantly diverse from those they aspire to convert.

Here at Lospalos the Italian fathers were living like Neapolitan peasants – and who could fail to respect them for it? The one luxury that might have tempted them was an electric generator. 'We always seem to be kept busy,' Father Palomo said, 'and it would save time to have one.' But there was no generator, and therefore no electric lighting, no fridge, nor any of those small pleasures of the world that would have sneaked through under the fathers' guard in the generator's wake. And, as was to be imagined, there was no store of meat air-lifted from Canada, no stocks of canned foods, no crates of 7-Up, Pepsi or Dr Pepper, no radio-transmitter to keep them in touch with a missionary headquarters – which in any case did not exist – or in an emergency to call for a Missionary Airforce plane.

There was the faintest possible aroma of Italy in this house, but it was hard to guess at the elements in its composition. One of the fathers had been puffing at a thin, black, straggling cheroot at the moment of our arrival. Perhaps that came into it, as even the odour of spaghetti, cooking too slowly for Father Ernie's liking over a faltering wood fire. He popped out and came back with a handful of twigs, snapped from a moribund garden tree. 'Sometimes a woman comes in when we have friends,' he said, 'but I do not trust her with the pasta.' The water in the pot boiled in fits and starts and he shook his head in a pretence of frustration.

No mention was made of the case of Selina, and we sensed that it was a subject to be avoided. Father Palomo had probably gone as far as it had been safe to go by introducing us to the problems of the relocation at Maupara. The co-operation of the fundamentalists with self-imposed authority was absolute. A heroic prudence had been forced upon the Catholics. They may well have witnessed the murder of members of their flock in circumstances comparable to those facing their predecessors at the time of the Nordic invasions in the European Dark Ages. Of this, had it been so, not a word was said. Even Christ had been tricked into a situation where only diplomacy could save. 'Is it meet', the Centurion asked, 'that we should render tribute unto Caesar?', to receive the reply, 'Render unto Caesar those things that are Caesar's.' It is certainly the recommendation the fathers would have made in similar circumstances, for a more direct expression of opinion could easily have put an end to the mission.

ELEVEN

WE HAD BEEN taken by Sister Marlene to register with the police who turned out to be extremely courteous. The sister explained who we were and what we were doing in Venilale and they shook hands with us in order of rank. The police station reflected the drive by Jakarta to improve its image in East Timor. It was brightly furnished, like a tourist office in the capital, with coloured views of outstanding scenery in less troubled parts of Indonesia: a line-up of Japanese gawking at the slaughter of buffaloes in Sulawesi, a cremation in Bali, a tidied-up long-house in Kalimantan. Besides these there were wall posters illustrating the ideal Indonesian policeman and policewoman – both of them tall, of slender build and impeccably uniformed. They stood to attention to face the viewer, their faces imprinted with sincerity and resolve. *The Policeman and Policewoman*, said the notice in translation, *are servants of Pancasila, our national ideal, and the guarantors of the freedom of the people.* The NCO in command said he had no objection to our wandering about the countryside, if that was what we wanted to do, but was concerned for our sakes, and offered to detail one of his men to accompany us on such expeditions. From this offer we extricated ourselves as gracefully as we could. It was hard to imagine any of these mild-mannered men in the situation of the policeman friend of our taxi-driver in Bali, who had volunteered for service in East Timor, then on being told of 'secret enemies' in the village, dealt with this possibility by executing all the males.

There were no difficulties in country walks taken in the neighbourhood of Venilale, although they usually turned out to be a melancholic form of exercise, through wide, silent landscapes imprinted with blond leaves of banana plants growing in gardens where the house had vanished. In one case a stylish portico rescued from a ruin had been stuck imposingly across the front of a standard government 12ft x 18ft shack.

We set out to walk southwards in the direction of Bibeleu, the second sacred mountain, appearing at a distance of six or seven miles as a mist-washed isosceles triangle at the back of a rolling heathland, braided here and there with juniper thickets. It was a lonely place, the only sound apart from that of our voices being the falsetto despair of the constantly repeated call of an unseen bird. The jungle thickets we found, on closer inspection, contained occasional trees, from which the lower branches had invariably been stripped. As such mutilations were illegal, they had been done in a way that produced no more than the effect of a crazy bonzai styling. The first thicket we investigated contained a soldier of eighteen or so in a brand new and wonderfully pressed uniform, and with a trained vacancy of expression, who may well have been just keeping out of the way. Now, with a relaxation on movement, the village deforesters were everywhere and the ten years' growth was being hastily lopped away. Next to foodstuffs, wood had become the most important commodity in the Venilale market, and we were informed that a species of female mafia had already sprung up through which this valuable trade was controlled.

The young guitarist from the *passeio* had taken to accompanying us on these outings. He had been recommended to us as possessing a smattering of English, which he hoped to improve, but in our short acquaintance produced a single intelligible sentence, which even then fell short of conveying his meaning. 'Last week my brother and sister died,' he said, after a period of agonised concentration. 'No, no,' said the nun who was acting as interpreter, 'it was not last week, but last year.' Thomas, as he called himself, was a Tetum-speaker, throwing into this mellifluous and expressive tribal language a few thorny words of Portuguese. Once in a while he produced a small square of slate upon which someone had chalked words he was hoping to add to his vocabulary. *Boot*, *hedgehog*, *horsewhip*, *2-stroke motorcycle*. He was an unobtrusive and diffident presence, tailing along behind at a distance of three or four yards and occasionally twanging urgently on his guitar to draw our attention to some feature of the sinister wilderness through which we were trudging that had sparked off strong emotion. He possessed a range of theatrical grimaces of the sort exhibited in the Chinese theatre, which speak more than words – but only for those holding the clue to them. A twang of the guitar might be a signal for the eyebrows to shoot up over widened eyes and the corners of the mouth to droop in a sort of depressed smirk. We followed his eye, wondering what could have happened to provide fury or grief among a largely featureless spread of thickets, cunningly pruned trees and sallow rocks at this particular spot. The road, hardly better than a track opened by the gnawing of goats, twisted through the contours of the low hills. Once in a while we saw teams of emaciated women dragging branches (stripped from forest trees like huge combs) through the scrub on their way down to Venilale. Once only were we able to identify the cause of Thomas's excitement, when a spar of charred wood poked through the undergrowth on a ridge over a shallow valley. This had been a village, but no more of it remained than the Romans had left of Carthage. The cemetery down in the valley had escaped interference. Low walls of rock enclosed the old burials, with their inscriptions and even the faded remnants of the photographs intact. The recent mass graves had been squeezed in between: little anonymous mounds sprouting numerous five-inch-high crosses. The cemetery was kept tidy, with not a weed to be seen.

Not enough of the original population remained to rebuild such villages, but every mile or two we passed a shack put up for a family relocated by the roadside. The road had been engineered in such a way as to provide the speediest possible drainage of torrential rainy-season water into the valley below. Thus the gardens provided for the shacks were on dry, barren soil. In one of these, a woman whose pregnancy was grotesquely defined by her fleshlessness was at work with her three small children, extending by a few metres her cleared and planted area, for this purpose gouging out tufts of deep-rooted, sabre-toothed grass. We noted even the youngest of the family, a child of no more than four, tugging desperately at the deep, resistant turf.

'How old are you?' I asked the woman.

'Twenty-nine.'

She would have been thirteen when the great storm swept her childhood away, compelling her to adapt to a normality of hunger, or perish. Nothing in this thin body served any other purpose than to foster survival, and nothing about it was wasted. Her sharp nose, almost deprived of nostrils, was drawn to a point over the cartilage. The lobes of her ears had gone, and shallow hollows like the fluting of a column had been gouged in her neck. She had hands of iron with dark muscular swellings over the finger joints like those of a climbing animal. With these fleshly economies and adjustments nature had protected her, just as it had permitted all the old of the island to be culled. 'Husband?' I asked her, and she shrugged her shoulders. No husbands. Few men. Yet half the girls pregnant, and no shortage of children. Strange.

'Don't people steal your cabbages?'

The question seemed to embarrass her. My impression was she was pretending not to understand.

'They're all hungry, aren't they?'

She considered the matter then nodded her head. 'They are hungry,' she admitted grudgingly, as if in answer to an eccentric question.

'Don't they take the cabbages from your garden for themselves?'

'Take?' she asked, 'take?'

'Steal, I mean. Rob you.'

'No.' She shook her head. It might have been incomprehension or it might have been the true facts of the case – that however powerful the persuasions of hunger, the poor here did not steal from the poor. I was inclined to believe that with these tiny cabbage patches left to look after themselves, often miles from their owner's hut, this must be the case. That family's possessions, apart from fourteen cabbages, were the usual magnificently strutting cockerel and his hens, and a starveling dog, fiercely repelled by the cockerel as soon as it attempted a timid approach. Poultry-keeping could be the salvation of such households, yet here again dietary prohibitions of the kind imposed by so many brands of faith forbade it. Somehow on this not quite barren hillside the chickens managed mysteriously to support themselves, and to appear in excellent condition, but they are *leluc* – sacred according to the Tetum religion. Neither they nor their eggs may be eaten, and it is said that the truly orthodox Timorese will see their children die of hunger rather than breach this taboo.

Back in Venilale we were caught up in the mild hysteria of excitement over the promise of a festa to be held again after so many years. The seven chieftains now on the verge of their submersion in a quiet takeover by the Church had sent representatives and all the appropriate materials that could be gathered by way of contribution to the decorations. Many of those we saw were strikingly different in appearance from the Timorese of Venilale, giving rise to the speculation as to whether separate racial ingredients were involved. Much of the gala attire was striking indeed. Horsemen rode in wearing gilt dunce's caps with eruptions of feathers bursting from their tops, and there were dark-faced knife-carrying women in crimson sarongs. A line of splendidly got-up joggers slowed for respectful salutations as they passed. Many of these people seemed thrown off balance by contact with an almost unmanageable freedom, reminding me of the bewilderment of a previously impoverished pools winner who is unsure how to handle wealth. Three or four years before men had been shot on the spot for being found out of their houses at night. Now, after the long, claustrophobic years, unaccountably and at a stroke, twelve hours had been added to the day. For years the villagers had been penned up at night in squalid little shacks. Determined now to make the most of a concession that might at any time be withdrawn, many refused at first to go to bed, wandering about in the darkness, gazing up with wonder and relief at the stars.

Sleep was at an end at 3 am when drummers went into action by torchlight in the cleared space next to the orphanage HQ. By dawn this had been taken over for rehearsals by stern-faced women, like those at Bercoli, marching smartly forwards and in reverse. Next on the scene were the boy dancers of the cockerel cult under the leadership of the aged shaman in his wonderfully tied turban and navy pullover. It now appeared that there was a triangular association here not only with a totemistic rooster but with the moon, seen by its votaries as a cockerel under another aspect, in token of which these eight- or nine-year-olds now wore moon discs on their bare chests, and sickle moons on their foreheads, both stated to be of beaten gold. From that time on, in whatever part of the town we happened to be, we constantly ran into the shaman and his team going through the vigorous contortions of the dance, to the shrillest fife music I have ever heard.

We had been told by the nuns that Venilale, and probably all the small towns and villages of East Timor, were virtually free of crime. It was to be taken for granted that all such consideration of the problems of morality were based upon the ethic imposed by Moses on his descent from Mount Sinai, as set forth in the Book of Exodus.

The Timorese, the sister said, were weak on all the commandments handed down by Moses dealing with their obligations to God – but very strong indeed with those concerned with one's duty to one's neighbour. They were outstandingly observant in the commandment calling upon them to honour their father and mother, so far as they had survived, and no fathers or mothers anywhere were better off in this way. The murder rate, she believed, was infinitesimally small, compared say to the United States. It was hard even to make a Timorese understand what the ruling against bearing false witness was all about. Adultery? 'Well,' she said, 'I'd have to think about that one.' This left covetousness and theft. She shook her head. 'You have to remember this is an egalitarian society,' she said. Status was determined, she thought, in Orwellian terms, in being more equal than the next man. No-one wanted to live in a big house. No honours were conferred upon an accumulator of property. 'You could say that covetousness is unknown in East Timor. And theft.'

Yet suddenly in this almost crime-free society a competitive urge had insinuated itself. The forthcoming procession was a religious occasion, when it was incumbent upon participants to wear headgear composed of the longest cockerel plumes to be obtained. The first hint of what might happen occurred to me when an acquaintance made on the *passeio* asked, 'Did you bring a cockerel with you, sir? If so, I should keep your eye on it.' In fact all cockerels had been placed under close surveillance for the period and it was a matter of local outrage when on the day before the Bishop's arrival an exceptional bird with which someone had presented the orphanage was found to be bereft of its tail.

Two days went in the scurrying ant-like labour of every spare male to be found to strip the fronds from all the palms and to cut, twist and weave them into miles of complex roadside decorations. On the third day, to the spreading outcry and the great dinning of drums, both far and near, the Bishop arrived. Absurd hopes that he would be mounted on a white horse foundered as a Toyota truck so heavily enshrouded in garlands on the radiator and sides that little of it but the wheels was visible, trundled into sight.

The Bishop stood on a platform fixed behind the front seats, arms at his side and the palms of the hands turned outwards in the 'standing Buddha' posture to been seen in Burmese temples. An archway had been built at the entrance to the town where Claudia and I waited to take photographs, and here, both for ceremonial reasons and because steam was hissing from the Toyota's radiator cap, the cortège came to a halt. A rush of tribesmen for a closer view of their leader was momentarily impeded by Claudia's wondering encirclement by a small crowd of those who had never before seen a fair-haired girl in a white dress. We stood our ground and snapped shutters. The tribesmen blew on their archaic horns, clashed cymbals and shrilled their flutes. Nothing moved in the Bishop's features; he gave the impression of an awareness not wholly dependent upon vision, of a kind shared perhaps with the most practised of card-players. The radiator calmed, the Toyota jerked forward and, the Bishop having miraculously kept his balance, the procession moved on.

With this, the musicians who accompanied the shaman's cockerel-dancers renewed their tremendous squealings. They had been placed not in front of the Bishop, as promised by the nuns, but immediately behind. The purpose of the dance was to invoke the awe-inspiring vitality of a fighting cock in combat with a challenger, and both the young boys and old man, eyes staring furiously from their heads, leaped high into the air, twisting their bodies in a half-second's mid-flight before dropping back to earth. Thus, for a moment the pagan symbols of the moon were displayed within view of the cross. In theory such ritual performances, unless held to be devoid of all but tourist attraction, are ruled out by the monotheistic Indonesian *Pancasila*. Yet here the Church was prepared to show not merely tolerance in its handling of the animist competition, but had sided with it in the face of government disfavour. As another sister had said, 'The shaman is on the side of the people. He shows them sympathy and love, and there are times when he can be of material help. Most people cannot obtain medicines, but many of his herbal cures are effective. His influence is for good. We are coming closer. Soon we believe he may ask to attend Mass.'

'And after that – will the cockerel dance still go on?'

'Yes, of course. If this is something the people want, let them have it.'

But what of the significance of the dance? What of the dance as an act of worship? Those were questions I would have liked to ask, but quicksands stretched ahead, and I drew back. The procession moved on a few hundred yards then stopped once again to allow the Toyota's engine to cool and for a break from marching in which the dancers could whip themselves into a brief frenzy. Everyone who had survived in this wasteland and had retained necessary strength had rushed to Venilale. Even the old king, supposed to be at least 110, tied to a bed in his shack and caught up in the delirium of approaching death, had called for ex-subjects to carry him into town, and volunteers had been forthcoming although in the end the idea was dropped. In these hold-ups the dancers went running up and down, foaming at the mouth, and waving their tin swords, with the stewards in charge of the groups sprinting after them to drag them back into line.

A small earnest man I'd not seen before, and never saw again, although he must have known us, cornered me to explain such wild performances. 'They've all been inside for years,' he said, 'and when you come out you go to extremes. When they took me to Atauro prison they put me in the coffin for four months. It's dark. You hear nothing, you see nothing and it just fits your body. When you come out all you want to do is run about. Sometimes they made you drag an iron bar to quieten you down. Even now I want to run around with the dancers. Four years in Atauro, then another four in Cai-Laco. It leaves its mark. You're never the same again.'

The stewards had hustled all the dancers back into line, and the procession jogged forward, the women marching backwards at its head, followed by the Bishop on his platform in the Toyota, very erect with eyes narrowed to search the distance. Now, with the church in sight, the elderly regulars from the *passeio* watched keenly from the sidelines – the aristocratic gentleman with cane and spats, an old soldier of the Portuguese army wearing medals bought at a sale of effects, a *senhora* in a print frock salvaged from the thirties with a maid indifferent to the happenings, her bereaved eyes fixed on the Soul Mountain lifting its incandescent mass from the heat mist spread through the valley.

A stage had been knocked together outside the church, and from this the Bishop delivered an immensely long, eloquent and moving speech in Portuguese. It was dedicated to the six virtues, of which he placed justice firmly in the lead, quoting Saint Thomas Aquinas saying that it was 'the firm and constant will to give to each person what is theirs'. Nothing could have been clearer than that the Bishop was convinced that this had not been done; and his audience were unanimous in their agreement.

That evening, to our huge surprise, we were invited to the banquet to be held in the incompleted building of the new seminary. Since notice of this was only given two hours ahead of the event, there were panic stations over the matter of refurbishing the now impossibly soiled and travel-worn white dress. The seminary building occupied part of the site of the ruined school, having a large, bare refectory which in spite of its size had managed to retain an atmosphere of austerity appropriate to a semi-monastic building. In this, benches had been placed all round its walls, seating about 200 Catholic supporters in the neighbourhood. A long central table would accommodate headmen whose domains were to be absorbed in the spiritual unity of the new parish, intermingled with church dignitaries; the Bishop and those close to him were to be seated at the cross piece at the table's top.

We arrived at a moment of intense excitement and the pleasurable chaos to be expected in a situation where no public function on this scale had been held for so many years, where everything was in short supply, and nothing could be found. Timorese notions of hospitality forced people to rush about in all directions, trying to find cutlery and plates and chairs for each other. An emergency raid on the orphanage kitchen produced a supplement of tin plates, but an alarmed outcry was immediately raised when it became known that these were the green-painted platters reserved for the sufferers from tuberculosis.

Crisis raged in the adjacent kitchen. Two days earlier we had been present at the nuns' headquarters when a boy of fourteen who had inherited the position of pig-killer for such celebrations arrived with a long knife and a small porker wrapped like a gift parcel. This, following Sister Paola's indication, he had carried out of sight behind a statue of a saint in ecstasy, while we made ourselves scarce. The best of the cadaver had been expertly converted by the sister into a hundred-odd slices of salami, which were hung over a fire for a specified number of hours to smoke in readiness for this occasion. Then suddenly the wind had dropped, the fire could not be persuaded to smoke, and the planned epicurean heart of the feast had suffered annihilation.

A goat was to have provided the basic sustenance of the repast, but it had gone adrift en route from pasture to table, calling for frantic improvisations on whatever edible was to be found. Slowly a vulnerable calm began to assert itself and I settled to the problem, when it would have been inappropriate to take notes, to impress the details of this scene upon the memory. I was surrounded by faces, both young and old, from old-master paintings in which a succession of emotions were reflected, briefly but with the utmost clarity, before their return to innocence and emptiness.

Here again were the splendid, stiffly perambulating waxworks figures from the *passeio*: the three oldish ladies in their re-made curtains, chattering in high-pitched ventriloquial voices and bestowing dazed smiles; the *Primeiro Cavalheiro* in his cricketing blazer worn with a winged collar; the *Capitao das Festas* with his badge of office depicting Silenus, drunk and riding on an ass. Three guitarists, faces bloated with embarrassment, had been unearthed and dragged here to sing unsuitable songs in which the word *amor* was repeatedly heard. Our white-moustached patrician who had just drifted up to exercise a few sentences in Johnsonian English settled our doubts. 'There is no carnal significance, sir. This song symbolises the love of Christ for his Church.'

These people had learned to live for the moment – or perhaps they had always done that. Pain, in East Timor, was rarely indelible. My interest in them was returned, although with discretion. We were always the objects of side-glances and conjecture. Bland as their expressions remained, we knew that our Timorese friends had never wholly recovered from the startling novelty of our appearance, our bleached skin, outlandish clothing, and the sound of our faltering speech. What – we knew they asked each other – could have brought us to such a place as Venilale? Perhaps it was something to do with the British alliance with Portugal of old. Those in this gathering who had reached middle age and had learned their history according to the Portuguese myth, remembered with admiration the English piracies in the early centuries of the New World. England had been able once to roll over all forms of opposition. Surely it could still make its voice heard? Perhaps we were the emissaries of the British government who would report back after hearing the story of their miseries from their own lips.

Perhaps it was the strength of this rumour that had placed us at the head of the table seating the village notables, and a few feet from the Bishop himself; who, when our eyes met, nodded and smiled. So close were we that it would have been impossible, despite the festive tumult from the further end of the room and the rousing ballads of the guitarists, not to overhear snatches of his conversation with his clerics, appearing to be concerned wholly with routine ecclesiastical topics. When the banquet was over he came up to speak to us for a few minutes. He was enormously relaxed and easy to like, small – as men so often are who fill the great roles in history. He shrugged in the direction of his escort of priests. 'There are so many people,' he said. 'Please come to see me next week.'

This we would much have liked to do, but next morning we were due to return to the capital. We considered the possibility of postponing the flight back to Bali and Jakarta for a few more days, but as it turned out these arrangements could only be made in Díli itself.

Next morning the nuns gave us a lift in the truck to Baucau, where we caught the bus to Díli. In East Timor buses have the agreeable custom not merely of depositing passengers in the town of their destination but of delivering them at their street address. In such countries where savagery is predominant, the ordinary citizenry seems so often to be kinder than elsewhere, and in this case the bus driver had not only insisted in our sitting in the front seat, but took us to the Turismo by a circuitous route so that we should see as much of the town as possible. In this way we passed through outskirts that had escaped brutalisation. There was rain in the air that had softened the edges in this scene and had turned the tender sea-washed greys and greens down by the shore into an old Caribbean aquatint.

Our reception at the Turismo lacked the good humour displayed on the occasion of our previous arrival. Quite unintentionally I had fallen into the habit of speaking Portuguese, and now, in picking up the keys of the rooms, the word *obrigado* slipped out. The reaction was startling. The girl receptionist who had been pleasant enough at our first meeting, let out an angry shout: 'Obrigado!' causing a member of the staff seated nearby to jump out of his chair, and one of the caged parrots noted by the correspondent of the *Figaro* to utter a piercing squawk.

Having dumped our baggage we drank a Coca-Cola and went for a walk along the front, watched the woolly-headed children chasing land-crabs, and a man with a sledge-hammer trying to break a useful lump of iron from one of the beached landing-craft, then returned. The receptionist, who appeared to have calmed down by now, gave us a thin smile. This seemed the moment to try to organise a delay in our departure, but she shook her head.

'There are no seats.'

'That's what they told us in Bali when we came here, but the plane was half-empty.'

The grimace of anger returned. 'There are no seats.'

Our keys were not on the board, and there was a longish wait before the key to Claudia's room was forthcoming. The room had been turned over in an amateurish fashion, but nothing was missing.

The same receptionist was on duty in the morning when we left for the airport.

'Salamat jalan,' she said with some emphasis, meaning in Indonesian, goodbye.

'Adeus,' I replied in Portuguese, and she shook her head as if troubled by a fly.

The waiting taxi driver had heard this exchange and showed his delight. 'Vivan os companheiros,' he said as I got in. Long live our friends.

We caught the plane back to Bali, where we parted company. Claudia returned to Java to attend a medical conference in Bandung. For me the long-planned experience of Irian Jaya was about to start.

IRIAN JAYA

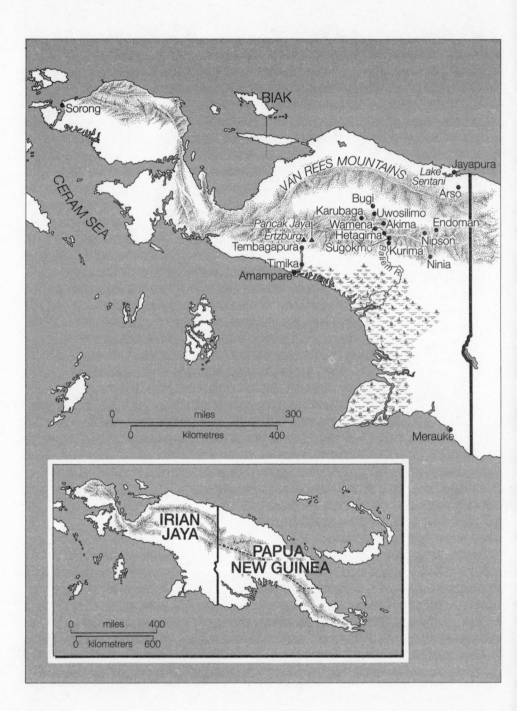

TWELVE

I TOOK OFF for Jayapura two days later and after a six-hour flight over an empty ocean landed for refuelling at Biak island in the north-western corner of Irian Jaya – a principal US base in this theatre of World War II, but long since devitalised by peace. Both the moments of coming to land and those following take-off offered a view that was memorable. Biak in the local language means coral town. It was from coral that the village now become capital was largely built, and the coral spread in all directions like contoured mist through the shallow sea. Until recently, inaccessibility had helped Biak to hold its place among the undiscovered paradises. There was an exciting wildlife in forests that so far had escaped the loggers, including such rarities as marsupial cats and tree-climbing kangaroos. Enormous bird-wing butterflies sucked at decaying fruit fallen from the jungle trees, and a bird sanctuary teemed with parrots, sulphur-crested cockatoos, and pigeons said to be as large as geese. All these pleasant things lay under sentence, for, said the *Jakarta Times*, the best of Biak had been acquired by compulsory purchase by a consortium which would now develop it as a resort for Japanese tourists, making a start with seven hotels, and as many golf courses as thought essential by the Japanese developers.

A short flight from Biak brought me close to the great uninvestigated swamps of West Papua, a milky, green frontier creeping towards me over the sea. Here I was about to touch on the edge of what has remained, after the Polar regions, one of the least known areas of the globe. The forest first appeared as veinings of deeper colour in this vaporous surface, then a mould or moss that broke up the flashing reflections of the swamp, then at last came the trees that had rooted in solid earth, hundreds of thousands of them, although still no more than a crimped vegetable pattern stretched over most of the land in sight. It was a pattern without variation or interruption. To the south the faintest of pencilling sketched in the outline of the Van Rees Mountains. I was flying parallel to the shore and through the opposite cabin window a metallic ribbon of beach divided the trees from the flushed coral sea, upon which in a hundred miles not a single craft had been seen.

Something remarkable in the way of a city might have been expected as capital of this great unknown. As an outpost of colonial power in conquered territory it should have been full of the remembrance of things past, of jaded pretention, of the stage scenery of a tropical fin-de-siècle and dignified decline.

Nothing could have been further from the case. The Dutch had established themselves here in 1906, when almost at an end of their colonial tether, in the hope of keeping the Germans from sneaking westwards over the frontier of their sphere of influence in New Guinea. They put up a minimum of government buildings, sentenced a few unpromising civil servants to a piteous exile, ordered the natives to cover their nakedness and to keep holy the Sabbath day, called the place Hollandia, and settled with sophisticated awareness to await the end. The city's inability to develop a personality has been underlined by its three changes of name since those days.

The impression it still gives is of a temporary civic arrangement. Just as Charles V of Spain agreed to the siting of his new capital at Madrid, where it was easiest to use it as a centre to reach other important places, Jayapura was probably kept in business after the Dutch pull-out as a convenient staging point, already in possession of at least the basic furniture of a city. Nevertheless the atmosphere is one of impermanence, and there is a feeling of restlessness and nomadism in the air. The crowds of men drifting past the booths and stalls lining the streets that largely replace shops are like seamen on shore-leave. People seem obsessed by time, and perhaps that is a symptom of something or other. The roadside stalls display cheap watches galore, and citizens are everywhere to be seen wearing two watches – sometimes three – on their wrists.

An unevenness is instantly evident in Jayapura's adaptation to the modern world. Stepping from the raucous street through the still portals of the Import Export Bank, the customer finds himself in a temple of Muzak and computerisation. Here he encounters wonderfully uniformed hostesses who receive him with the grave or smiling acquiescence, according to the merits of the case, of geishas of finance, which indeed they are. But strictly speaking, the twenty-first century is about to dawn only at street level, and access to the bank at the time of my visit was across a plank laid over a hole – one of dozens – in the main street's shattered pavements. This revealed a section of gully in which sinister-looking shapes – some undoubtedly of animal origin – were steeped in black ooze. An evening stroll without a torch down the Jalan Yani was a hazardous affair, and one soon became aware of sly nocturnal movement on the edge of such pitfalls and a shadowy scuttering then disappearance of an animal seeming to be larger than a rat.

A few guerillas of the OPM (Free Papua Movement) were supposed to be holding out somewhere in the central highlands, giving sufficient trouble until the last few months for a police permit to be necessary for a visit to Irian Jaya. Relaxation in this matter had been so recent that while the Indonesian Embassy in London ruled that permission still had to be applied for in Jakarta, it was only on arrival in the capital that I learned that this was not the case. A *surat jalan* (permission to travel) could now be obtained from the police office in Jayapura, situated most conveniently next door to the Maloc Hotel where I had booked in. Unfortunately, having arrived on a Saturday after office hours, I was faced with a wait of two days at the least before travel into the interior could begin.

Jayapura had no attractions. The reception clerk at the Maloc smiled incessantly as he demolished hope. There was nothing, nothing, nothing; no restaurant where a man could take his wife, no night club, no casino, no gymnasium or public swimming bath. A cinema, yes, but only showing B-grade Indian films. Also a Rollicking Bar. This was the way it was named but he would not recommend hotel guests to pay it a visit.

Consequently, the Maloc offered the only possible respite from the city's tremendous tedium. Mr Beringis, an English-speaker who had something to do with tax-collection, smiled and said that Indonesians saw Jayapura as the Siberia of the tropics. Slowly I was beginning to separate the Javanese smiles. The reception clerk had the congeniality of a man with a splendid digestion. Mr Beringis's rueful smile covered up for *You see it is necessary for someone to be sent to Jayapura, but the belief of the man who is chosen will always be that he has fallen foul of the boss and head office.*

'No wife can agree to live in such a place,' he said. 'So I must face the world alone.'

'Are the beaches here any good?'

'They are lacking in shade, and the sea is dangerous.'

'Pity.'

'Speaking for myself, the fact is I am not a beach man. Well, there it is. I have two more years to serve. Oh yes, this is a sentence. I feel myself in prison.'

Mr Beringis thought that the main tourist attraction of the town might be of some interest to me. This was a crocodile farm where baby crocodiles caught by the locals were grown to a commercial level. The skins went to Paris and the meat to Singapore and Hong Kong, where the

Chinese ate as much of it as they could get, as a cure for asthma among other ailments.

'The smell of the surrounding area is very bad,' he said. 'Shortly after I came to Jayapura I made the acquaintance of a lady and took her to this place, offering to buy her a skin for a bag. She did not wish to take the skin. I think this outing was not a success.'

'Tell me, Mr Beringis, do marsupial rats exist in this part of the world?'

'I am ignorant of animals, Mr Loosidge, but opinion is that most kinds are of the marsupial variety.'

I decided to give the crocodile farm a miss and devote the rest of the day to finding out what I could about the interior of the island, and the travel facilities that existed. From this emerged the striking fact that no-one I spoke to had more than the foggiest idea of what went on beyond that rampart of low scrub-covered hills that debarred the city from the relief of cool breezes and separated it from the rest of the country. Whatever was required for the establishment and maintenance of so many settlements behind the vast emptiness of the mountains, forests and swamps was unloaded here in the docks to be flown a hundred miles or so to Wamena, sometimes described with a patronising smile as the highland capital. A passenger plane went there every day carrying government officials and technicians and bringing them back, and a number of commercial flights transported thither everything from corrugated iron by the ton and even dismantled steam-rollers to the endless catalogue of essentials for survival in an area that produced nothing.

Only the persons directly involved in these operations, as it seemed, ever went to Wamena, and once arrived there saw no point in exploring across the boundaries of this hastily put-together town. The technicians from Jakarta were hygienically lodged in company barracks. Merpati air-crews returned the same day to Jayapura, where they were comfortably lodged in the Maloc, with air-conditioning that really worked and a colour television in every room. Thus the highlands, a half-hour away by air, full of strange men, beasts and birds, remained in Jayapura the great unknown. No member of the staff at the Merpati office, entitled to travel on the company's planes at one tenth of the normal fare, had bothered to make the journey. The Protestant Mission Centre to which I was directed as centre of all information relating to the interior had nothing to offer but devotional books. The government information office was closed. This almost total lack of contact between the mountains and the coast worked the other way, for in the two days I spent in Jayapura not a single Papuan was to be seen. Perhaps they were kept away by the police, for it seemed probable that the appearance in these streets of one dressed in the normal tribal nakedness would have startled the public as much as in Jakarta. A tobacco kiosk tucked away in a corner, displaying postcards of highlanders in feathers, paint and penis-gourds, was never without an assembly of giggling boys.

I was to have continued my enquiries next day, but found the whole town closed down, for although all physical evidence of the Dutch occupation had vanished, awe of the Sabbath remained. So silent, so devoid of activity, so shuttered and deserted the town appeared, one was tempted to wonder whether the locals had decided that the best way to deal with this Dutch legacy was to stay in bed. With the onset of this strange calm – the disappearance of the snorting Japanese motorcycles from the streets, the silencing of the Hindu roarings from the cinema loudspeakers, and of the Muzak whisperings at the entrance to the bank – the city's mood had changed, and for a moment Jayapura proclaimed itself as part of South-east Asia. Feeling in need of exercise, I began a brief exploration on foot. The wind had turned round, and down by the port the odours of crude oil had been pushed aside by an ancient mangrove smell of roots fermenting in mud, and seabirds with long tapering wings had settled on the cranes.

Thereafter I investigated the north of the city and where the road to Sentani Airport began to wind up into the hills. Above this was an area where people who had gone a little wild with destitution had tucked their shacks into whatever niches in the mountainous landscape they could find. Encouraged by the Sabbath desolation they had come down to where the streets were about to end, and were picking through the packaging materials used to protect imported machinery that had been discarded at this point, prior to charging themselves with enormous loads, perhaps to be used in house-refurbishing, and humping these back uphill.

At exactly 6 pm, in a moment of gathering gloom, all the lights of the town went on. Here the Sabbath was confined to the twelve daylight hours. Now it was at an end; doors and windows were flung wide, and the population poured out of their houses. In a matter of minutes the streets and the town's many haphazard spaces were filled with gamblers. Groups of hard-faced punters squatted in circles to join in the unidentifiable card games and contribute sounds like the snap and whimper of hunting jackals to outcries of triumph and despair on all sides. 'Find the Lady', embodying all its routine trickeries, was played with small discs of polished stone. Jayapura is celebrated for its extreme population mix – the seafaring mélange from the islands, its Minang merchants, Chinese laundrymen, Indian vendors of junk jewelry, Javanese officials, and a variety of technicians and mechanics kept busy with the electricity supply and the shattered drains – and here with the collapse of the Sabbath they had come together to play bingo. Contestants had settled by the hundreds between the holes in the pavement and within feet of the streaming traffic in the road. In response to numbers called through a megaphone they marked the squares of paper they had been given. In reality, it seemed, only the middle class were debarred from Jayapura excitements.

Apart from the gaming, a great rush to the shops was a feature of this no man's land of time between the demise of the Sabbath, and business as usual on the next day. Both the smaller shops and the supermarket next door but one to the bank, which was also reached by planks across a black chasm, were crowded with eager shoppers. On offer everywhere were sporting trophies in the shape of cups of all sizes with lavish and often dismal embellishment. The public had formed a tight cordon round the supermarket's central display, commenting excitedly on the maenads, tritons and cherubs, before making their choice, capturing the attention of a busy assistant, and being accompanied to the check-out. The shimmer of silver and gold misled. It was far and away the largest collection of such objects I had ever seen in one place, but all were of plastic, although indistinguishable at a distance of two or three yards from the real thing.

A sprightly young assistant, later identified as son of the cinema owner, just back from college, explained the public enthusiasm for such implausible purchases.

'You see normally these cups are being awarded for achievements of many kinds. For running like greyhound. For throwing ball into net. For lifting heavy weight with separate class for lady competitors. Always the purpose is to encourage athletical success.'

'But not today, you say?'

'Today is special occasion for giving such cups as presents to good friends. This, in Jayapura, is friendship day. If friendship is big, cup must be big. Oh yes, a man who receives much admiration may fill a room with them.'

'But for every one he gets he must give one in return, isn't that so?'

'That he must do. That is natural thing.'

'Well at least it's good for business.'

'Oh yes. On friendship day we are being given shot in arm.'

Sentani, a flat spot in the foothills above Jayapura, is Irian Jaya's busiest airport, and having collected the necessary travel permit from the police I went up there on Monday morning to investigate the availability of flights into the interior. As in Irian Jaya's few other small towns, Sentani contained a number of tribal people, who were always Danis. To get to the primitive Yali tribes, you had to travel far into the interior, and the only means of transport in this case were the light planes of the Missionary Air Fellowship, which very rarely carried anything but the missionaries themselves, their supplies, and the occasional government official. A traveller motivated presumably by nothing better than curiosity could buy himself a seat in a missionary plane, but having reached his destination could normally expect, at best, nothing more than a hut in which to shelter. Few of these remote outposts had mission houses with resident missionaries, and where these existed it had been made known that visitors were not welcome. It was a situation calculated to bring the insistent traveller a little closer to the Stone Age than almost anywhere else in the world, for a few of these areas in which the Yali and Dani tribes live have come under missionary influence only in the last 10–15 years. In these, in some cases, stone implements are still in use to cultivate the fields.

The missionary in charge of the offices of the MAF could provide little enlightenment as to the practicalities involved. His manner was cold and distant. 'Why did you come here?' he asked. 'What is the purpose of all this?' I tried without success to make him see that I was not involved in some ridiculous and probably discreditable adventure, but my lack of evident motivation dumbfounded him. 'I can tell you nothing. I have only just arrived myself,' he said. He passed me over to an exceedingly polite and genial Indonesian clerk, who – however much he may have felt it – showed no surprise at being asked to recommend a primitive village. 'You better go to Endoman,' he said. He had never been there or to any other Yali village, but someone had told him the people were pygmies, which he found very interesting, and was sure I would, too. 'I was told they were eating each other when we got there,' he said. He followed me out and we stood to admire the sparkle and sheen of the missionary planes, mathematically lined up on the tarmac; the soft cool breezes of the efficient air-conditioning played upon us even outside the office. It's kind of hard to think of pygmies as cannibals,' he said.

There was no hope of being able to go anywhere that day, so he booked me tentatively for Endoman for the next day, recommending me to talk to one of the pilots to find out what to expect. As it turned out they had all gone home by this time, so I left him and took refuge in a losmen quivering at the edge of the airfield in the noise of the planes. It was a row of rooms tacked together in a wasted flower garden with a frieze of pink geckos, like tiny plastic toys, round the ceilings and the light switches hanging from the walls. The fussy little Indian who owned it promised to brighten the next morning for me with a 'real English breakfast'.

The night was filled by the sound of the junketings of huge rats, perhaps of the marsupial kind, thumping and thwacking over the tin roof. The calm morning view through tousled flowers was of the rise and fall of fishing eagles over the wide and splendid lake of Sentani. As promised, breakfast arrived, taking the form of fried plantains tasting like glue, and sandwiches with a filling of powdered chocolate. Rejecting this, I hurried over to the MAF office, where the pilots, all of them missionaries as well as pilots, were uncommunicative and aloof. One of them had been discussing the purchase of that day's food with his wife, and a Dani woman had emptied an assortment of vegetables carried in her head-net to display what she had for sale.

The wife poked disconsolately with her toe at what was on offer. 'Hon, we need any yams?' she asked.

'Not for me,' the man said.

'Funny they can't do any better than this,' the woman said. 'Anyone can raise chickens, for example. Why can't they?'

'Lack of imagination,' he said.

'Don't you want to take any photographs?' she asked.

'Nope, not right now. I have to get a new film.' He seemed irritated and broke off to talk to me. 'Yeah?'

'I'm hoping to fly to Endoman today. Can you give me any idea of what sort of place it is?'

'What sort of a place? D'ya mean to get in and out of? It's an all-weather strip. No overnight stay. We drop in there once in a while when there's a hole in the clouds. What's the interest in Endoman anyway?'

'I'm a writer out from England. I was interested to see something of a typical primitive Yali village.'

'Well, you certainly picked the right place.'

'I suppose there's a water supply? And can I buy food?'

'You're OK for water. River down in the valley. If you don't go for yams better bring your own chow. Check on the weight though. Limit's twenty kilos per person. Anything over that gets left behind.'

Next morning the flight to Endoman was confirmed. It was arranged that I was to be picked up there by a missionary plane when weather permitted and flown direct to Wamena. There was a last-minute rush to buy provisions: biscuits, dried noodles, instant soup, tea, sugar, powdered milk, kerosene and a stove.

John Strawser, the pilot, seemed more relaxed than he had been when I had met him on the previous afternoon. We climbed into the plane, and he became suddenly genial and confiding. I settled in the seat behind him and he raised his baseball cap in a little ceremony that concluded a routine last-minute check, addressing his maker in a strong and cheerful voice. 'OK, Father, we thank you for this time. We thank you for the beauty you have created here and we are able to see on this flight, and we ask you to protect us and give us a safe flight as we travel. We do pray this in Christ's name, Amen.'

The beauties of divine creation were imposingly on view within seconds of the take-off. There was a stunning view of Lake Sentani spread among purple hills, with sea-eagles drifting by, and its many small islands ringed with what at that height appeared as gem-stones in an over-opulent setting but which were in fact circular corrugated iron roofs.

Freed of some earth-bound tension, John opened up. He was proud of his Helios Courier plane and the aeronautical tricks it could be induced to perform if necessary. This short take-off, short landing missionary-special could land at 35 km per hour and take to the air in the length of two planes. If you crashed a Cessna you might at best end up with a number of splinters in your skin. The Helios encircled the cockpit with an iron frame. If they pulled you out of it alive you could expect to be intact.

The élite of the Missionary Air Fellowship, John said, were ex-Vietnam. He had just missed out on that great experience due to his youth, and had done what he could to compensate for this by his readiness to take on missions in areas only recently opened up, where a little more effort was demanded and there was a pioneering feel about the work. Take the case of Endoman, he said. It was one of the last Yali villages to be reached, and that made it interesting. The chart he used (Endoman was not yet on the map) showed it on the edge of a swirling contour enclosing what the chart called the 'limits of reliable relief'. After that there was a certain amount of guesswork in the mapping owing to insufficient exploration on the ground. Places like that had to be more interesting than others where all the work had been done twenty or thirty years ago.

And there was no doubt that even from the air the magnificence of this pristine jungle of Irian Jaya set it apart. It was impossible to withdraw the eyes from these instant changes from peak to ravine, from the savage conflict of colours, the black alpine forest stifled with moss, the razor-sharp mountain ridges glinting with malachite and quartz, the yellow rivers, the dark, rancid greens of the swamps. 'Know something?' the pilot said. 'Whenever I come over this run I give thanks to the Lord.'

There was a rent in forest texture surrounding a rectangle of a soft green, quite alien to the hard colorations of the jungle. Tiny straw-colour cells clustered at its edge to form a new pattern, but of a natural kind, at one with the environment. The nose of the plane dropped towards a sagging ridge-line between two peaks ahead, forming of this mountain the outline of a tent. The airstrip passed out of sight to the rear as the plane lifted itself over the ridge, and dropped to the left into a tight valley wooded with high trees. Here it banked sharply to the left again round a ferny, sugar-loaf hill, then faced upwards towards the airstrip which suddenly swung into sight, clean and sharp in an up-slope with a black shed and a couple of huts, and motionless black figures along the edge of the grass.

We bumped up to the top of the runway where more black figures awaited us. These I at first took to be teenage boys – perhaps even pygmies – but they turned out for the most past to be grown men, although considerably smaller than the Papuans of Jayapura and Sentani. Most of them were naked except for curving yellow penis-guards. There was a surprising absence of excitement. Three women, bare-breasted with swinging grass skirts, approached in single file and passed without so much as turning their heads. I unloaded my gear from the plane's hold and the pilot told me to carry it down to the black shed. At this point some of the watching Yalis, who up to that moment had hardly moved a muscle, came foward to help with the packages and bundles.

With that, a group of men made a slow and dignified appearance. These were the village chief, who was the smallest and most dignified of them, and his notables. The chief was an unsmiling man, very straight and slim, who could have been in his sixties. I shook hands with him, and he said most politely in Yali, 'I prize your faeces.' Each man of this group wore nothing but a penis gourd of identical length, and slanted slightly to the right.

'Well this is it,' the pilot said. 'Apart from us missionaries you're the second white man they've ever seen.'

'Would you describe this as being still part of the Stone Age?' I asked.

'Well I guess so. In a way,' he said. They still use stone tools to chop around in their fields. They're sure backward here.'

At this instant there was a brief glimpse of colour at the back of the little group of naked bodies as a grubby T-shirt came into view.

The pilot said, 'As soon as you get fixed up, you should ask for a meeting to be arranged with the chief in his house to get his permission to stay in the village. Right now give him and the other fellers a hank of that tobacco you brought along. You'll find the chief's OK. He killed a lot of men in his time, but he's a nice guy these days.' I handed out the tobacco, which was received with no evidence of emotion other than slight smiles. The chief and his retinue then withdrew, moving in step slowly and gracefully across the close-cropped green sward of the airstrip towards a high stile in the fence closing off the main part of the village. This, despite the bow and sheaf of arrows carried by each man in his right hand, they vaulted weightlessly, one after another, to pass out of sight.

Catan now took over. He was a Yali trainee-schoolmaster speaking fragmentary English and by virtue of his government post one of the authorities in the village. He and the headteacher, who hovered in the background, were the only males in view to wear Western clothes: track suits in extreme contrast with the otherwise general nudity. He was a more substantial man than the villagers I had so far seen and there was something in his complex expressions as well as the garments that hinted at a fairly successful detachment from the inconveniences of the Stone Age.

After consultation with the pilot it had been proposed that I be put up in the black shed by the airstrip, the dwelling of the first missionary who arrived in Endoman in 1980, which had latterly served as a schoolhouse and was now rapidly approaching dereliction. It was made from woven bamboo, with floors that flexed and creaked loudly under the tread. Catan showed me through its darkly theatrical interior and I settled myself in a cubicle which might once have been the headmaster Mattius's study. A notice in sprawling capitals, ORA ET LABORA, had been fixed to a wall; a number of the kind of random curiosities that schoolboys collect shoved into corners, and a narrow three-legged desk held a dozen or so exercise books that were to be, or had been, corrected. Two of the subjects taught at Endoman, simple arithmetic and the Indonesian language, were to be expected. The third, Moral Philosophy, came as a surprise. The headteacher's problem, Catan said, was that so far he had been unable to learn the Yali language, and while attempting to remedy this he had removed himself to an Indonesian-style house built for him outside the village.

'Big house. Very modern,' Catan said of the black shed as we crossed its swaying floors to inspect the amenities. It possessed, he claimed, aiding speech with grimaces of satisfaction, Endoman's most reliable water supply. Nearby a tiny stream trickling down from the hill above fed through a spout into a pool. It was available for drinking, washing sundry articles, or personal ablutions, and apart from a faintly sulphurous odour in its vicinity, which might have been all to the good, I noticed a yellow sediment the water carried. A more pressing problem was that of the latrine. The house was surrounded by a fence of stone-hewed palings, enclosing in addition to the building a strip of uneven land about fifteen feet in width. This sloped more and more steeply, eventually becoming a precipitous climb down a hillside, leading in the end to a length of ragged planking over a ravine. To attempt to negotiate this at night, I believed, would have been a perilous adventure. It was a problem aggravated by what I had read somewhere of the intricate inhibitions of Yali society, and the taboos imposed upon the desecration of a holy place (which could be anywhere) by faeces, urine or blood.

With the inspection at an end Catan reminded me of my interview with the chief the next day. 'You come morning.' It was impossible to fix an hour when I was expected, and at that moment I realised that for the Papuan peoples clocks had not been invented, and time as we understood it did not exist. As I later discovered there was a first part of a day and an end of a day, and no more than that. Thereafter, even the days that followed, so uneventful in their unchanging routines, settled into a simple compost of things past, and I suspected that from dawn until midday at least, the chief would await me without impatience.

Catan went, and suddenly I was terrifically alone. I made tea and sat outside the black shed scanning the valley, feeling myself in a species of quarantine. The first thing I had learned about the Yali was their capacity for total, purposeful inaction. A hundred yards away three boys had placed themselves against the village fence, and the positioning of heads, arms and legs had not changed since the plane touched down. Further away still on the slope of the airstrip, Catan and the headteacher stood together, garish in the poster colours of the track suits against the soft, green monochrome of grass and jungle. I turned my head, and with two hours to go until sundown, saw the slow steady encroachment of the fog, moving down towards the village through the trees. The silence was absolute.

THIRTEEN

THE SPECULATION AS to the best time to call on the chief ended with the appearance of Catan shortly before sunrise. I had failed to realise that he lived with his wife and child in a conical thatched hutch within yards of the end of the black shed, but now remembered vague disturbance in the night through the sound of coughing, and the outcry of someone – probably Catan – troubled by a nightmare. He had brought water boiled up by his wife, and I made tea, and we munched biscuits from Sentani, which set his eyeballs rolling with pleasure. Dawn was dramatic. There was a great combative upsurge of glowing mist from the darkness, and a greenish aurora overflowing through a cleft in the eastern peaks. In the interior gloom of the black shed, luminous stars shone on Catan's shirt. 'Let us take biscuits for chief,' he said. I grabbed some, and we set out to see Yurigeng.

Endoman, which had frequently been attacked in the course of never-ending ritual conflicts, had been built for reasons of defence on the slopes of a steep hill, with the chief's house near the top. It was reached by narrow, precipitous and circuitous paths involving, in addition, the negotiation of slippery stepping stones placed in a stream. These obstacles to easy access were designed to complicate an assault by surprise attackers. A minor aspect of the long catalogue of village protocol was that the chief's *yegwa* could only be approached from below, and those attempting to reach Endoman from the mountain slopes above were assumed to be enemies.

All the habitations of Endoman were of roughly the same circular design and appearance, differing mainly only in the matter of size. The very smallest of the women's huts could have been hardly more than six feet in diameter; an average hut would have been about double this size. All were made of stout stone-hewn planks bound together by rattan, with pandanus thatches drawn up to a central pole. A number of villagers had been able to build huts with double walls. This provided a narrow circular corridor with a floor raised about a foot from the ground, and was for the occupation of the pigs at night.

We climbed a short ladder to enter Chief Yurigeng's hut, and found

ourselves on a circular first floor about sixteen feet across. It possessed a
narrow gallery on which we settled ourselves facing the chief, who was
seated on a species of dais, flanked by five notables who, Catan said, had
distinguished themselves in the wars. All were naked except for penis
gourds of roughly the same size and colour. I was immediately struck by
the fact that, whereas the five notables had recognisably Yali faces, with
slightly Mongolian traits, Yurigeng was the image of Haile Selassie, with
the Emperor's small, spare body, his upright posture, his long, thin nose,
his downcast eyes, and his faint imperial expression of refined contempt.
Catan introduced me and explained the reason for my presence and
Yurigeng swivelled his eyes slightly in my direction and repeated the word
'*weh*', meaning welcome, five times. Someone added more branches to
the fire smouldering in the hearth, the smoke thickened, and two of the
notables began to cough.

There were the questions to be asked, but with what degree of formality or
informality, I wondered, and how were they to be framed? Was the subject of
cannibalism to be touched on? I decided against it. It was impossible to
imagine these Yali patricians, their faces full of reflexion and calm, gnawing
human bones. With Catan as interpreter I made an obviously hopeless
attempt to discover the chief's reaction to the enormous changes to which he
and his people had been subjected since the missionaries' arrival in 1980,
their destruction of the old order symbolised by the ritual house in which the
hitherto sacred objects had been kept, and the proclamation of the role of
Jesus Christ. It was a delicate topic and Yurigeng was well aware that
whatever he said would soon reach the ears of those civil and religious
authorities to which he was now subject.

Doubtfully I put my question. The answer was mumbled in a liturgical
monotone. Yurigeng was supposed to have said something to the effect
that things were much better now that the Lord Jesus had taken Endoman
into his care.'

'In what way?' I asked.

Clearly nothing had been prepared to deal with this. The chief cobbled
sentences together as a child might have done following a badly learned
lesson. Once again it was only possible to discern the gist of what
Yurigeng had to say in the dark verbal labyrinth of Catan's translation.
There followed a garbled and hesitant account of an attack by enemies in
the bad old days, in which one of Yurigeng's two wives had been killed.
Jesus had driven these enemies away.

I had the impression that Catan was steering the chief towards a
confession of a blameworthy past that he had now put behind him. 'He say
kill many men in wars,' Catan said.

'How many?' I asked.

Yurigeng's eyes met mine and suddenly there was an unmistakable flicker of interest – perhaps even the ghost of a patrician smile. He spoke firmly and without hesitation, and I could detect no evidence of contrition in his voice.

'How many did he say?' I asked Catan.

'Twenty-seven,' Catan said.

It was an insight into an aspect of the Stone Age still surviving here and there in tiny remote pockets of human isolation. Notwithstanding government and missionary efforts, Catan said, there had been battles in the last eighteen months in the neighbourhood of Endoman, with some sixteen deaths among those who had taken part. These were limited wars fought under ancient rules of combat in hard places like this where there was never quite enough in the way of resources to keep pace with the population. In Endoman people were very poor.

By night and at an altitude of nearly 6,000 feet and enswathed in chill mists it was a cold place, and fires burned in the huts. I asked Yurigeng why his people did not wear clothes, to which he replied that they would if they had them, adding that he himself did not even possess a shirt.

More branches were laid over the embers in the hearth, blue smoke curled up, eyes watered and soon the coughing became general. The moment had come to present the chief with the radio set I had brought him. He took it, was assisted to remove it from its box, twiddled with the knobs, found a snatch of Indonesian rock from Wamena, and after a moment of indecision passed the set to a friend at his side, after which it went the rounds. I wondered if this could be the first present he had ever received, and whether this little ceremony of giving and receiving marked yet another step, along with the putting aside for ever of his spear, in Yurigeng's transition to the new culture of possessions and the accumulation of wealth. The chief owned nothing but his reputation, his hut and his now obsolete weapons. Any pigs belonging to him could hardly be defined in terms of sole ownership because when a customary celebration called for a pig to be killed, the flesh would be divided between the members of the community, and by supplying the pig Yurigeng did no more than add to his prestige. It was my impression that the chief was totally at a loss what to do with his radio, which he would have been happy to cut into small pieces and share out like a pig. Thereafter one or another of the villagers – never the same man – could be seen tinkering with the set. Perhaps Yurigeng's turn came round again in the end.

When I left, Yurigeng came with me, and as we walked, his child's hand in mine, down the hill, across the stream and the airstrip to the black shed, where he left me, I wondered in what circumstances had this tiny black Alexander of the White Mountains killed so many of his enemies.

Endoman and its setting were exceedingly beautiful. The necessity to keep fires going in the huts meant that fuel was constantly in demand and this must have modified the original landscape, for few large trees were left. Instead, there were secondary growths of all shapes and sizes, spindly saplings often of enormous height, lianas dangling avalanches of tangled stems, plants with huge leaves patterned like medieval banners, and vigorous pandanus palms providing excellent thatching as well as tolerable fruit in season. Strangely enough, the crisp green rectangle of the airstrip seemed by no means out of place among this rich assortment of jungle colours, and the vast black shed did no more than add an acceptable touch of theatre. The airstrip had become a sort of promenade where young males put themselves on display with their bows and arrows and their spears and above all a missionary handout of a T-shirt featuring Donald Duck, and naked babies tumbled about the close-cut grass in perfect security. There were no orchids to be seen on the kind of trees left in the jungle by the village wood-cutters, but full sunshine on the strip had encouraged the appearance of a spectacular terrestrial variety ranged along the grass verges and growing to a foot in height. Endoman was spruce and clean. There was no mess anywhere because nothing was thrown away. Every single component of what we regard as litter would have been seen in this village as valuable.

The most striking features of these mountains were its mists and clouds. They surged up suddenly from the valleys or toppled over the mountain tops, diaphanous and brilliant and constantly in motion. Within minutes they dismembered a landscape, leaving a peak afloat in the whiteness here, a patch of forest there. A moment later these vanished and other scenic features appeared briefly in windows in the vapour before being blotted out in turn. During the night it rained steadily, but by day there were no more than spasmodic, freakish spatterings, and once I was showered by heavy droplets from a clear, lemon sky. Most days the sun shone but there was always a lurking dampness that took over at sundown and the insides of my sleeping bag were never quite dry to the touch. On my first morning in the schoolmaster's house I found that a billowing white fungus like moulded rubber had grown overnight all along the base of the fence, and this nightly growth proved to be a regular phenomenon.

The women did all the hard work in this village. They hacked the turf off patches of jungle, dug the soil with their digging sticks, planted, tended and harvested the sweet potatoes and yams. It was they, squatting on their haunches and with their babies miraculously balanced on their shoulders who slashed away at the grass with their machetes to keep the airstrip almost as smooth as a bowling green. It was a task for which I was never able to find out if they received a reward. The menfolk's function was little more than decorative now that the government, at least in theory, had put an end to the chronic inter-tribal warfare that had plagued these parts. Until recently they had been kept busy planning surprise attacks and ambuscades and keeping their warlike skills up to the standard called for by these affrays. Now, when such encounters were unpublicised and rare, they had time on their hands. I came to the conclusion that the first Yalis to settle in Endoman had only chosen to tuck themselves away in this narrow valley for reasons of defence. Otherwise it had little to offer. The zone was one of recently formed mountains prone to earthquakes and landslides that had destroyed many villages. The soil was poor and the climate harsh, and it was said to take twice as long to grow a crop of vegetables in this unfavourable environment as in the fertile valleys. Even then the results were small and poor. The men hunted in the jungle but killed little more than small birds and the occasional forest rat. These they ate themselves on the spot, because the vital essences of a living prey sharpened the eye of the marksman and toughened the spirit of the warrior. The women had to resign themselves to an unremitting diet of starch which no more than developed a fraudulent corpulence that concealed undernourishment. It was the spartan qualities developed in ritual warfare, the taboos outlawing all things endangering survival, and subservience to the rule of the ancestors that had ensured the Yalis' continued existence for unimaginable thousands of years. The government, with missionary aid, had released them from the ancient bondage, but it was hard to see what would become of them now.

Conflict was inseparable from the emotional lives of these Papuan mountain peoples. Three to four days on foot away to the west, the Danis of the Baliem had based their prosperity and developed their extraordinary gardening techniques on a forty-mile sash of alluvial soil approaching in its richness that of the Nile Valley. Dani families fill themselves on sweet potatoes, either steamed in leaf-bundles or baked, several times a day – an apparent vegetarian excess which can only have contributed to their fine physique. Their neighbours, the Yalis, who are obliged to eat much less of roughly the same thing are by comparison puny and unimpressive. There was food in abundance for everyone in the Baliem in an egalitarian system, with no internal dissent or fear of outside invasion. No necessity existed for warfare, yet this was – and is – a warrior society purely because racial memory harked back a few thousand years to the days before the Baliem, when the Danis had once battled with unyielding nature and numbers had to be trimmed to match meagre rescources. Limited battles staged between clans were invented to accomplish this.

It is not quite the same with the Yalis, who share an almost identical culture. The Yalis are poor and still living in the hard times from which their neighbours successfully extricated themselves perhaps ten thousand years ago. The Yalis cultivate pockets of soil in largely barren mountains containing little in the way of game. They need the battle casualties which the Danis certainly do not, and the families of no more than the two children to which most Yalis limited themselves. In their case it is something more real than a cultural hangover that drives them into battle. Now that such conflicts are virtually at an end, life has lost its point for warriors trained in the belief that the only honorable occupation is war.

It was against this background of boredom and restlessness that Catan took me by surprise with a proposal that the unemployed village warriors should stage a mock battle to be followed by a mock victory dance. This was by no means entirely for my entertainment. Mock battles were an accepted feature of Dani and Yali culture, a better-than-nothing opportunity for keeping warlike capabilities up to the mark with no more than accidental bloodshed, thoroughly enjoyed by participants and spectators alike. The authorities looked on them with a jaundiced eye, because a percentage developed into the real thing, and they were banned by most provincial governors, in particular the Bupati of Wamena, in whose territory most of them happened. 'It is forbidden,' Catan said. The clandestine encounter he had already mentioned had started as a sham of this kind, but resulted in the death toll of sixteen. Nevertheless, all the able-bodied males in the village, Catan assured me, would be happy to take part, and he seemed to suggest that it was an occasion when such persons as Mattius the schoolteacher might be induced to look the other way. By general agreement, then, the mock battle was to be staged on the following morning.

That evening brought about a change in the weather. A mist overbrimming suddenly like a sea of swansdown set all the conical thatches of the village afloat before unrolling itself down the airstrip, then spreading its tissues into all the gulches and gullies in the neighbourhood of the old schoolhouse. With the gathering of dusk huge moths settled around us, of a purple so dark that until a torch was shone upon them I assumed them to be black. They were of a kind I had already seen, attracted to the effluents of decay dribbling from under the supermarket in Sentani. Here they packed themselves, wings spread but absolutely still, under the overhang of thatches offering protection from what I supposed were eagle owls that flapped just above my head after dark.

Later the rain fell in brief torrents, a fence of water floodlit by the constant flickering of lightning. I was to discover in the morning that it had brought out the insects everywhere. Spiders with enormously long legs rushed about and rolled themselves into defensive balls in a hopeless attempt to escape Catan's sprightly cockerel, and his harems of blond hens covered the *yegwa* roofs in the compound, scratching a version of lice among the thatch. One hour of sunshine was enough to dry the grass of the airstrip, but mist, from which only a triangle of peak poked through, still drowned the lower slopes of the mountain. The mist was always different. This morning it swirled and twisted like an animal caught in a trap. It was thick enough to oblige the birds to strengthen their piping, muffled in fog. Then it weakened and drifted away in sashes and tatters, leaving as always only a small smokiness in the thickest of trees.

The first of the warriors began to arrive, bounding into sight over the five-foot-high fence with the airborne agility of a *corps de ballet*. Their black bodies glistened with grease, penis gourds curved to the height of breast-bones, and each man carried a bow, a sheaf of arrows having various uses, and a spear.

A minor crisis now arose. It had been understood that those taking part should dress in traditional style, wearing no more than their customary ornaments, such as neckties of cowries, bracelets of graded boar's teeth, trimmed white cockatoos' feathers in the hair, armbands of selected shells, and sometimes a hat of the fur of some rare animal into which a few feathers from a bird of paradise might have been stuck. It was a prospect that excited the villagers, and all the participants had fallen into line with the arrangements, decking themselves out in a manner reflecting wonderful natural taste. Only a small handful had not understood what was required of them. These, grinning triumphantly, had tried to outdo their friends by turning up in Donald Duck and Bugs Bunny T-shirts, which Engen, who kept a tiny missionary shop, had recently added to his stock. When asked to remove them they showed disappointment but no displeasure.

There was a small problem, too, with Catan, who ran up against his wife Apina's scornful resistance when he proposed to appear dressed, like all the rest, in a penis gourd. 'I can't bear to see him in one of those things,' she said, shaking her voluminous posterior in disdain under its covering of a grass skirt. From this remark it seemed possible that he had taken to Western garments before their marriage. However, it was clear for the moment that Catan had ceased to think of himself as a minor official, and was determined to recapture the excitements of even make-believe combat; the track suit came off and the *koteka* went on. Now, suddenly, barefoot and traditionally priapic in feathers and shells, he had undergone a quite extraordinary transformation, a subtle, physical change, even right down to the shape of his elongated almond eyes. In this moment of exaltation, and the resurgence even of natural valour, caution was thrown to the winds. Having fitted a well-made arrow to the string of his bow, he jokingly pointed it at me. His expression was suddenly thoughtful. 'Good you come here now,' he said. 'You come before missionaries' time, we eat you.' I could not be sure whether this, too, was to be taken as a joke.

According to the account of the happenings of eighteen months before, the battle appeared to the onlooker as much a ballet as conflict. With each man well-separated from the next, and placed like the pieces on a chess board on the slope of the airstrip, the two sides formed lines and rushed to the encounter, merging and intertwining in symmetrical fashion with their opponents. In this manner, however rapid the movement, the combatants remained separate. There was no infighting. Racing at top speed the warriors waved their spears, shot their arrows high into the air, formed figures of eight, carried out their serpentine forays through the enemy's lines, advanced and retreated. They took long shots at running adversaries they had little chance of hitting, and no-one came under fire at point-blank range. And this was much what I observed, too, with a single casualty at the end of a prolonged skirmish, and the battle called off when it came on to rain. Something must have gone wrong with the arrangements in 1981 when so many had died.

Karl Heider of the 1961 Harvard Peabody Expedition wrote disparagingly of these Papuan archers. They had never learned to feather their arrows, so could not shoot straight, nor had they learned to shoot off volleys, taking pot-shots here and there at random in such a way that the arrows could be watched in flight and thus easily avoided. Heider, who had probably seen the film purporting to portray the efficiency of English bowmen at Agincourt, seemed to ignore the reality that the Yalis and the rest of them were not in the business of efficient slaughter, and indeed were even at pains to avoid it. Yali arrows had a simple bamboo point, and it normally took a number of them to kill a man. The redoubtable Bruno De Leeuw, cornered by the Yalis on a fetish-burning expedition, had collected five of them – one in the intestines – but simply yanked them out of his flesh and threw them away. The Yalis were not interested in conquest or extermination but in population control, and rival battles fought with not very lethal weapons were part of a programme which also banned sexual intercourse for three years after the birth of a child, thus contributing to the same end in a less spectacular way.

The mock battle merged into a victory dance, with little to distinguish the two phases, except that, with no arrows to be avoided, the dance was a simpler affair. The action was accompanied by monotonous chanting. Closing my eyes I could imagine myself at Highbury at a cup tie, for these primeval sounds were to me indistinguishable from the atonal baying of an excited football crowd exhorting their team to 'come on you reds'. Thus, and in an almost comparable situation, a triumphal outcry from the dawn of humanity was to be matched with one of our day.

Nipson nestled to the west of Endoman at the foot of the mountains in the next valley and had been pointed out by the pilot as we flew over it as a place of singular interest. As it happened I knew something of its history, for it had achieved a macabre celebrity in 1974 following a massacre in which a native evangelist and his twelve assistants engaged in conversion of the local people had been killed and devoured. I would have liked to visit Nipson but abandoned the idea after Catan's warning of a two-day walk through difficult mountainous terrain, with rivers to be crossed. I found it curious that he should have been the first to broach the subject of cannibalism, yet a discussion of the history of Nipson should clearly have been taboo, for he went on to say that it was a place of no importance which he had only heard of two years before.

The Nipson episode belonged to the final explosive stages of a war between tribesmen and the missionaries following over-confident missionary thrusts into new territory for the building of airstrips prior to the establishment of permanent bases. These lightning forays into *terra incognita* were undertaken by exceedingly adventurous young zealots with the backing of a government who recognised them as specialists in the pacification of tribals.

A widespread fury over the appropriation of tribal land was intensified by the missionary custom of destroying village 'spirit houses', and their contents, regarded as sacred by the tribal people. A typical incident in the course of the evangelical campaign is described in a missionary publication, *Lords of the Earth*, by Don Richardson. It took place in 1967 at the beginning of the great missionary drive, and Stanley Dale and Bruno de Leeuw, pushing blindly on into the unknown, found themselves in the village of Ninia. They discovered some flat terrain of the kind which, 'with a little grit and three or four months of hard work could be coaxed into an airstrip'. But the co-operation of several hundred Yalis would be required, and they seemed undisposed to help. Their reluctance may

have been due to the fact that, as usual, gardens and dwellings stood in
the way. Stan and Bruno carefully listed the names of their owners,
presumably for eventual compensation. 'Lord, you knew,' Bruno prayed,
'when you created this valley, that this conflict of interests would arise.
You could have provided a slope for an airstrip somewhere else, or you
could have prevented the Yali from choosing this site for a spirit house.
Since you didn't, this conflict of interests must be part of your plan.
Perhaps you intended to work through it.'

And it was with this assumption that the pair went into action,
dismantling the village houses with the aid of the native converts they had
brought with them. Stan and Bruno found the Yali's stone-hewn boards
to be of 'excellent quality', and promptly used them to begin new and
larger dwellings for their own need. They were short of wood to finish the
job. 'No matter,' Stan said. 'We'll dismantle that spirit house on the knoll
tomorrow. It has to go because of the airstrip, in any case. And it will yield
plenty of good large boards to finish our own dwelling.'

It seems incredible that hundreds of Yali, noted for their combative-
ness, should stand meekly by and watch the destruction of their village
and their crops and do nothing to prevent this happening. Richardson
explains why. Stan and Bruno, unlike their fellow evangelists, had been
at pains to study Yali culture and traditions, and had unearthed a belief
that powerful ancestors would appear again on earth reincarnated as
whites. It was a credence that was put to good use on this occasion. The
Yalis looked on in bewildered dismay as those they took to be their
illustrious ancestors Marik and Kugwarak wreaked their havoc. It has
been suggested elsewhere that this imposture had served its purpose on
other occasions.

Next year Dale, with a fresh partner, Phil Masters, set out once again to
push back the missionary frontiers, trekking into the Seng Valley, one of
the few remaining areas without an airstrip. Here, while in the process
of measuring out suitable ground, they were intercepted, killed, and
subsequently eaten. This act of cannibalism provoked the inevitable
police reprisals in which a number of warriors were shot. Thereafter war
with the missionaries escalated until the final holocaust several years later
at Nipson.

A sharp-eyed chronicler of this period and these events was Robert
Mitton, an Australian geologist who was in Irian Jaya between 1970 and
1976 investigating its mineral resources. Outside his professional geology
Mitton interested himself in every aspect of the local culture, its history,
botany and anthropology. The maps he made for his company were in
demand by missionaries and government officials. He collected Asmat art

for museums and took a crash course in medicine enabling him to undertake paramedical work among tribal people up to a time when, as a result of an illness which proved fatal, he was obliged to return to Australia.

Of the remote valley where Stan Dale and Phil Masters met their end, Mitton wrote to a friend in 1971:

Today we went into true cannibal country around Nipson and the Seng Valley. So aware of the fact was everyone that we carried a shotgun in the helicopter. The thought of me standing over Dave with a loaded gun while he did his geology was mildly absurd. Dave and I were dropped into a creek to take a sample, and the pilot, instead of hovering, left us for forty-five minutes. We were a trifle hypersensitive and when I looked up at one point I noted with an 'Oh shit' that we had company. Anyway, all the visitor wanted was to trade his stone adze. Later we became quite uncomfortable when the village across the river began to empty in our direction. Dave and I began to lay bets on the odds of their reaching us before the helicopter. With flare guns loaded with our last flare (the shotgun with everything else was in the helicopter) we sat down and waited. Fortunately the helicopter came first, but not until Dave had stated that 'we could have been dead and defecated by the time it got to us'.

The geologists' problems among the angry and now dangerous tribes-people continued. 'Angurak was opened up and a strip begun by the Dutch Protestant missionary. Not long after, a flu epidemic went through the area and many people died. The natives blamed this on the missionaries and passed out the word that if the missionaries came back they would be killed and eaten.' However, the missionaries returned and were attacked. It seems to have been quite a battle. Once when a missionary plane came under attack and the pilot took off with arrows hitting the plane, 'it then proceeded to dive-bomb the attackers while Kujit (the local missionary-in-chief) held them at bay with a shotgun. At the same time there was an attack at Angurak which resulted in eight attackers being shot. It will be interesting to see what happens next'.

What in fact happened was the massacre at Nipson in May 1974. As Mitton puts it: 'the locals had had enough of the Good Word, burned down the missionary's house, and ate his Biak preacher and 12 of his assistants. Fortunately for them the missionaries, including Kujit, were in the United States on leave'.

It was not all aggression and retribution. A month later Mitton noted that a Missionary Aviation Fellowship plane crashed near this spot. 'Of six or seven people aboard only a ten-year-old boy survived, who was taken care of very tenderly for some days by the Seng people until the rescue party arrived.'

FOURTEEN

I HAD COME to Endoman in the expectation of discovering Stone Age remnants in an otherwise transitional society committed to the future of the Indonesian racial amalgam. This proved far from being the case. Catan, who said that no-one had bothered to count the exact number of the inhabitants, thought, after a surreptitious use of fingers to aid calculation, that a figure of 200 might be about right. Of these it was clear that five had moved with the times. They were Catan himself, his wife Apina, Mattius the headteacher who could not speak the language, Engen the native preacher who also ran what was called the shop, and an Indonesian with a soured and fugitive expression who drifted occasionally into view wearing as a badge of authority an American Airforce peaked cap. This was the government appointed shadow-chief, of whom nobody took the slightest notice. Of the rest of the population it would have been reasonable to say of them that they were as solidly embedded in the Stone Age as they and their ancestors had ever been. One of the pleasant things in Endoman was a walk out of the village, when I would meet tiny men on the path, armed to the teeth, who just happened to be passing through, and we would exchange broad smiles, clasp hands and perhaps walk a yard or two together before going on our own way. Could it be that once they would have eaten me on the spot? I doubted it.

It was impossible not to think of the naked if charismatic Yurigeng, doing his best to share a radio with approximately 195 persons, and freezing in his hut at night, as anything but a product of the Stone Age. What else could be said of the aged, toothless, smiling men who squatted all day long outside his hut and had no contact with the products of any age but the far past – with the exception of the ball-point pens stuck through holes in the septums of their noses? What also of the womenfolk of Endoman who did all the work and were hermetically sealed off at the day's end in women's houses, debarred from all contact with males except for the purposes of procreation. Only Apina had been wrenched out of the arduous and restrictive past. Catan had taken her to live with him in the hut next door, and she faced the world with an expression of permanent astonishment and embarrassment in the brown and yellow squared-off jogger's top, which – despite her insistence in concealing her enormous buttocks beneath a grass skirt – admitted her to membership of our age.

Money was the talisman chosen by the missionaries to break the hold of the past, but its uses were still hardly understood in the village and I suspected that what little of it there was in circulation remained in the hands of the five leading personalities. Cowrie shells and above all salt had been the old mediums of exchange. When Stan Dale and Bruno de Leeuw had taken over much of the village of Ninia for their airstrip and calculated it would take 'a hundred or two Yalis three or four years to complete the work', salt was the inducement offered. 'As Stan, Bruno and the Danis (converts the missionaries brought with them) fell to the task of dismantling the nearest Yali *yegwas* and *homias* (men's and women's houses)', Don Richardson the missionary historian tells us, 'no-one paid much attention. All were hungrily nibbling the *duongs*' salt as if they had never tasted true salt before, and might never have the privilege again.' It was a situation detrimental to trade which was quickly ended. Cowrie shells imported in vast quantities from the Pacific were dumped on the market, and unlimited supplies of salt quickly provided. Communities such as Endoman were to become trading partners with the missions, and all deals were for cash. I noticed that the plane carrying me into Endoman was loaded up with ground nuts for the return journey. Exactly how the partnership worked I was never able to discover, although Catan produced some interesting figures. The missionaries, he said, paid between 600 and 700 rupiah (approximately 20p) per kilo for the nuts, which were resold in the shops at about 2,000 rupiah. But did the villagers receive cash for these sales? I asked, and at this point Catan became vague. The missionaries, he said, bought the things they needed, and in addition were paying for a new school. Yet cash was in circulation, as I observed when Catan inadvertently produced a wad of rupiah notes from his pocket. Engen's shop, too, sold for cash such requirements as soap powder, aspirin, packets of dried noodles, and above all T-shirts. Tiny leaks, I suspected, may have opened up in the mainstream of income, in whatever direction it might be flowing.

The picture Endoman presented was of penury and neglect borne with stoicism. Inevitably the children were worst off, although I only once heard one cry. They had the advantage over the children of civilisation in that wherever the mother went, and in whatever posture she worked, her baby was always carried in a net on her back. Many babies' stomachs were dreadfully distended by parasites, and children as a whole normally suffered from inflamed eyes, sores, a variety of disconcerting skin conditions and incessant coughs. Did they receive no medical care? I asked Catan. He took me to see what he called the dispensary. Evidence of benefits derived from the trading partnership eluded me. With some reluctance Catan admitted that it might have been better had the women spent the whole of their time growing food for hungry people, rather than dissipating so much of their energies in what seemed to be a dubious commercial adventure.

When travelling in Latin America and the Far East I had found that the medical profession of late had developed a new respect for the skills of practitioners of certain herbal and traditional remedies, so much so that in some countries orthodox physicians have openly turned to them for assistance. What had happened in Endoman? Did traditional healers still exist? I asked. The answer was – as I knew it would be – that they had been driven away under the government ban. One or two remained, although hidden deep in the forest, where they were out of reach by those who most needed their services.

The problem of shortages arose. I had concentrated on a supply of powdered soup and dried noodles not because I had any faith in them as nourishment, but because they were practically weightless. The heaviest item was a case of water in sealed plastic bottles. Tea and powdered milk had been remembered but there was not nearly enough sugar.

The mountain climate of Endoman seemed to stimulate appetite, and therefore dissatisfaction with chicken or mushroom soup with noodles twice a day. John the pilot had advised on any problem in the matter of provisions that might arise. 'These guys actually like yams,' he said. 'It's the only thing you're sure to find. Sago is OK if it's cooked right, and the same goes for sweet potatoes. Trouble is these people don't grow too much of anything. Anyway, you're not going to starve.'

After the third meatless day I spoke to Catan about the possibility of buying a chicken, and he said he would look round for one. Chickens in plenty used to parade with their young up and down the airstrip, but they were exceptionally handsome birds, and kept, I suspected, largely for their ornamental value rather than for food. Catan made it sound as though chickens were rare, although that evening he turned up with a shapeless and partially defeathered black hen. This was instantly killed in my presence. It seemed extraordinary to me that the Yalis, who are known for killing their enemies without compunction, should have shown squeamishness at a time like this. It upset them, Catan said, to have to listen to the squawkings of a dying bird, so they avoided this by a deft manual operation to destroy its vocal chords. With this, appetite for chicken stew left me, and once again it was soup for supper.

Following the growing concern over food was the discovery I had forgotten the replacement torch batteries. My torch was already showing signs of giving up, so for twelve hours at a stretch I was at the mercy of absolute and impenetrable darkness. Being warned of what was about to happen to me I took to switching on a glow-worm illumination for no more than two or three seconds at a time to establish my position in the geography of the night and to check the time in the pink halo encircling my watch. The loss of sight sharpened the other senses. The darkness that lay like a bandage on the eyes contained its own repertoire of noises, most of them faint but some remarkably loud, and all inviting interpretation. With every movement of the body the bamboo creaked softly, not only at the point of physical contact but here and there in response to the changes in stress throughout the building. Water dripped constantly from the pipe into the pool on the other side of the wall, but added to this familiar sound there were occasional inexplicable splashes. Something whirred like a tiny electric fan over my head; a metronome ticking started, stopped and went on again. From the sleepers of the Catan household clustered around the embers of their fire and drawing its smoke into their lungs the sound of intense coughing reached me, and, once in a while, a groan. The night, too, brought out new scents, above all the spiciness of mildew in the nooks and corners of the bamboo where the air lay undisturbed.

Morning, as ever, took me by surprise with its fanfare of birds, the orchids which had opened overnight in the ditch by the fence, and a sumptuous evanescence of clouds dissolving as I watched them in the pale vaporous sky. This was the day when I had agreed to accompany a party on a hunt for birds of paradise. I did this with misgivings, falling back, in attempted self-justification, on the argument that with or without me the hunt would in any case go on, that I might at least be rewarded with a good view of one of these extraordinary creatures, and that, as the Yalis ruefully admitted, the chance of shooting a bird was very slight.

The Yalis had always hunted birds of paradise, using their separate feathers as adornments for various parts of the body, or in the case of a powerful chief, incorporating the whole bird into a headdress. The birds had an exchange value against pigs, and it is believed that Chinese traders of old travelled as far as these highlands searching for them, along with kingfishers' breasts from Cambodia, to embellish the ceremonial attire of leading mandarins. Nowadays, pitched suddenly into a money economy, the Yalis hunted for cash. It was notable that every man in Endoman, when leaving the village for any reason, carried along with his bow not only arrows with a single point to deal with human adversaries but those having three points for small birds, and a third kind of arrow in which the point was replaced with a small plug. This was designed to bring down a bird of paradise without damage to its plumage. Such successes were rare. When, once in a while the hunters had the good luck to kill one, they would share out and devour the entrails on the spot. These were valued for their magical juices, responsible for the birds' inexhaustible promiscuity. After that the fastest runner in the group would be commissioned to take on the four-day trek across the mountains to Wamena where the carcase was worth a bundle of rupiah notes.

The potential value of such a bird in terms of money could be enormous, but wealth remains a hieroglyph of language to the Stone Age man. It is not understood, therefore it is not sought, and if by accident, almost – as in this case – it is come by, it is rapidly disbursed. An American I met in Jayapura was emphatic in his agreement that this was so. This, coincidentally too, was apropos of birds of paradise. 'A native in Biak offered me a Prince Rudolph in perfect shape. They net them and a good one fetches up to a thousand bucks. I started off with two hundred bucks. No deal. He wanted the watch I was wearing. "I don't want to let it go," I said. "It was a gift. I'll make it five hundred and we'll call it a day." He still wasn't interested. "That's about a million rupiah," I told him. "You could keep your family in food and clothing for the rest of their lives." He still wanted the watch, so I had to give it to him.'

Where were these famous birds to be seen? The answer to this question was that they put in a regular afternoon appearance round about 4 pm in a clump of tall trees mysteriously spared by the gatherers of fuel at the top end of the village, to which birds were attracted by the small fruit they bore. Experience had taught them that in the topmost twigs they were out of bow shot, and next day, placing myself at a discreet distance from the trees, I waited in hope. I had visions of the Emperor of Germany's Bird of Paradise that begins its courtship display the right side up, then tilts backwards until it hangs upside-down among its cascading plumes, of the Enamelled Bird of Paradise flying a series of between twenty and forty miniature flags from the two-inch plumes sprouting from its head, of the Twelve-wired Bird of Paradise extending an iridescent bib of bluish throat feathers up to and around its bill, before opening this to reveal the brilliant lining of its mouth, and of the Magnificent Riflebird, which, having spread its purple wings shaped like a Japanese fan, also displays the coral interior of mouth and throat, before uttering a call that sounds like the whistle of a bullet.

The reality of the experience was unexciting. At a couple of hundred yards – which sensibly enough was the nearest approach the birds would permit – distance had demolished any possibility of appreciating these splendours. The supposed birds of paradise tumbling anonymously through the trees' high branches might have been crows – to which they are closely related.

It was no more than a foretaste of what was to follow. My route with the hunting party was through a shallow valley continuing the slope of the airstrip along a path around enormous fern-embedded boulders to the river, overshadowed by substantial trees. At 5,500-odd feet, Endoman was placed above the level of the rainforest, although here and there an interesting mix of jungle trees had survived. Inevitably the demand for firewood and building materials had described a circle possibly two miles in diameter round the village in which most trees had been chopped down by the wielders of stone axes. A great influx of sunlight had replaced them largely with underbrush and scrub. Irian Jaya was supposed to possess an unparalleled richness of fauna, much of it extraordinary and unique, including tree kangaroos, the flightless cassowary, capable of disembowelling a man with a single kick, goliath frogs, giant marsupial rats, bird-eating spiders, a pigeon nearly as big as a goose and 70,000 species of butterflies and moths. They all inhabited the rainforest which spreads its shade through the largely uncluttered spaces between the tall trees. By comparison the secondary forest of Endoman was largely devoid of wildlife and the best it had to offer were the great owls flapping through the mists as night closed in.

Coming down from its source in the Snow Mountains in the south, the river, which was full of orange silt but quite empty of fish, ran brightly over porcelain rocks. It curled endlessly, sometimes almost doubling back upon itself in this rocky terrain. Where there were pockets of earth that tributaries feeding into the main river had been unable to leech away there were small groves of casuarinas and firs, most of them stripped of their lower branches. We saw no birds of paradise.

The one interesting feature of this unfruitful enterprise was a brief encounter with the moss forest. It is a phenomenon delicately adjusted to altitude, temperature, the swaddlings of fog and an absence of wind, and is widespread in a patchy fashion throughout Irian Jaya. In this case it covered a lodgement of flood-subject soil squeezed in between the river bank and a tall hill overshadowing it, and although elsewhere the morning had long since dried out, the mist still hung in strips among these sepulchral trees. We were confronted with a miscellany of tangled branches and wasted trunks under a vast, grey cobwebbing of moss through which lianas hung like hangmen's ropes. The mosses were of many kinds and they grew here in competition with one another. They invaded and fed upon sickly wood, flayed away coverings of bark, and climbed to hang in terminal bunches among the topmost twigs. When one growth that had sucked the nutrients from a colonised area died back, laying an inert blue carpeting between the trees, another broke surface to feed on its predecessor's decay. Fallen trees had turned over the years into ridges or banks without solidity, or fragile cylinders of embalmed wood, and scrambling over them they squelched and collapsed like pastry-crust underfoot. Whichever way you turned the moss hung in tattered curtains over the path. Mitton was much impressed by this speciality of the Irian Jaya landscape, but in carrying out his geological surveys he found it more of an obstacle than the rainforest; even of the highest mountain ranges.

Whatever the undeclared views on religious matters they may have, the people of Endoman follow the general Papuan custom of these days by going to church. Some may be impelled by genuine fervour, others by a yearning for distraction of any kind. In a village where men and boys would gather for hours on end to watch me washing up dishes or shaving at the edge of the stream, churchgoing was rich in the incidents it provided.

Endoman's mission hall was devoid of chairs, a plain affair rather like a well-scrubbed cow-shed – but it was at least the centre of some activity, some brief relief, particularly for the menfolk, from the slavery of idleness now the coming of peace had left them with so little to do. The first of the congregation arrived before seven in the morning to take up preferential positions, squatting in rows as near as possible to the platform from which, when the hall had filled up, Engen, having shut up shop for the day, would begin to preach. These early arrivals were properly clothed in accordance with missionary standards. The less important next-to-naked, who had been unable to come by imported finery, were placed as far out of sight as possible at the back. A few women, who were the last to slip through the door, ranged themselves carefully separated from the men along one wall, and were expressionless as ever. By about 9 am I would have said that apart from Chief Yurigeng and his small aristocratic following, whom I suspected of covert agnosticism, the whole male population was in attendance. Nevertheless there were few women indeed. Catan evaded positive explanation. Perhaps no-one had quite succeeded in convincing them that the mission hall was not an extension of a men's house from which by the old religion they had been ritually debarred. Those that had shown up had brought their children, almost all of them, like half the adults present, wracked with terrible coughs.

There were men in the congregation I had never seen before, and it was to be supposed that they had come from outlying hamlets, and were to be instantly distinguished by a certain rustic outlandishness in their appearance. At this point I realised that even in such basic and age-old cultures the townee distinguished himself from the countryman. The conservative poor wore nothing in the way of adornment but a necklace of graded boar's teeth or a few shells. Those who had taken a few paces towards our times sported T-shirts upon which the Disney animals could hardly be made out through the grime. The country-folk, who had set out to trudge here across the mountains before dawn, still thrust any small manufactured objects they could lay hold of, even the occasional key, through the holes bored in the septums of their noses, and forced two-inch plugs into their earlobes, in which trifling articles of value were carried. Eventually, in old age, the earlobes gave way, so that their ruin in the form of little ropes of cartilage and skin hung down each cheek. This was a sight from which the villagers averted their eyes.

What purports to be a religious service conducted in such an environment calls for extreme theological simplification. What possible contacts could the minds of these villagers have with the intellectual subtleties evolved in fourth-century Byzantium shortly after the Emperor Constantine's conversion to the new faith? How could the preacher Engen, peeping out through the shutters of the Stone Age, explain to them the mystery of the Holy Trinity, Redemption, Atonement, and the union of divine and human natures in the Hypostasis of Christ? Or, if compelled to fall back on biblical stories, what would a people who had always lived for the day, possessed no property, and shared whatever they produced, make of the idea of laying up treasure in Heaven, or of the many examples scattered through the scriptures of admiration for those who advance their own cause at the expense of the community.

The fact is that Engen may have been a first-rate raiser of sweet potatoes, and have learned to cope with trifling monetary transactions in the shop, but as a spiritual leader he was non-existent, reduced to repeating formulae which at best his congregation could accept as words possessing some magical association. It was a case of the blind leading the blind. The service took a liturgical form in which Engen chanted a sentence and the villagers chanted their response. 'Mathew, Mark, Luke, John,' trumpeted Engen through his nose, and a responsive roar arose among the coughing of the congregation. 'Mathew, Mark, Luke, John.' I was reminded of the experience of Henry and Maria Carradine employed by the Venezuelan government to carry out a census of its Indian population. They were carried by helicopter to a remote Panare community where a native evangelist was at work with the children, trying to inculcate the principles of Christianity. 'The village children were made to kneel down in a row. No-one could understand what was going on, nor could the evangelist understand. In the end he said, "Every time I say the word Jesus, you must bang your head on the ground," and this they did.' Of this experience Carradine said, 'Know something? They were quite happy about it all. Not much goes on in the Venezuelan savannah. It gave them something to think about.' And perhaps the service at Endoman did that, too.

Catan had been with me and seemed to have been revived by the chanting. I would have supposed from all accounts that a similar meeting conducted in the vicinity of the spirit-house in the old days might have been more dramatic, but this was entertainment of a kind. I took advantage of his evident euphoria to risk bringing up the subject of his own conversion and how it came about.

'They tell us', he said, 'to take Christ or burn in big fire of God.'

When the first white man in an aeroplane drops out of the sky to deliver this ultimatum, little but instant compliance is to be expected.

Next day the Helios Courier was to fly in to pick me up. There was no certainty about this arrangement, for the weather in these inconstant mountains followed no pattern and barometric probabilities were to be measured by hours rather than days.

On about one occasion in three a visiting missionary plane in search of an airstrip might be called upon to circle for a while before locating a hole in the swirling clouds, and on this day of my depature for Wamena in the Baliem Valley the prospects were at first dubious. An otherwise luminous night had spread great charcoal smears across the sky, translated by the dawn into mists. In the first hours they spread about the village like outpourings of smoke but then the sun broke through and tore them apart, and shortly the air-sleeve was run up by the strip to signal that the plane was to be expected.

With this the women responsible for the airstrip's maintenance scuttled into position, babies on shoulders and machetes in hand, and began to chop away with all possible speed at fast-growing weeds that had appeared on the surface of the airstrip during the few days I had been there. Following this, a stream of villagers was seen to be approaching for the ceremonial leave-taking. They were led by Chief Yurigeng holding the radio set in his hands like a sacerdotal object. This had long since fallen silent from battery exhaustion. Following Catan's suggestion my rubbish had been piled up within the fence, ready for removal. One by one my visitors bounded over the stile and began to examine opened sardine tins, powdered milk cans, and plastic bags. Every single constituent of this tiny pyramid of junk down to the last tin lid was found to be of value. Calmly, quietly and equably the division of the detritus was carried out, and I was thanked by universal smiles.

One of the grass-cutters waved her machete at the sky, and little high-pitched laughter broke out, with which our visitors showed their excitement as the Helios Courier turned almost on its side to round the mountain, levelled out, lowered itself on its enormous wings to the runway, and touched down with extraordinary grace.

Yurigeng passed the silent radio to a servitor, took my hand and, with two of his notables following with my bags, we walked together hand in hand towards the plane. Round this the villagers – including now even the women – had formed a wide, absolutely motionless semi-circle. John the pilot received me with a congratulatory smile. He had been a little doubtful if he could make it. He raised his baseball cap in prayer. 'Lord we thank you for opening up the weather this morning and for the success of our friend's mission. Right now we're taking off for Wamena. Happens there's a scheduled flight from Sentani to Wamena this morning with more passengers I'm aiming to pick up, and I ask you Lord to make their connection possible.'

The take-off was exhilarating. Endoman's neat assembly of bee-hives were suddenly snatched up and dragged away to the rear out of sight. Coming in to land the pilot had had to make his cautious turn round the base of the mountain with a wing almost brushing the tops of the pandanus, but the take-off was a full-throttle charge straight at the mountain, then an easy lift up over the low trees and the great white limestone crags at the top into the mist-free, crystal clear air, with the forest lying crinkled at its bottom like weed on the bed of the ocean. A single white cloud, swollen and bulging at its base, had settled on the top of a peak; gorges and waterfalls were spaced like a geographical exhibit on the mountainsides, and yellow rivers curled through the valleys. Somewhere, shortly beyond Proggoli, a mountain range with an 11,000-foot summit ridge had to be crossed. On a bad day, John said, we would have to zig-zag to get over, but everything was right with the weather to go straight at it, and this he did. A million or two years of alternative sunshine and frost had shaved the ridge to a series of cutting edges that flashed back at us as we skimmed over them. There followed an Alpine flatland with its crabbed and stunted and moss-laden trees only 200 feet below.

Forty miles of the Baliem Valley lay ahead, coming into sight as a glittering snakeskin of fields through which the river corkscrewed, narrowed to a thread and was blotted out in mist. The valley's bottom held gardens by the thousand created in the depths of pre-history. For the Danis are accepted as being among the world's most skilful and sophisticated horticulturists, although they are almost certainly cultivating their gardens in these days as they did thousands of years ago. Following what must have been a huge period of trial and error they succeeded in deciphering the secrets by which certain jungle root plants could be transformed into edible forms. Thereafter the brand of intelligence and ingenuity displayed by the Mayas and their development of corn was applied in this case to the sweet potato. The Danis devised a complex system of irrigation ditches giving the plants' roots constant access to water, combining this with the perfect drainage provided by raised beds. They enriched the soil by potash obtained by burning of underbrush, by mulches from compost heaps of weeds, and by the mineral-rich soil dredged up from the bottom of the ditches and spread over the beds. Apart from utilitarian ends they were and are concerned with appearances. The tops of Dani vegetables sprout from the ground in perfect line, each plant at a precise distance from the next. The beds' geometry will have won the approval of a critical eye, and, seen from above, the bold, black scrawlings of the ditches among sparkling vegetation recall the designs of an archaic vase-painter rather than the prosaic labour of men concerned only with harvests. Archbold, leader of the 1938 expedition who first viewed this astonishing prospect from the air was inclined to believe that they might have stumbled upon an ancient civilisation, a Conan-Doyle-style lost world that had remained hidden away here. For how could primitive people in the mere tillings of their fields have possessed such an enthusiasm for pattern and form? 'From the number of gardens and stockaded villages we estimated the population to be at least 60,000,' Archbold wrote.

He was increasingly amazed by these Stone Age experiences. So overwhelming, for example, was the Dani hospitality that when on a subsequent expedition on foot his party reached their first village the villagers refused to let them pass, and the convicts supplied by the Dutch as bodyguards had to shoot two before they would move aside. 'Never in all my experience in New Guinea have I seen anything like it,' Archbold said. And there was nothing comparable in those days – and very little since.

As we came in to land villages drifting into sight spoke of inflexible planning, and the exact placing and alignment of paths radiating from their nucleus recalled the linked molecules of a diagrammatic chemical formula. The arrival by air gave us glimpses of Wamena at its best: two naked men waving from a rattan suspension bridge over the river, fifty

children circling hand-in-hand in a pre-historic ring-a-roses, a newly
built compound with a man on each roof-top trimming the thatch, a
garden burnished with squares and diamonds of vegetables, irrigated
fields with emerald reflections skipping from ditch to ditch, then
Wamena's line-up of tin roofs and the small blustering whirlwinds
whipped up by the propellers on the airport.

Wamena produced so far nothing but excellent vegetables so everything from a steam-roller to the altar for the Catholic Church, and thence
down the scale to a one-inch nail had to be brought in – in some cases in
many parts in the hold of a plane. All round us these imports were stacked
up, providing useful material for a study of Papuan development along the
road to a future in a new age.

A massive delivery of lavatory pedestals had been invitingly lined up –
which even I was ready to accept as an advance over Endoman's plank
over a ravine. Behind them were piled lengths of drainpipe, and in the
background the ends of privacy and exclusion were to be served by
innumerable rolls of barbed wire. A small tree with big, glossy, unnatural
leaves and root-ball in sacking was ready to be dropped in its hole in some
upper-class patio garden. The Danis who worked at unloading the planes
were examining these objects with the greatest possible interest, and the
occasional outcry of wonderment. They were at least a head taller than the
Yalis, and of exceptional muscular physique. The prodigious hospitality
we had read of still existed. The Danis carried it to such lengths that they
were accustomed to visit the airport in the hope of running into newly
arrived visitors with nowhere to go, whom they would invite to their
homes.

The one thing that impressed me about the airport building at Wamena
was an enormous artificial flower placed in the path of arriving
passengers. This, a polystyrene Rafflesia fully four foot in diameter, had
been so painstakingly created that for a moment I thought I detected a
sickly floral fragrance in its vicinity, whereas the fact was that the airport as
a whole smelt of nothing but a powerful anti-mosquito spray in use. After
the flower came the information desk where I enquired for a taxi driver
called Namek who, according to a Jayapura agent, could usually be found
at the airport, and was the only Dani in Wamena who spoke English
reasonably well.

I was taken to the back of the building, where he was pointed out to me,
occupied at this moment with some tourists who were photographing him
in national garb. He was short for a Dani, with glittering eyes and a black
beard, and as he hurried forward at the end of the session to introduce
himself his limp translated itself into a skip. His flat fur hat, of the kind

once worn by Henry Tudor, enhanced a dignity by no means impaired by his nakedness. Apart from this head-covering he wore nothing but a two-foot yellow penis gourd, the *koteka*, held in the upright position by a string round the waist. The scrotum had been tucked away at the base of this, exposing the testicles in a neat bluish sac. After the nudity of Endoman this did not surprise; moreover, as the plane had taxied in I noticed half a dozen nude men unloading a cargo plane.

We shook hands. Namek repeated the greeting '*weh, weh*' a number of times, excused himself, and came back wearing ill-fitting ex-army jungle fatigues. It now turned out that the taxi, in which he had a quarter share, was the magnificent ruin of an ancient Panhard-Levasseur, formerly owned by a Javanese rajah. It now awaited us, refulgent with polished brass, at the airport gate. In this we travelled in some state to a losmen he recommended, the Baliem Vista, where we learned that no rooms would be available until a Dutch tourist group had vacated them later in the day.

As I had discovered during these travels, the losmen is a respectable Indonesian institution: a basic hotel, with neither frills nor nonsense; honest, cheap and usually clean, often run by a family who leave the imprint of their good humour on the atmosphere, take an interest in the well-being of their visitors, and send staff members scurrying round to keep them happy with free-of-charge pots of tea at odd hours of the day. By chance we had arrived in the midst of a minor crisis. The town had been showered overnight by large flying insects which, although harmless, were of menacing appearance. Many of them had found their way into the losmen, where they hurtled noisily across the rooms and down passages, colliding with staff and guests. Their energy then exhausted, they were swept into large piles until time could be found to clear them away. Namek took a gloomy view of this phenomenon, which promised, he assured me, a change in the weather that was likely to be for the worse.

We withdrew from this scene to settle in a species of porch, opening on the street – a typical feature of such an establishment – and here we discussed the possibilities of an investigatory trip into the interior of the Dani country.

'How do you come to speak English so well?' I asked him.

'My mother was killed in an accident and a Catholic father adopted me,' he said. 'From him I am learning English and Dutch.' He spoke in a soft sing-song, eyes lowered, as if soothing a child, then looking up suddenly at the end of each sentence as if for assent.

'Now I am registered driver,' he said. 'No other taxi has assurance. Also I work in my garden. Tomorrow I will bring you sweet potatoes.'

'Are you married?'

'I have two wives,' he said. 'My father had two handfuls. That is the way we say for ten. We are always counting on fingers.' He raised his eyes to mine with a quick, furtive smile. 'You see I am going downhill.'

'Catholic, are you?'

'In Wamena all Catholics.'

'Doesn't your priest object to the wives?'

'For Danis they are making special rules. It's OK for them to have many wives. I cannot catch up with my father. Times now changed. Maybe one day I will have one wife more. That is enough.'

There was a moment of distraction while the losmen's cat raced through and over the furniture in chase of the last of the fearsome insects. Namek showed me the muddled letter from the agent. 'My friend says you are wanting to see of our country. May I know of your plans?'

'I haven't any,' I said. 'This is just a quick trip to get the feeling of the place. What ought I to see? Merauke, Sorong? The Asmat would you say?'

'You may show me your surat jalan. Did you put down these places?'

'I only put down the Baliem. Can the others be added here?'

'No. For that you must go back to Jayapura for permission to go to these places.'

'In Jakarta they said it could be done here.'

'They are wrong. Go to the police office and they will tell you.'

'It seems a waste of time. Even suppose I go back to Jayapura – am I sure of getting the permissions?'

'Here nothing is sure. One day they are telling you yes, the next day they say no. They will not agree to tell you on telephone. Now also telephone is not working.'

'So what do you suggest?'

He was reading the *surat jalan*, going over the words letter by letter with the tip of his forefinger, each word spoken softly, identified, and its meaning confirmed.

'With this surat jalan you may go to Karubaga,' he said.

'And what has Karubaga to offer?'

'Scenery very good. Also you are seeing different things. There are women in Karubaga turning themselves into bats.'

'That's promising,' I said. 'How do we get there?'

'By Merpati plane,' he said. 'To come back we are walking five days. In Karubaga you may find one porter, maybe two. Also one bodyguard.'

'Why the bodyguards? Cannibals?'

The thick beard drew away from his lips as he humoured me with a smile. 'No cannibals. Sometimes unfriendly people.'

The many frustrations of travel on impulse had left their brand-mark of caution on me. 'What are the snags?' I asked. 'Tell me the worst.'

'Very much climbing,' he said. 'Heart must be strong. Surat to be stamped by police in five villages. At Bakondini no river-bridge. Porters may bring you on their backs across river, or rattan bridge to be built one day, two days – no more. Every day now it is raining a little.' As he spoke a shadow fell across us. Part of the porch was of glass, and through it I saw that where a patch of blue sky had shown only a few minutes before, black, muscled cloud masses had now formed. An outrageous flower of lightning opened in the sky. A single clap of thunder set off a cannonade of reverberations through the echoing clapboard of the town; morning darkened to twilight, and then we heard the rain clattering towards us over the thousand tin roofs of Wamena. Pigs and dogs were sprinting down the street, chased by a frothing current, then disappearing behind a fence of water.

The rain stopped, the sun broke through, and the steam rose in ghostly tattered shapes from all the walls and pavements of the town. Mountain shapes, sharp-edged and glittering, surfaced in the clear sky above the fog. 'In one hour all dry again,' Namek said. We came back to the question of travel. 'I'll think about Karubaga,' I said. 'Any suggestions about using up the afternoon?'

'We may go to Dalima to visit my smoked ancestor,' Namek said. 'For this we may bring with us American cigarettes.'

In Wamena they smoked clove cigarettes, and there was a long search in the market for the prized American kind that were rarely offered for sale. By the time we found a few packets, the shallow floods had already dried away, and the journey began. We chugged away on three cylinders into the mountains to the north, left the car sizzling and blowing steam at Uwosilimo, and trudged five miles up a path to Dalima. In these off-the-beaten-track places the Dani had held on to their customs until the last moment, cropping ears and amputating fingers years after such exaggerated expressions of bereavement following the deaths of close relatives had been stamped out elsewhere. Persons of great power and influence, known as *kain koks*, were not cremated in the usual way but smoked over a slow fire for several months and thereafter hung from the eaves of their houses. There they continued to keep a benevolent eye on the community for decades, even centuries, until the newly arrived Indonesians launched their drive against 'barbarous practices', took down the offending cadavers and burned them or threw them into the river.

Namek's ancestor had been one of the few successfully hidden away, and now, in a slightly more relaxed atmosphere, he could be discreetly produced for the admiration of visitors with access to cigarettes from the United States, which the ancestor had let it be known through a shaman was the offering he most appreciated.

The whole village turned out for us in holiday mood, the women topless and in their best grass skirts, and the men in *kotekas* of the local style, with feathers dangling from their tips. We distributed cigarettes and the current *kain kok* tottered into view, overwhelmingly impressive with the boar's tusks curving from the hole in his septum, his bird-of-paradise plumes and valuable old shells. Beaming seraphically he punched a small hole in the middle of the cigarette and began to smoke it at both ends. He was the possessor of four handfuls of wives, and of this Namek said in a sibilant aside, 'Now he is old, and his women play their games while they are working in the fields.'

At this point the smoked ancestor was carried out having been crammed for this public appearance into a Victorian armchair. One arm was flung high into the air, a malacca cane grasped in the hand. The other hand, reaching surreptitiously down behind his back, held the polished skull of a bird. The Tudor-style hat affected by all the clan's leading males was tilted jauntily over an eye socket, and the ancestor's skin, quite black and frayed, was split like the leather of an ancient sofa. His jaws had been wrenched wide apart by the fumigant, and now the old *kain kok* lit a Chesterfield, puffed on it, and wedged it between the ancestor's two molar teeth that remained. Behind him descendants of lesser importance awaited their turn to make similar offerings.

The scene was in part grotesque but abounding in good cheer. The women rushed at us giggling and happy to show off their mutilated hands. The village was a handsome one, scrupulously clean and well kept, and I was fascinated to see that the villagers had uprooted trees in the jungle and replanted them in such a way that they drooped trusses of fragrant yellow blossoms over the thatches of their houses. These attracted butterflies of sombre magnificence which fed on the nectar until they became intoxicated, and then toppled about the place like planes out of control, and were chased ineffectively both by the children and the village dog. In such Dani communities it is more or less share-and-share-alike, and it seemed that in the allocation every child over the age of seven had been given a half-cigarette. These they were puffing at vigorously, and the village was full of the sound of their jubilation.

Namek was free next morning, and when I mentioned my interest in horticulture to him he suggested a trip of ten miles or so down the valley to Megapola (the name means 'big delusion'), a village a few miles to the south of the capital where, he said, the best of the gardens were made. Megapola was another beneficiary of the simple, one-family housing idea, and here, as elsewhere, such dwellings had remained closed and shuttered and the equatorial sun had stripped away most of the coats of yellow paint applied to the wood. What was singular about this village was its new school where the Dani children, at the time of our arrival, seemed to be having a remarkably good time. The principal goal of these schools is to integrate culturally diverse populations into the Indonesian nation. A start is made by teaching minority children the state language, to be followed by other aspects of *Pancasila*, including – as I had observed at Endoman – an Indonesian brand of Moral Philosophy, and probably in this case a readiness on the part of the homeless to take up residence in Megapola's empty shacks. Yet, extraordinary as it seemed to us, the children we saw were being taught skills that had no business in *Pancasila*, although of exceptional value in the traditional life of the Dani people.

Across the road from the school was an acre or so of land seeming, possibly as a result of past troubles, to have been abandoned and which in consequence had grown a covering of coarse grasses interwoven with a low-lying shrub resembling heather. Schoolboys between the ages of perhaps eight and fourteen had been set to clean this and restore the terrain to cultivation. They had been split into working groups in the charge of a Dani junior master with dark spectacles and Bermuda shorts. Everyone engaged in the project was in a state of hyper-activity – the schoolchildren brandishing their garden implements sprinting about in all directions and the master racing after them, bounding over walls and across ditches and roaring instructions to which little attention was given. Standing at the top of the school steps, the Javanese head, who might not have spoken Dani, looked on with an approving smile. He wore a flowered shirt, crocodile skin shoes, and a cap of the kind favoured by the President of the Republic. Occasionally he gestured authoritatively with a cigarette holder, although without effect, at some aspect of the operation calling for his assistant's attention.

A gang of the older boys armed with adzes were hacking with a vigour that came close to ferocity at the close-knit covering of weeds, loosening it, then peeling it back in the way of a butcher flaying the hide from an animal carcase. A younger group, having worked off steam by running in circles and shouting at the top of their voices, were chopping with their adzes into the soil thus laid bare, while teams of even smaller boys raced into sight carrying armfuls of dry vegetation to be burned off before incorporating the valuable ash into the top soil, which had been thoroughly dug over to receive it.

At this point one or two Dani bystanders who had stopped for a chat could not resist shouting advice to the youngsters and then scrambling over the field to snatch the tools from the childrens' hand and demonstrate how the work was properly done. This brought the junior master, furiously protesting, on the scene. He called the interferers 'saboteurs', using a fashionable newcomer to the national language, which was employed, Namek said, to denounce anyone disliked by a government servant on any grounds.

Suddenly, after adzes and clenched fists had been raised in fury, it all died down. The head, imperturbable as ever in true Javanese style, came down the steps, shook hands and handed out cigarettes to the disputants, and no face was lost. The children, who for five minutes had been an undisciplined mob, calmed down a little and settled with unabated enthusiasm to their jobs. It would take them a week, Namek said, to provide Megapola with a splendid new vegetable garden.

Ultimately this was to no purpose according to those who controlled the national thinking. Not only was subsistence food-production contrary to national policy, but it was bad for the producers themselves. There was a school of thought, attracting much publicity, that attributed the backwardness (as they put it) of 'isolated' tribes such as the Danis to what they ate. 'Their lack of mental alertness, lack of concentration, and reduced intelligence', as one of the government publications said, 'is largely due to their eating habits, and their ignorance of the facts of nutrition and hygiene.'

Like Megapola, all sizeable villages in the Baliem are Indonesian – that is Javanese – in architecture and style. Except in the case of public buildings, houses are made of wood, devoid usually of paint and adornment, and in general aspect a little dull. Their occupants are outstandingly fond of flowers and squeeze little flower gardens into every hole and corner in an effort to brighten them up. The police do this in some style. Whenever the blow falls and they are told of the posting to Irian Jaya, there is a rush to the nearest garden centre to buy all the pot plants they can carry. The first thing I saw upon arrival in Megapola was the policeman at the post there watering his plants. Strident colours are preferred: cactuses exploding with fiery blossoms, scarlet salvias thrusting like bayonets from the earth, dahlias, canna. The schoolmaster had gone in for miniature decorative firs from Scandinavia, and had planted a copse of them round his door. Danis in from the country and faced with these displays, Namek said, would invariably ask what the plants tasted like and there are reports of their being stewed up for use as an appetiser with sweet potatoes. Nevertheless, while mystified by pot plants, the Danis

fussed continually to beautify their traditional villages. They would
tolerate no mess of any kind about the place, and there were flowers in
plenty. These were invariably those of flowering trees transplanted from
the jungle.

They was a tiny market here, only for the benefit of the Javanese
settlers. On display were some of the most spectacular lettuces and celery
I had ever seen, and carrots weighing a pound and over, eighteen inches in
length. The Danis had been under pressure, Namek said, to grow these
for the market, and did so, with some reluctance. They called them 'silly',
he said. 'Do you like these,' I asked one of the market people. 'No,' he
said. 'We eat them sometimes for medicine. They have no taste.'

The most interesting feature of my association with Namek was that he
was the only person who had spoken with nostalgia of the cessation of the
almost continuous state of warfare in the highlands of Irian Jaya and who
had actually fought and been wounded in a battle. In theory the warlike
operations inseparable from the culture of all the mountainous region of
New Guinea had been suppressed in the Indonesian area shortly after
1961, when the Harvard Peabody Expedition wandered backwards and
forwards without hindrance through the ranks of the contending sides
taking several thousand excellent photographs of the last of the major
battles in progress. Nevertheless, local conflicts have continued to crop up
regularly since then. In Endoman the principal topic was of the small war
in the area shortly before my arrival. The year 1988 saw hostilities spread
over several months in the south Baliem with a death toll variously
estimated at between 30 and 140. In Easter 1992 fighting broke out on the
southern outskirts of Wamena itself causing possibly a dozen deaths.
Such happenings receive no publicity, and it is unlikely that tourists ever
come to hear of them.

In *Gardens of War* Robert Gardner, one of the leaders of the Harvard
Peabody Expedition writes: 'The Dani fight because they want to, and
because it is necessary. They do not enter into battle in order to put an end
to fighting. They do not envisage the end of fighting any more than the
end of gardening or of ghosts. Nor do they fight in order to annex land or
to dominate people. The Dani are warriors because they have wanted to
be since boyhood, not because they are persuaded by political arguments
or their own sentimental and patriotic feelings. They are ready to fight
whenever their leaders decide to do so.' It is an evaluation remarkably
endorsed by the experiences of Namek, who, despite his hybrid culture,
his fair degree of fluency in two foreign languages, his habitual use of
Western clothing and his third share in a dilapidated car, had found himself

spear and bow in hand on a mountainside near Kurima, the place of his birth.

Probably as a result of his partial Westernisation, Namek had left his first wife and some land he cultivated in the Kurima area and had gone to live with a second wife near Elegaima in the north. Here, news reached him of a dispute in the old homeland over a piece of land claimed by two clans, to one of which he belonged. The quarrel, Namek said, was artificial. This land had remained untended for years. It was an agreed no-man's-land overgrown with weeds and sapling trees and had been fought over many times before, only to be instantly abandoned by the side that had finally taken possession of it. There was no better confirmation of Robert Gardner's dictum. A barren field was the perfect and instantly available pretext for war.

A formal declaration was issued by those Namek now referred to as the mountain people. The challenge was accepted by the valley people, a provisional date set for the battle, and a call-up sent out by both sides. Namek found himself in a quandary. He had been born in one of the valley villages involved in the dispute, and had married a woman who still lived in the village and was registered there as his wife. Although it was ten years since he had married his second wife and moved away to Elegaima, he was still caught up in a complex clan arrangement with the valley people of the South. It was in Elegaima that the equivalent of his call-up papers reached him. These his strong-minded new wife urged him to ignore. He wholly agreed with her. He had never seen the land in dispute, nor did he wish to do so, and his life had become remote from that of the clans of Kurima.

He regarded himself as possessing a calm, quiet temperament, and was in instant agreement with his wife's advice when she said, 'Perhaps they will come for you. You must go away and hide.'

Namek's wife talked him into leaving the house for the period of the emergency and moving into a shack he had built in a vegetable garden in a spot well-sheltered from casual view. He worked there comfortably enough for two days cutting an irrigation ditch before being overtaken by a feeling of anxiety of a kind familiar to Danis and attributed by them to ill-intentioned ghosts. Voices scolded him in the night, and the years spent as a child and adolescent in the mission had not been long enough to silence them. These he was obliged to accept as an ancestral summons to the battle.

On the evening of the third day he stripped off his Western clothes, fixed his penis gourd in position, grabbed up his spear and bow and set off for the place near the Wauma bridge in the south of the Baliem where the battle was to be fought. To be sure of avoiding capture by the police in his fighting trim he was obliged to skirt villages, and keep away from roads and tracks. The ghosts had been accurate in their monitory timing, for, having run for most of the night, he arrived at Wauma shortly after dawn – in time to report to the valley people's chieftain just as battle was about to be joined. His bow was tested, his spear measured for length, and a bundle of arrows issued to him. At this point the minor chief in charge of these details happened to mention that his uncle was fighting on the other side.

What followed throws perhaps another flicker of light on the character, psychology and motives of ritual warfare. By now about 300 men had taken up battle stations on each side: the valley people on the lower frontier down by the river of the area under dispute, while an equal number of mountain people were mustered some hundreds of yards away across the hillside above. On both sides the heads of families were receiving their last-minute orders from the 'big men' whose prestige had been staked on the outcome of the battle. The forthcoming fight would be at the farthest imaginable extreme from modern warfare in any of its guises: a delicate, light-footed exercise in feints and subterfuges, ambushes, surprise attacks and withdrawals carried out by young athletes moving at the speed of Olympic runners. In this moment of frenzied tension, among the shouted challenges, the Papuan catcalls, the threats, the cries of derision, when the impetuous young warriors had to be physically restrained by their comrades from suicidal single-handed ventures, Namek's case had to receive consideration. He was permitted to cross no-man's-land, find his uncle among the enemy, take him aside and formulate a plan by which they placed themselves in the battle in such a way that it was not possible to kill each other.

The extreme poverty of a shared vocabulary prevented Namek from sketching in more than the barest outlines of a battle which clearly reproduced in general pattern the one illustrated by the photographers in Gardner's book. The camera depicts every stage of the similar encounter in Kabela in 1961, recording hand-to-hand combat, thrusts, the agony of the wounded, the fearful primitive surgery. Nevertheless drastic action is hamstrung by the rules. This is warfare in which men are killed, but it is also a game.

As at Endoman in the mock battle, bodies of men advance waving their weapons and leaping high into the air before hurling their spears and retreating. The effect is choreographic rather than belligerent, and little blood is shed. This is not warfare as we understand it. Arrows that are not feathered inflict only accidental damage. Gardner noted at Kabela that half the fatalities arose from infections in minor flesh wounds. The spear-throwing and bad archery appear as hardly more than military histrionics, but in the separate combats in which the warriors confront each other after adopting the postures of Japanese wrestlers, deaths sometime occur. To kill a man is a costly business, involving the victor in feasts with clan members of his vanquished adversary, which in the end he will probably pay for with his own life. In such fights a weakened opponent was given a chance to survive. Rarely was a man speared in a frontal bodily area where the soul was supposed to reside. There were conventional manoeuvres in which he could be encouraged to turn away, or retreat, and then skewered in the buttocks or thighs.

It was such a manoeuvre that put Namek out of the battle, with a spear thrust in the back of the leg just above the knee joint. Although crippled and defenceless, no attempt was made to inflict further damage upon him. The old man kept ready to take the wounded in charge wrapped a cloth round his head to prevent identification by one of the ghosts attracted in such scenes by the scent of blood, then put him on a makeshift stretcher to be carried by nightly stages back to his home in Elegaima. Here after three months of treatment by native remedies he had recovered sufficiently to be back at the wheel of his taxi.

FIFTEEN

THE BALIEM VISTA exposed its guests to a series of mild oriental experiences which the Javanese who stayed there probably did not notice, and the foreigner at first accepted as all part of the fun. Apart from these Javanese expatriates connected with local ministries or businesses, the losmen was frequented in the main by Dutch package-deal tourists who stayed four days and did the sights, such as they were, before their return to Jakarta – usually, by all accounts, in a state of physical and nervous depletion. There are many small things wrong with the Baliem Vista, the first being the interminable wait for meals which, when finally served, were almost certain to be not as ordered. The locks on the room doors jammed constantly in such a way as either to lock guests out or lock them in. In addition an obscene-looking tail-less tomcat pounded endlessly up and down the passages in pursuit of large marsupial mice, and having caught one would immediately present it to the first Dutch lady it encountered.

Among the small advantages the Vista had to offer was the pint of tea left at frequent intervals outside the room door. It was pleasant, too, as evening approached, to relax in the wide, glass-enclosed porch serving as a lounge, to watch the lively mix of street scenes, and the missionary joggers panting past at half-past five according to their invariable custom. At exactly a quarter to six the moment awaited by all arrived – a transfiguring radiance illuminated the plaster façades and tin roofs and conferred upon Wamena a moment almost of dignity. Minutes later the day was at an end.

When I was there the Dutch group were in the charge of an extremely bright and beautiful Indonesian courier. She was compelled at this hour to listen to the complaints of tourists who had been upset by the sight and sound of pig-killing in a ceremony she had taken them to. They had been caught in heavy showers, tipped into shallow rivers by the porters who had carried them on their backs, chased by dogs objecting to their smell, had got flies in their eyes, and in one case a leech between the toes. There were more complaints about the long wait for dinner. One of the guests, on wandering through into the kitchen, had found it to contain one wok, one electric ring, and one cook to prepare dinner for twenty-one persons, each meal being cooked separately. He described this predicament to the rest of the Dutch who sat along one wall of the porch, with the Javanese along the other wall facing them. The Javanese had brought hundreds of family snaps in their luggage, and these were doled out and passed round to be admired, as the Dutch already knew, for hour after hour. Most of the people here could expect to wait several hours for their food. The Javanese threw up their hands in wonder at the family snaps and nodded and smiled incessantly, while a low murmur of discontent arose from the Dutch. Shinta, the courier, had studied the Yogyanese classical dance and had taken part in the Ramayana Ballet – performed on nights of the full moon at the Prambanam Temple near Yogya – with her head still full, as she admitted to me, of celestial visions of enchanters and demons and the divine thunderbolts hurled by the gods. An attempt to interest the guests in such things, in the long drawn-out pause until the first of them would be beckoned to table, failed, and they drifted away to the patio where the reception was better for the transistors pressed to their ears in an attempt to pick up the news on the BBC World Service. As soon as they could be interrupted she presented each of them with a leaflet headed *Let Us Smile Together*, which explained how visitors to Indonesia should best confront certain frustrations that might arise. *In all circumstances remain calm. Thus you will earn respect. It is typical of the national personality that there are six ways to say YES, but great efforts are made to avoid speaking the word NO. Let us smile together. Let us remember to say YES whenever we can.*

Shinta had other problems on her mind. The first was to protect her charges from the stealthy approaches by football-shirted Danis with bottles of lethal Baliem whisky for sale. The second was the absence of an adventurous Mr Enquist, who owned a bus company in one of the Dutch cities. He had gone off with a local guide and was long overdue.

Eventually he showed up plastered in yellow mud and avoided Shinta to take me into his confidence, and I gathered by the odour on his breath that he had discovered an outside source of Baliem Old Highland Stag. 'Also,' he said speaking of the guide, 'this man was keen to sell me his wife. I think maybe he could not work out the price in dollars, so he said it would be two small pigs.' He slumped into a chair and yawned.

'What time may we expect to be served dinner?' he asked.

'In theory seven. In reality about nine-thirty,' I told him.

'Ah yes. Yesterday it was the same. Chicken with rice.'

'I assume so.'

'Yesterday there was a beak in my food. Miss van Steen discovered part of a foot.'

'Shinta has a leaflet to show you which covers situations like that,' I said. 'It says: "Public criticism of others will cause you to lose face." '

'Ya,' he said. 'That I heard already. Why don't they give hutspot or maybe boerenkool? That we are used to. It is easy for them to make and for us to eat. Maybe now I will go to bed. Also the walk today was not interesting. If you are keen to see this, at Bugi there is a female dried baby. But you must walk half a day, and now I am tired.'

Enquist went to bed and one after another the Dutch were shunted into the dining-room to do what they could with the chicken with fried rice, and I was left along with Shinta. 'These people can only think of food because they are bored,' she said. 'I am accustomed to a programme, there *is* no programme. We do not offer enough.' Previously she had taken tours to the island of Sumba to see the villagers spear each other on horseback. Also the Komodo Island where the package included the provision of a goat to be slaughtered and left in a ravine up which the dragon would come scrambling to tear it to shreds. 'These were strong programmes,' she said. 'For some there is poetry in the shedding of blood, but I think always drama.' Would it not be possible, she wondered, to arrange an entertainment similar to the Komodo Island one based on the gigantic lizards she had been told existed somewhere in the mountains north of Wamena?

I was sure, I told her, that if there was money in it something could be done. At this she seemed much encouraged, and decided that she would call on the government tourist office next day and discuss the possibility with them.

Almost brainwashed by the losmen into patience and calm, the Dutch bundled up their souvenirs and were carried away. With their departure the minor points of punctuality inculcated by the latest guests were forgotten, wailing Javanese music demolished silence, the evening meal reverted from rice with chicken to just rice, and the impressive but harmless flying beetles that found their way through open doors or holes in the mosquito netting were frankly ignored.

The Ludwigsons then arrived, a vivacious smiling woman and her two daughters who had recently escaped from the routines of wealth in Palm Beach, where they occupied a sea-front mansion next to that of a famous film-star whose name I have forgotten. They had come here, Mrs Ludwigson said, with a touch of defiance in her announcement, in search of innocence. It would have been easy to mistake this family for a trio of handsome sisters. The girls, Sandra and Lucille, were in their late twenties. Edwina, their mother, would have been a beauty in her time, and at forty-eight she was exceedingly well-preserved. They crammed as much information about themselves as possible into the first half-hour of our acquaintance, at the end of which we were all on first-name terms. It was easy to talk to the Ludwigsons. They radiated friendship, were avid for new experiences, and were confident from all they had heard that Irian Jaya was well-placed to supply them.

'We talked this thing over,' Edwina said, 'and decided the time had come for a let-up from the scene back there. Listen, there I was with this house, a really great family and a load of good friends, and I was asking myself, where do I go from here? What am I doing with my life? For God's sake, I just felt superfluous. Norman, would you please level with me. I have this feeling I'm getting old. Do I look old? I want you to be frank.'

I told her sincerely that she did not, although there was planning in her features and expression that muffled the spontaneities of youth. 'My girls wanted to come along. They don't like to let me out of their sight. That's the way it is in our family. We stick together, we always have done. Oh, just look at those two guys dancing back there. Would those be people who work here. Don't you just love this place?'

Now the pressure had been taken off the kitchen staff, a noise from that area suggested a dance might be going on, and presently a couple of the staff burst through the swing door giggling and fencing at each other with ladles. Edwina's attention was diverted from this spectacle by a procession containing a hundred or two tiny bugs curling away from us across the floor on some mysterious communal errand; she shook her head in pleased wonderment at the sight.

'So what are your plans?' I asked.

'They aren't necessary,' Edwina said. 'What we stand in need of is fresh day-to-day experience, and it doesn't matter how it comes. No planning. No clocks. We were living in a prison house of our own making. The time comes when you have to say to yourself, "Right, this thing stops here and now." We're taking another direction. What we need is a culture shock, and that's something you can't plan for. Mistakes? Sure we'll make mistakes, but we'll be getting some place with a new view through the window. You get what I mean?'

Sandra, the prettier of the girls, said, 'Do they have a bar here?'

'They have a bar,' I said, 'but there's nothing to drink. Irian Jaya is dry. You can't even get beer.'

'Do you suppose they have soft drinks?'

'Normally, but I know they've run out. They get deliveries of Sprite from Jayapura on Tuesdays. That's tomorrow. You can get bottled water.'

'Well, that's good to know,' Edwina said.

'I'll check to see if any's on ice,' I said.

'For me it doesn't matter one way or the other. I guess ice is something I need to forget. I'm quite happy with whatever's going. Back home you need something – you crook a finger, and that's bad for anyone. What do they feed you on here?'

'Fried rice.'

'Is that on Mondays only?'

'No, that's every day. They stir a few different odds and ends into it according to the days of the week, but it's always fried rice.'

'Well, I have news for you, Norman. I happen to like fried rice. How about you girls?' Sandra and Lucille agreed that they, too, liked fried rice, but with less conviction than Edwina.

'Fruit do they have?' Edwina asked.

'Yes, bananas.'

'Nothing but?'

'No.'

'Well, I like bananas, too. How about that?'

'If you can get by on a diet of rice and bananas, you've nothing to worry about. They're always on the menu.'

'Talking about food,' Sandra said. 'How long is it to dinner?'

'It'll take about a couple of hours after you order. Best get your order in now.'

'No hurry in my case,' Edwina said. 'I have an inner dialogue going. This place draws me out. Why didn't we come here before?'

Apart from the shortage of legitimate drink, it happened to be a good day to arrive in Wamena. The rain had held off, with the promise of a fine, clear evening. The joggers had already passed, and the flush spreading through the sky was about to disguise the extreme banality of the town in a brief interlude of charm and distinction. Middle-class Javanese settlers who were susceptible to such things had hurried into the street for a stroll in the brief romanticism of the setting. With the fading of the light a party of them, bags and pockets stuffed with family snapshots, descended on the chairs in the losmen's lobby, and we found ourselves split up.

Now I found myself seated next to Lucille, who was quieter but more intense than her sister. The Javanese women smiled and chatted. 'What do you suppose they're talking about?' Lucille asked.

'Their children,' I said. 'All Javanese conversations are politely non-controversial. When you meet someone for the first time you could ask what is their favourite colour.'

'That's interesting,' she said, 'mine's yellow. Listen, I wanted to talk to you, this place is supposed to be pretty corrupt, isn't it?'

'From all I hear, yes.'

'Can you get hold of booze, for instance?'

'If you feel like paying the kind of price they ask for it. A whisky boy shows up most nights. He'll sell you what he calls scotch.'

'I suppose it's really bad.'

'I've never tried it but we had some Dutch here who took a chance. So far as I know, none of them went to hospital, but it's a wonder to me they didn't. It's said they cook up the alcohol with palm sugar and wood shavings. It smelt like herbicide.'

'I have to tell you,' she said. 'We have a family problem. It's not something I want to talk about. Can I leave it at that? What time does he come?'

'About seven,' I said.

'What I'd like to do is make sure we're in our room. Maybe you could tap on our door when he's left. Say "dinner's ready", or something like that.'

'Certainly,' I said. 'No problem.'

The Javanese pocketed their family photographs, made an end to their prolonged leave-takings and went off. The Ludwigsons retired to their room for evening aerobics and meditation, and I decided on a short stroll in search of the evening breeze. In a matter of minutes the town had emptied of light, and as if someone had pressed a series of switches, one after another all the affable daylight sounds – the slap of running Dani feet, the grinding of bicycle chains, the soft twanging of Papuan Jew's harps unlocated in the velvet gloom, the gentle smokers' coughs provoked by Baliem cigarettes – were silenced. Fifteen miles away in the mountains, lightning flickered on and off like a broken electrical contact. It was one of those night when the moths were flapping stealthily everywhere.

I plodded back to the losmen with its dim lamps, evening inertia, and the patina of stale kitchen odours.

At first there were no signs of life, then I heard movements in the patio and found the whisky boy there picking dark objects off the floor. Someone had left the street door open, and a few moths had come flapping through it, drawn to the lights. The whisky boy showed me one held very gently in the palm of his hand. The moths had fierce, bold eyes on their wings to deter the predators of the night, and soft bodies which curled away, twitching, in sensitive repugnance from the shining pavement surface upon which, in their confusion, they had either alighted, or fallen. A recognisable insecticide odour polluted the air in the vicinity of the whisky boy's head. He was drunk, and his expression as he handled the distressed moths, was one of alcoholic compassion. He was the employee whose job it was, after an invocation of the merciful Allah, to cut the throats of the chickens that later featured in the *nasi goreng*, yet at this moment he was obsessed with the problem of carrying moths to the safety of the patio shrubs and persuading them to settle there. I asked about the whisky, and he said that a woman had cleaned out his supply.

With this there was a rattling of pans in the kitchen, and within minutes the familiar smell of rice frying in coconut oil. Knowing that culinary operations in the losmen were careful but slow, I gave them a half-hour before knocking on the Ludwigson's door. In a few minutes they came down and we went in to dinner. As sometimes happened with new guests, the management had gone out of their way to put a little extra effort into this occasion, and there was a first course of tough little segments of disjointed chicken cooked in sate sauce, which for all its pungent fragrances was unable to suppress the spiritous odour that had followed the Ludwigsons to table. The suspicion dawned that the whole family had been hitting the bottle.

They seemed almost ominously cheerful, and tore enthusiastically at the ligaments and muscles of a bird specially toughened for local taste. Edwina had picked up one of the Let Us Smile Together leaflets. 'Isn't that great,' she said. 'Isn't that just great?'

The waiter was thanked as the leaflet said he should be. 'If you enjoyed your meal you should go out of your way to express your pleasure. A desirable compliment might be *Makanan yang enak sekali di restoran ini* (Dishes are particularly delicious in this restaurant).' Mrs Ludwigson, overbrimming with graciousness, seemed to make an understandable job of this, for the waiter pressed his hands together, beaming, and the cook in turn was called to the door to take a bow.

With the electricity supply failing fast we were dependent upon the spiralling glow-worm in a low-wattage lamp, misted by mosquitoes, suspended over the table. The waiter removed the debris left over from the first course, then returned to light three small candles. This pleased the Ludwigsons, who appeared happy to snatch at small pleasures, and full of nervous, brittle jollity, producing laughter at the smallest excuse, or for no reason at all. Everything was funny; the tooth-cracking chicken sate had been a joke disguised as food. They had read in the leaflet that the polite way of calling the waiter's attention was by flapping one hand down beside the table, which they did whenever he put his head through the kitchen door. This was uproariously funny. Spurred on by such frolickings Edwina remembered an episode at the airport when a man waving the Stars and Stripes had pounced on them and thrust into her hand a barely legible computer print-out. ' "American friend, please no touch baby's head, no kick dog, no telling you bastard for Indonesian man." Doesn't that really kill you?' Sandra asked.

In the early stages of this meal I took a deep draught of Jayapura bottled water, noticing only when it was too late an unusual chemical flavour and then an odour that revived the memory of long-forgotten school experiments. It was only to be concluded that the bottle's contents had been tampered with; almost certainly blended with Old Highland Stag. As far as it was possible to do in the slightly hysterical environment, I settled to await possible effects, and immediately the imagination took over. Perhaps I was very slightly drunk, perhaps not. I have noticed that imagination often enters into the processes of intoxication. The only suspect symptoms at this time seemed to be an enhanced concern with details of our surroundings of which less and less could be made out due to the slow wasting away of the light. For the first time, although I had been in this room on a number of occasions, I noticed the tide mark left by the last flood all the way round the sea-green walls. Why should it be, I asked myself, that although I had sat as I did now within feet of the carved ancestor from the Asmat hanging from a wall-bracket I had never been repelled by his priggish expression? The only picture in the restaurant was of a blue-eyed, cross-carrying Christ, mass-produced possibly by the million in Japan, and at this moment it was something that seemed extraordinary to me, as did the fact that it should be prominently displayed here by the owner, who was a Javanese professing the Muslim faith. The background of these musings was the Ludwigsons' merriment, and the crackling of the wood cooking our food.

Suddenly the *nasi goreng* was there, overbrimming steaming platefuls, brought out of a kitchen now illuminated only by the fire under the wok. Obsessed by shallow philosophising, I had overlooked the coming and going of the waiter. The candles burning down magnified the shadows huddled about us. Perhaps the management saw my American friends as being more valuable customers than the members of the Dutch package-deal groups who usually filled most of his rooms. At all events, although *nasi goreng* previously served here had been a simple affair, this time the ingredients were more varied, although in this light not identifiable. Edwina, sitting opposite, plunged in her fork and in the next instant plucked something from her lip, stared at it in obvious horror, dashed whatever it was away, let out a high-pitched, keening cry, jumped to her feet, and rushed from the room. Chairs went over as Sandra and Lucille followed her. I went round the table to examine the rice-bedaubed raggedness she had found in her mouth. This was recognisable as a moth that had fallen into the wok.

SIXTEEN

THERE WERE TWO celebrities to be seen in the Baliem, the first being Da-Uke, built up in recent years as unofficial figurehead of the Dani people, although otherwise, in reality, of little interest except as son of the great war-lord Kurulu. The father had been described with respect by Mitton, Gardner, Heider, etc., classic observers of the Papuan scene, who saw a great deal of him at a time when he had already entered a robust old age. Dispassionately he embraced and perfected himself in the art of warfare inseparable by immemorial custom from trimming population to resources. Apart from his supremacy as a strategist, he was seen as possessing all the manly qualities. He was loyal, chivalrous, magnanimous and bold; a Papuan Galahad whose strength was as the strength of ten, although in the end the fire-power of a modern army proved too much for him. By the time of the Harvard Peabody Expedition in 1961 the old man's shadow empire was about to fall apart. The expedition observed the last of the great ritual battles, with members completely at liberty to potter about the battlefield, to photograph various phases of the action, the attacks, withdrawals and the wounds. Kurulu died, and his son Da-Uke took over, although there was no evidence that he had inerited his father's remarkable qualities.

Kurulu had come up from nothing. He was a *kain kok* – a man of influence, of the kind typified by those who led the 'old' Sicilian mafia, the 'men of honour' existing before the decline into total gangsterism after the sixties. The seizure by these men of secret power was traditionally unaided by birth, parental influence or inherited fortune. In the argot of the place and time, a mafioso 'made his own bones' – a notable case of this grim self-conditioning being that of Minasola, an illiterate shepherd who held sway for some years from behind the scenes of a sizeable part of Sicily.

The Danis, too, in theory went it alone. At a man's death his meagre possessions were divided up to be shared among members of his clan, and his sons started from scratch. This, and other aspects of an extreme form of democracy, came under the pressure of invasive cultures, first of the Dutch, then of the Indonesians. Effortlessly Da-Uke became a rich man and has continued to be one.

Kurulu's custom had been to hold a great pig-feast every four years, designed to cement friendly relationships, win over opponents, and bring about reconciliations. It was also a convenient opportunity to celebrate marriages, carry out the rites for delayed funerals, and arrange for the initiation ceremonies of young boys. It was this last ingredient of the feast, just about to be celebrated once again, that offered the major attraction so far as I was concerned. Such rites tend to share a remarkable similarity throughout the primitive world, not only in tests devised to gauge the participant's understanding of tribal morality, his physical resistance and his martial skills, but as a measure of courage, and resourcefulness when confronted with an unexpected emergency. In the Baliem the initiates were seized suddenly by the arms and legs and thrown into a bonfire. The temperature was carefully regulated by dousings with water to see that no serious burns occurred. Nevertheless it was regarded as the most important of the ordeals suffered, and the boy's reactions were carefully watched. By its nature this had to be a secret affair, from which outsiders were debarred. Perhaps it was an indication of the way things were going that since Da-Uke's accession word had leaked out that in the coming feast ways might be found of getting round the ban.

The centre of Da-Uke's domain remained, as it had been in his father's day, at Akima, a few miles north of Wamena, an area of wide green meadows with saffron ponds encircled by explosions of ferns. This immediate vista was backed by an amphitheatre of mountains usually feathered with white cloud. The road twisted round low easy hills, chosen on many occasions as a battleground upon which ritualistic manoeuvres could be comfortably performed.

Kurulu's compound, now Da-Uke's, was the only one permitted to retain a watchtower – once a feature of every village – on which sentinels watched every day from dawn to dusk for signs of enemy activity. It was under this rickety affair, outside the compound's walls, that I was asked by one of the chief's men to wait until Da-Uke and his right-hand men had completed their toilet and were ready to receive me. Ten minutes or so transpired before one of the principal wives came out to lead me into his presence. She was wearing a jumper and a flowered skirt and walked rapidly towards me in military style, holding out her hand to introduce herself. She did this in such a way as to conceal the fact that a finger had been removed in a ritual amputation. In talking to me she averted her head, so it was not immediately evident that half an ear had also been removed. She was accompanied by a charming piglet that was also much spoiled and squealed piteously whenever she put it down. Her daughter, who trotted at her heels puffing a cigarette, was about six. I asked the mother her age, but she did not know. In Baliem this was to be expected.

The compound was the largest I had seen; a wide oblong with the men's house closing off the far end and flanked, as usual, by a women's house, a house for the boys, a kitchen, and in this case, exceptionally, two houses for the pigs. All these buildings were of identical structure and in immaculate condition, with recently renewed and carefully trimmed thatches. The wives had been placed in rank, seemingly in reverse order of age, at the compound's entrance, presenting themselves erect, unblinking and staring straight ahead, as if for a military inspection. All were topless, the first few the possessors of firm and enormous young busts, but thereafter the years had taken their toll, and a cursory glance at the senior lady at the far end seemed enough. One of the younger wives had been a mourning and in consequence forced to promenade daubed with dried yellow clay for at least a month. Of the clay, little remained, and I suspected that around the eyes a few glittering spangles among the yellow detritus had been added by way of maquillage.

Da-Uke, regally corpulent, awaited at the entrance to the men's house, decked out in feathers and shells. Standing on his right, his second-in-command had attempted to amend an essentially mild expression by fixing in the aperture in his septum the largest boar's tusk I had ever seen. The bellicose effect of this was reduced by his brand new T-shirt bearing the lettering Natural History Museum of Chicago. Da-Uke was extremely affable, welcoming me with the polite phrase still in use among tribal patricians, 'I prize your faeces,' and wringing my hand over and over again in the way Western statesmen do in their meetings with representatives of unfriendly governments. Da-Uke was seen as having become very much an establishment figure. He had been invited to meet the President at Jakarta, had been lumped in with a delegation of high-ranking Somalis on a quick trip to the United States, and had recently been honoured by the Governor of the Baliem with the gift of a Toyota pick-up. In this he was said to travel wearing eye-shades, a blue blazer, and bracelets of interwined pig's scrotums to ward off the ghosts.

A polite interrogation of a standardised kind was now expected, but I had been unable to locate Namek that morning and so was obliged to make do with an interpreter who was new to the game. This man had attempted to squeeze through the language barrier by learning by heart a number of sentences that might fit into a routine of probable questions and answers. Such conversations, for example, were bound to open with a polite query into the number of wives a man possessed. I started off, and

Da-Uke held up his hands with one of his thumbs tucked away out of sight. It was 'less than two handfuls', in other words, nine.

Next, I understood Da-Uke would expect to be questioned about his record on the battlefield. Without batting an eyelid Chief Yurigeng had claimed to have killed twenty-seven men. In Da-Uke's case the question seemed to give rise to some uncertainty. 'He say many,' reported the interpreter, hugely impressed, but at that moment Da-Uke's expression, probably as he remembered the government's attitude to ritual warfare, was suffused with a dubious piety. There was a quick reshuffle of words and the hecatomb was reduced to a number of warriors Da-Uke had *seen* killed.

Thereafter the conversation became a matter of a sifting of verbal clues in a search for meaning. What came out of it was that Da-Uke had an obsession on the subject of fetiches. These are objects of the kind a child would collect – stones of unusual shape, fossils, or the remains of animals displaying some genetic freakishness – and are generally supposed among Papuans to enshrine magic power. Fetiches are not worshipped, at most held in respect and regarded as 'lucky', but they were banned by Protestant missionaries, who burned, buried or simply threw them away by the thousand. It was a course of action that often determined what brand of faith a convert would accept. The Catholics tolerated fetiches. Notables like Da-Uke were allowed to keep them and they are still regarded with a mixture of awe and affection throughout the Baliem. Here, the Danis, in so far as they have any religion other than ancestor worship, have largely remained at least nominally Catholics.

Da-Uke was immensely proud of his fetiches and it was his belief that such collections as his could be promoted to become a major attraction of the Baliem Valley of the future, which he saw as being in the main devoted to tourism. With much effort and occasional lapses into total incomprehension the interpreter managed to get across his special introductory offer to me. Normally, he said, he charged 2 million rupiah (approximately £700) for allowing visitors to see his 'sacred' objects, but in my case, as a special concession, this would be reduced to 50,000 rupiah (approximately £17). I did not take him up.

The second, and more interesting notability I managed to see was Chief Obaharok, who in 1973, while already the possessor of two handfuls of wives, claimed briefly the attention of the world's press by taking as his eleventh the American anthropologist Wyn Sargent, then forty-two years of age and the mother of a fifteen-year-old son, Jmy, living in the United States. When asked his opinion of the new marriage in the course of a press interview, Jmy said, 'My mother knows what she's doing.' Of this verdict Wyn wrote in her autobiography, *The Headhunters*, 'no mother ever felt so proud as I did when I read my son's words'.

Apart from the interest inherent in details of the wedding ceremony, this book provides first-hand information about the resistance put up by the Papuan people, who had been internationally assured after the departure of the Dutch of their right to self-determination, on their discovery that the promise had been a delusory one. Ironically, Wyn Sargent's presence in the Baliem Valley followed a pressing invitation issued to her by none other than President Suharto in person, who seems to have been a fan. He received her in the Disneyland Hotel, Anaheim, California, and the picture offered of this meeting of the cultures is a homely one. Suharto sat stocking-footed in the Presidental Suite . . . 'the little muscle between his brows was pinched up because his feet hurt'. He and Madame Suharto had just returned from a peregrination of many miles round Disneyland. 'West Irian,' said President Suharto, 'West Irian is the place you should go.' She did, and appears bitterly disillusioned by what she found.

Wyn Sargent was working in the Dani area in 1972, during the troubled times of the establishment of Imperial authority. She was quick to take sides.

> When I learned of the brutality and maltreatment inflicted upon the native population by the government police, schoolteachers and military, I was overwhelmed with a desire to help the Dani. The people had been beaten, burned and sometimes broken, their pigs as well as their money stolen, their women raped, and many had been subjected to forced labour. I wrote letters to government officials requesting the return of stolen goods, a stop to the beatings of the people, and the granting to the Dani of the rights and liberties enjoyed by all other human beings.

At this point Kurulu is heard of again. Obaharok, whom she only knew by reputation, had formed an alliance with three other chiefs she had come to know and respect 'to resist the increasing domination of Kurulu', but when it appeared that the alliance was gaining the upper hand in the conflict that followed she accuses Kurulu of calling in the Indonesian military. From all we know of Kurulu's character and motives this seems hard to believe. Thus for Wyn Sargent Obaharok became the people's champion. She met him and seems to have been overwhelmed by his physical presence. 'Obaharok wore a ring beard on a face that told the truth, and his eyes reflected great friendliness because he had a desperate desire to make everyone he knew happy. Behind that face and those eyes was a mind that was filled with honesty, wisdom, charity, courage and heroism.'

Obaharok undertook a short-lived private war against Indonesia. 'To show the great might of the man, Obaharok in July 1972, outraged at the sometimes murderous methods used on his people by the police and military officials, tried to put down the whole Indonesian government. He simply could no longer bear to see the physical sufferings of his people at the hands of those who were supposed to be "helping". But Obaharok's bows and arrows were no match for the government guns fitted with live ammunition and realistic counsel prevailed.'

The admiration Wyn Sargent felt for the chief must have been returned, for in January 1973, after a few weeks of courtship, they were married. Despite her long experience of such tribal matters, Wyn seems to have been surprised that there were no formal speeches, and that all that was required of her, apart from a simple announcement, was to put herself on display before the tribe wearing a *yokal*, a married woman's skirt, the equivalent in the Baliem of a marriage document. Picturesque in its simplicity as this arrangement undoubtedly was, certain drawbacks soon appeared in Wyn Sargent's case. The *yokal* as worn by Dani women leaves much of the buttocks and pubic region in sight, and it is a mystery to most newcomers including myself how it is ever kept in place. Notwithstanding her sympathy with the culture into which she was marrying, she found this garment more than she could take. 'To accommodate my Western modesty,' she says, 'the *yokal* was remodelled. I wanted the skirt high and long.'

It took the ladies of the village eight hours to accomplish this. Each strand and fibre had to be placed in a certain way, and although, she says, the result was beautiful, the fibres scratched and itched, and the skirt weighed seven pounds. 'To marry a common man was one thing,' Wyn says, 'but to marry into royalty another.' Status obliged her to wear fifteen ceremonial carrying nets suspended from the forehead down the back, each net weighing two pounds. 'Walking was more in the nature of shuffling than anything else. I had to be steered by four women.' She also refused to surrender her brassière, but the Danis put up with this, and it even started a brief fashion for bras among Obaharok's women.

There were attempts at a ritual distribution of Wyn Sargent's Western garments worn prior to her marriage, and presumed to retain a residue of magic power. Kelion, one of the sub-chiefs, was after the shirt worn before her adoption of the *yokal*. ' "Since you are my sister," he said with sad, innocent eyes, "you must give me a piece of your old clothing. This is the custom. Girls give their *thali* (virginal grass skirts) to their families when they are put in *yokals*. "You can give me your shirt." He settled for a pair of socks.'

The wedding ceremony was officially over when the last *yokal* knot was tied round my waist and Obaharok had killed his pig . . . It was a glorious event which continued for nearly one month . . . During that month the tribes of Kolo, Keliom, Walek and Obaharok streamed across the valley to attend the pig feasts which celebrated the wedding. Many of those previously hostile warriors became brothers, an accomplishment achieved through the Dani cultural laws.

Alas, Wyn's strident championship of the Dani cause inevitably put an end to the tribal peace ushered in by this symbolical union of divergent cultures. The order of banishment from the valley was delivered by a policeman who fired two gunshots over the village. She flew out and next day the Indonesian Antara news agency, quoted in *The Times*, reported that 'she had been ordered to leave the jungle where she lives, because her activities are detrimental to the development of the region'. The agency said: 'Miss Sargent had created a stir by announcing that she would shed her Western clothes and wear only leaves and strings to follow the customs of her husband Obaharok, chief of the Mulia tribe. This infuriated community leaders who said her action would hamper efforts to civilize the region. Miss Sargent, aged 42, from Huntingdon Beach, California, had been in West Irian for four months to conduct researches on the sex life of tribes there.' Antara also said she claimed 'that her marriage to the already much-married chieftain was not based on love. It was intended to bring together three opposing tribes near Wamena in the mountainous interior of the province and also to promote relations between Indonesia and the United States. What had attracted her most, she said, were the art and culture of the West Irianese rather than the sexual life of the tribal community.'

Obaharok's territory lay to the north of the valleys beyond the frontier of the rich Baliem harvests, and on my way to visit him I passed through a borderland where the surroundings departed from the trim good-order of the Wamena area to become a little untidy. Nevertheless they possessed great charm. No-one seemed to have staked out claims in this region of sparse woodland, ponds topped with the enormous leaves of aquatic plants, trees mantled to their topmost branches with ferns, and swamps to be crossed, with some small hazard, over slippery, half-submerged logs. There was a constant coming and going of men – Danis have never become accustomed to their nakedness – hugging themselves against the mountain chill. Women were much better off in this respect, with their grass skirts and layers of fat. All were exceedingly pleasant; the men in particular rushing to the rescue when anyone happened, as in my case, to slip off a log. The women were on their way to market with piglets in baskets and it was here for the first time that I saw a woman suckling one. The sight was all the more unexpected as she appeared well into middle age. The Dani interpreter took this up with her, to receive the good-humoured reply, 'I can't produce milk any more, but this keeps him quiet.'

A brook curled through the invisible frontier dividing rich valley soil from sparse mountain fields, and I crossed this on a swaying rattan bridge that inspired little confidence. Ahead almost treeless terrain sloped away into the far distance, where that majestic escarpment known as the Mountain Wall seals off the Baliem from the alpine tundra of the north. Clouds lay, as they would all day, like dimpled snow between the peaks. This was a new world of new colour. The Baliem was green and black – the black of rich, freshly upturned earth, and the green of new growth sprouting everywhere. In the Obaharok territory ahead polished ribs of limestone showed through the earth's surface, and great swathes of weeds flourished, turned yellow and died. Obaharok's land was the colour of pale saffron, with the great cobalt shadows of the clouds drifting across the fields. It had been spoken of as a hard place to live in, and it produced men, like the chief of the Mulia, who were tougher and more inclined to assert themselves than the valley people.

After an easy couple of miles uphill I found myself among Obaharok's fields, enclosed in their scrupulous drystone walls, and soon the compound came into sight. It was hardly distinguishable in arrangement from Da-Uke's, although on a lesser scale; a village in miniature with women busy at small tasks, naked children chasing each other, and lively, skittish pigs trotting in an orderly way in one direction or another. Obaharok awaited me in a species of arbour newly erected at the entrance to the men's house. Normally the floor of such a construction, as in the case of the houses themselves, would have been strewn with fresh hay, but on this occasion, probably due to the heat of the day, I was invited to join the chief and chosen members of his household, who were reclining on a bed of damp leaves.

Obaharok was a man of striking appearance, possibly in his late seventies, with the first signs of wasting in an athletic body, an exceptionally high forehead, grey, divided beard, a reflective expression, and – for his age – the most astonishingly white and perfect teeth. Age often seems to lessen the separations of race, and in this case I was reminded of the face of a Western saint carved in its niche in a cathedral façade. Nestling close among the leaves was Acu, the youngest of his wives – now reduced to five – who wore a new *yokal* correctly showing a four-inch division of the buttocks. Smiling notables presented themselves to be introduced, among them an excited dwarf covered from head to toe with monstrous ganglions. We all prized each other's faeces.

Obaharok had been promised a meeting with an English warrior and I suspected a certain perplexity in his manner as he studied my face and physique, tried to sum me up, and drew his own conclusions. But good manners quickly vanquished doubt and we launched – in so far as a tenth-rate interpreter permitted it – into an amiable discussion of his life. Previous experience had prepared him for a fresh raking-over of the coals of the Wyn Sargent affair, in which some degree of banality was hard to avoid.

A problem for the foreigner arises among country-folk of the Baliem Valley owing to the absence of any of the trivial abnormalities of daily life that ease the flow of conversation elsewhere in the world. The weather is always the same, there is no news and there are no problems to discuss; in the absence of seasons, crops grow all the year round, gardens produce an unvarying yield of four kinds of vegetables which fill the stomachs of those who grow them to repletion. There are no noxious animals in the valley, even destructive rabbits are absent, and plagues of locusts are unknown. Previous to this I had accepted the common theory that ritual warfare was nature's method of adjusting population to resources, but now I was becoming inclined to the view that it could also be a defence against ennui, and that it was long vacuums of experience that encouraged the Dani extravagance of conduct in other directions: the wildness of their delight, the uncontrollability of their grief, the strength of their friendships, and their taste for long-delayed Mafia-style revenge. It occurred to me that even Obaharok's flamboyant and eccentric marriage to a young anthropologist may have been another example of the Dani battle with vexation of the spirit, an attempt to recreate the excitements of his vanished campaignings in the field.

In the total absence of small-talk Wyn Sargent still held the field as a conversational topic, so I took the easy way out, plunged in and asked Obaharok if he had news of her. With obvious regret he replied that he had none. Like all the Danis, time, for which they had so little use, had come hardly to exist. The nineteen years that had passed since her departure had been shortened by lack of incident. There were no longer guarded watchtowers over his fields, and the blood debts incurred in the local wars had been settled. It was clear that he was trying to focus the date of her going among the other events scattered in the deep space of his mind. Her presence had made its impact, and left its mark. He thought that she had stayed in the house he had specially built for her for about a year. The marriage, he said, had been very happy. She and the ten other wives had lived together in the greatest imaginable harmony. This he repeated several times.

Acu, the current senior wife, seized on this matter of harmony in a polygamous household, when – inexplicably to her – it might have been called into question. They all lived together, worked together and brought up their children together in complete happiness, she insisted. Wyn had only been given a separate house because that was the way foreigners lived, but she would have been more than welcome to join the other wives in the women's house. And this may well have been the case, according to Father Lieshout, the Franciscan missionary whom I saw later. Harmony in a Dani compound, he assured me, was the normal thing. Sexual jealousy was rare, and he believed (as others had reported) that sexual activity was in any case maintained at a lower level than in Western societies.

Obaharok seemed to be tiring. We broke off for a while to stretch our legs and dry off the patches of clothing made damp by contact with the sodden leaves. Small pigs, grunting and whimpering in ecstasy, fussed around us like dogs. (There is a tendency in such Papuan communities to overindulge them until, having tied them in a position offering the best target, the archer approaches with bent bow.) The dwarf with the ganglions capered about us waving his arms. A large long-legged spider leaped on me, scampering up to my chest before being cuffed away, and even then, to the huge amusement of my Dani friends, returning twice to the attack. Women with bunches of twigs were brushing away to remove every fallen leaf, every alien speck from the floor of the compound. Two young children who had a come by a box of matches were striking them one after another and sniffing at the smoke. Obaharok wandered round on the arms of two of his friends. I had presented him with a radio which he believed to be a camera. He started to talk about the wars, although what came through in translation was largely gibberish. He promised to show me his fetiches, which as a Catholic he had been allowed, like Da-Uke, to keep, but this he forgot.

It was the personality of Acu that counted in this little community. She was extremely genial, lively and nimble, although old enough to have a grand-daughter who was an expert sniffer of matches. Acu kept her hands out of sight, giving rise to the suspicion that she had suffered ritual mutilation in the mourning rites of childhood – a possibility strengthened by an unusual arrangement of her hair with which she covered her ears. She was in no way averse to a discussion of this matter, probably even eager to ventilate a topic that had been dismissed from mind for so many years. There was a trace of almost ghoulish satisfaction in her description of childhood sufferings – although it later transpired that the details illustrated by theatrical gestures had largely been forgotten. Acu was on her feet, eyes starting from her head, as she recreated phantom images of a child's terror, the spurting blood, the snap of a stone axe on shattered bone. Between us, as always, stretched the barrier of language, with the interpreter rummaging among a tiny vocabulary to come up with the wrong word used in the wrong place and a result that so often came close to absurdity. The following is the simplest possible version of what was said.

N.L. How did you come to lose your fingers?

AKU I had four cut off when my grandfather died. That left only two for my father. I don't know how old I was. I was just a very young girl.

I had read that it was usual to reduce the pain of such operations by tying the finger with a ligature below the joint to be severed; then immediately before the amputation striking the elbow over the ulnar nerve. I asked if this has been done.

AKU No nothing. These four were cut off all at the same time. Like this . . . One by one they were cut off. My grandfather was a good man and I loved him, so they cut off my fingers. When he died I put my hand on a piece of wood like this, then one by one they were cut off. This was done because I was sad, and to appease the ancestors.

N.L. What was used to remove the fingers?

AKU A little stone axe. With this they chopped and no-one held me.

N.L. But Acu, you've lost your ears. What happened?

AKU We are only allowed to lose six fingers, so when my grand-mother died I gave an ear for her. I took a bamboo knife and with this I cut off one ear. The other I cut off when they stole my pig. This was a pig I loved, so I lost my ear.

N.L. But can you work with only two fingers on each hand?

AKU It makes no difference. I can work in the garden, cook and pick up small objects, and that is enough.

The staggering thing was that although Acu preferred not to take sides in the arguments over finger amputation, there was no doubt in an informal conversation that she approved of the custom so recently abolished. Danis had learned to be cautious in advancing an opinion on such topics, but Namek too, as soon as I got to know him a little, expressed approval for such aspects of the culture suppressed by Dutch reforms.

Over the question of Wyn Sargent she proved herself a staunch ally. Coming back to the subject she said, 'She was very good to Obaharok. Wyn and I used to do everything together. We'd go to the fields and we'd work. That's why I was sad when she left. I wish that Wyn Sargent was still here so that her relatives would come and visit her. When white people like you come to visit we feel very sad, because you remind us of Wyn Sargent.'

SEVENTEEN

I RAN NAMEK to earth in the Excelsior Cafe, and we sat together on seats wrenched from a crashed plane. The atmosphere was of that special bewildered emptiness so familiar in countries on the threshold of change from which purpose has been withdrawn, and nothing sucked into the vacuum to take its place. The attempt to brighten up the surroundings had underscored an entrenched bareness. A lizard that had clearly gone mad was scuttling in a distraught manner over the surface of a Fanta advertisement; the one-arm bandit had ceased to work, and a pool table attracted no players because the Dani guides and hangers-on who frequented the place still failed to understand the purpose of competitive games. Stray sounds emphasised a chronic silence: the scratch of a branch on the tin roof, the distant maracas rattle of a helicopter. A Dani tribal who had wandered in by mistake stood motionless in a far corner. He glistened from head to foot in the oiled silk of his skin, and a blue feather had been stuck in his penis gourd. After a while, perhaps from embarrassment, he emitted a deep sonorous giggle, then effortlessly, as if released from a spring, was carried at a bound through the window and out of sight.

We sipped sweet, lukewarm tea. I pushed a packet of clove cigarettes across the table and Namek took one with a flutter of the fingers, like a bird alighting on a twig. In the way of all the Danis moving into the new age, he was in a flux over the matter of clothing, and had dressed himself on this occasion in army service jungle fatigues – a miniature parachutist, short on aggression.

I had hoped to persuade him to tell me something of life as it had been for a Dani in the troublous period described in Wyn Sargent's book, but the moment I broached the subject I felt the loss of contact. The direction of his gaze has shifted and he appeared to be listening. He raised a finger to his lips in a gesture valid in every part of the world. Ears were cocked, it signified, behind these thin walls. 'Soon we go for a ride in car,' he said.

He was here to meet someone who might or might not show up. Punctuality was unknown, not understood in the Baliem. Nevertheless time came more and more to establish its dominance. All the Dani guides now wore wrist-watches from which, even in Namek's case, they had detached the hands. 'We must wait a little,' he said, 'then we go.'

It gave me the opportunity to tackle him on the subject of polygamy, from which strenuous campaigns mounted both by the missionaries and the government had been unable to dissuade the Danis. Namek, possessing two wives, was a suitable informant. 'How do you cope with them?' I asked. 'How do you keep them quiet?'

'On Thursdays I take first wife out in taxi,' he said, 'on Sundays second wife for nice ride. I am giving sugar almonds from Holland to both.'

'Do you make them work in your garden?'

'No, I am Catholic. The Dutch father who adopted me say not to make wives work. This why I am driving a taxi, but now I need a new tyre.'

I asked him the routine question, if Dani men marry ten wives or more how can there be enough women to go round?

'There are enough,' he said. He nodded his head in vigorous emphasis. 'A man may work until he has pigs to give. When he has pigs there is always wife.' This was the routine answer.

We were interrupted as the door burst open with a crash, and a number of Dani guides, taxi drivers and hangers-on in football shorts and singlets of garish colours rushed into the room. They yanked in succession with peals of high-pitched laughter at the handle of the one-arm bandit, picked up cues to jab at the balls on the pool table, went through a joking pretence of sparring and digging each other in the ribs, and dashed out again.

'Where do the pigs come from in the first place?'

'The man he works for will give him pigs. Then the wedding may be arranged.'

'Take the case of your friends who've moved into town,' I said. 'Surely they're no longer into working for pigs. How will they manage?'

'They will manage. Now they are working with Dutch tourists. These tourists say them, OK, so we give you money. You buy pigs.'

'And do they do that? Has anyone actually bought pigs for cash?'

'No,' he said, and his small, negative smile, launched with a nervous uplift of the eyes, warned of a threat of muddle.

'Why not?'

'Because village big men will not allow. These are men saying yes or no. They say all pigs now being saved for five-year feast coming. Pigs not to be given for money.'

'We're back where we started,' I said. 'Your friends have the money but the big men are hanging on to the pigs. So what are they going to do? A pocketful of money, but no pig, no wife. They're up the creek, aren't they?'

'Not up creek,' he said. 'Now there is pig shortage because of feast. After feast small pigs begin to grow. Soon big men will say, OK, let them take money for pigs. My friends must wait.'

'Those big men of yours,' I said. 'What is the largest number of wives any of them has?'

Namek held up a hand. 'I am counting by fingers,' he said. 'The one that has most wives has five handfuls. Maybe a little more. Every two years this man is taking one wife. Two houses he must build to hold them all.'

'How old is he now?'

'We do not know ages. He is very old. This man lives all day on a blanket outside hut. Friends come with brushes to clear from him the flies.'

'And I suppose his latest wife is a young girl?'

'She is young. He gave many pigs for her, and she put on marriage skirt for him for first time.'

'It's a problem for all concerned,' I said. 'Including him.' This was dangerous ground. According to the anthropologists the Danis usually clammed up over matters of marital relationships. I took the bull by the horns. 'We're talking about sex,' I told him. 'This girl isn't really married at all. Here's an old man lying on a blanket all day and the flies crawling all over him. Where does the marriage come in? Doesn't his wife do anything about it?'

His face had emptied. This was a Stone-Age face again, straight out of the compound. The widest of grins, or a frown, and between these extremes of satisfaction and discontent nothing showed but a graven passivity. Early associations and influences had rendered Namek's features susceptible to small invasions of expression, at the same time depriving him of the capacity to register deep emotion. I pressed on and a pseudo-European liveliness returned, and I knew I was in the clear.

'Sometimes,' he said. 'Yes, she does.'

'So what happens?'

'In compound nothing. Many woman are there cleaning up, cooking. Babies everywhere. Young women go out to work in gardens. Men are in gardens digging ditches. I would not allow my second wife working in gardens.'

'I wouldn't have thought they offered much in the way of privacy,' I said.

'There are sacred places with trees. These we call wusa. No-one must enter to cut wood, because ghosts are in trees.'

'I thought Dani ghosts were invisible.'

'These ghosts not seen but shoot with arrows. I have seen one man wounded in this way. When people come close to wusa place they cover their faces. Men are digging ditch on one side. Women plant sweet potatoes on other side.' I was the recipient of his nearest equivalent to a smile, with all the nuances of suggestion that an outright Dani grin could not contain. 'So that's how it's done,' I said. 'What about the ghosts and their arrows? Doesn't anyone ever get shot?'

'This place is not wusa for blind people, or one leg shorter than other leg, or for people we call geruba, meaning they are not strong in the head. Ghosts sorry for this boy and girl.'

'It's a sensitive attitude,' I said. 'Is it generally known in the compound that this goes on.'

'They don't say, but they all know.'

'Even the husband on his blanket, being eaten by the flies?'

'Yes, he knows also, but he will not say. I tell this to you because you are a foreigner and soon you will go away.'

The tourist Namek had been expecting failed to appear and in the end he gave up and said we might as well go. He wanted to show me the place where he had been born, south of Wamena near the Megapola road sloping gently down towards the river. Mornings in the Baliem are burnished and luminous before slowly the skies turn sullen in the afternoon and the clouds build up with the rain. At this time the outlines of the Mountain Wall were scratched across the sky, and a distance of twenty miles had turned quartz to aquamarine.

This was the scene of one of Namek's earliest memories. A helicopter – the first flying machine he had seen – had dropped out of the sky and smiling men had descended from it. They had handed out steel axes, knives and salt to the assembled villagers and one of the smiling men put a bar of chocolate in Namek's mouth, which he took out and gave to his father. The newcomers announced that they had been sent by God, with the instructions to build an airstrip there. They explained how this was to be done, and set the villagers to work. Namek's next memory was of the smiling man's departure. The airstrip going through part of the village gardens was finished, and then suddenly the men were gone, and were seen no more.

It is to be supposed that these were members of the expeditionary force dispatched by Lloyd Van Stone, a Texan, claiming that he had received a 'mandate from Heaven' to invade the Baliem and bring the Danis to God. Van Stone found Catholicism as introduced by the Franciscans unrecognisable as Christianity, burned several thousands of captured fetiches in a bonfire 200 metres in length, and encouraged defection to his brand of faith by the distribution of goods such as those Namek had described.

These lavish offerings were attributed by the villagers to successful ceremonies performed by members of the Cargo Cult. Namek was unable to explain why, after the missionaries departure, the village and its gardens had been abandoned.

There were police posts every five or six miles along the road, and a foreigner passing any of these for the first time had to check in for an inspection of his *surat jalan*, a routine questioning, and the entering-up of his personal details in the register. One of these posts was at the village Sugokmo. It had been built, as wherever possible police posts were, on a hillock with a good view of whatever was going on in the flat, surrounding countryside. The policemen were from Java, with supposedly little appetite for life in Irian Jaya, and here, once again, was a typical police-post flower garden. It had been raining at Sugokmo and the hill was covered in mud. 'Don't fall down,' the policeman said when he had finished writing my details in his register, and he told a naked Dani who was polishing the plastic flower pots to look after me. This he attempted to do, but we both skidded and sprawled in the mud, a scene that produced uproarious laughter and put everyone in a good humour. Namek's taxi always required a push start, and seeing this from their eyrie above, the two policemen, still grinning happily, came down to give a hand.

As reported by Wyn Sargent, the Danis had revolted and suffered repression immediately prior to her presence in the Baliem. In 1973 Robert Mitton commented on the harshness of the new regime:

> The Indonesians aren't particularly liked in the Baliem valley . . . they have resorted to violent suppression where their popularity is very low; Sengeh, Arso and the border areas. According to our pilot who has flown in the region there are literally no people left. Their villages have been totally destroyed and they are hiding in the bush, have fled to Papua New Guinea, or are dead.

In this way the Papuan people demonstrated a continuing resistance to the Indonesian presence and, being virtually without arms, suffered the consequence. The United States had backed Indonesia from the first as a potentially valuable ally against communism in South-east Asia. A moral problem arose, for the Western Allies had just emerged victorious from a war fought to put an end to territorial aggression by the strong against the weak. The dilemma was solved in a meeting between President Sukarno and Bobby Kennedy at which it was agreed that whether West Papua joined Indonesia or not, was to be an 'Act of Free Choice'. By this time the

Indonesian army had taken up its position in the territory under dispute. A referendum was announced, the votes to be cast by 1,025 delegates selected under Indonesian military supervision. Their voting was unanimous, athough it is alleged that a single dissenter was converted when a gun was pointed in his direction. West Papua passed under its new title of Irian Jaya into Indonesian control – a *fait accompli* upon which the UN hastened to confer its approval.

The major insurrection in the central Highlands took place in 1977, when Danis armed with spears and bows and arrows planted stakes in the runways of Wamena airfield and took on Indonesian commandos, but were still bombed and machine-gunned from the air. Many villages such as Sugokmo suffered aerial attack, in which traditional Dani dwellings were burned to the ground, to be replaced eventually by the government's standard 'healthy houses'.

Sugokmo village was down by the river seen through a screen of casuarina leaves, backed on its mountainside by great, smooth viridian rocks appearing to have been balanced, as a result of some ancient cataclysm, in a position from which one day they would come crashing down among the houses. It was full of life: men digging ditches for the fun of it, Namek explained, and others filling them in, friendly and intelligent pigs trying to ingratiate themselves with us, women at work in their gardens, and children galore. An Indonesian official had lived in a house of a better kind, leaving a gardenful of dahlias at their last gasp, and his Dani neighbours were in the act of tearing them out at the moment of our arrival.

There was a smell of money about this place, suggesting that some of its menfolk had drifted away to Wamena to pick up odd jobs. Mess strewn everywhere established its claim to a progressive attitude: a seat stripped from a plane wreck, matching the one in the Cafe Excelsior, flattened soft-drinks cans, an engine block about to submerge in the mud. One or two football shirts were in sight, and when we tried to talk to a group of villagers, someone went to find a spokesman who put on a miner's helmet before joining us. This man had worked for years for the Americans at the Freeport Mine and had picked up the best English I had heard spoken in Irian Jaya.

A row of government healthy houses had been built close to the river, all of these apart from one appearing to be empty. With our arrival on the scene this occupied house became the centre of scurrying activity. The man with the helmet explained that this was the officially tenanted house. He seemed to suspect me of being an inspector, but when Namek told him I was no more than an inquisitive foreigner, there was a cordial invitation to look over the place. Inside we found a woman with a pair of teenage daughters bustling nervously around in a pretence of occupying themselves with household jobs, and a pig that had trotted in after them was hastily kicked out. 'The deal is this,' the man explained. 'If a family takes on one of these houses the village is officially settled and we're left in peace. Some of my friends have three wives and two handfuls of children. Even to get them in here they'd have to be packed like freight on a plane. We keep a few odds and ends in this place and the women take it in turns to cook a meal or do the washing. If it looks like someone lives here that's all that matters, and so far we've got by.'

A few square yards of garden went with the healthy houses. The old-style *honais* with their low, thatched roofs and divisions by which ample space was shared between families had been shoved into the back of these, screened as much as possible among bushes and trees. In this way Sugokmo was slowly returning to what it had been when Archbold, flying over the valley in his sea-plane had expressed such astonishment and delight at what he saw.

Why are we here? I wondered. 'What happened at Sugokmo?' I asked.

'You asked me about nineteen seventy-seven. You want I show you these places. In Hetegima too many people die. Also Kurima.'

'In nineteen seventy-seven.'

'Yes, in that year. Next we go to Elegaima where I show you something. I tell you the story of this place.'

We set off again, but there was a stop at Kulagaima where Namek had learned en route that something was afoot. The chief's compound here was even bigger than Da-Uke's. He had twenty wives, said Namek, and, despite Dani restraint reputedly practised in sexual activity, forty-two children, of which a favourite son was accepted as the finest archer in the Baliem. He was about to demonstrate his skill in a noteworthy fashion, for Namek had now ascertained that there was to be a grand feast at which he would be called upon to kill all sixty pigs with a single arrow apiece shot through the heart. The chief, who had contributed handsomely to the dedication of a new Catholic church in the vicinity received us outside the men's house. He was a man infused with the dignity of power, a conservative with correctly blackened forehead and cockatoo feathers curving down from behind ears close-cropped in token of some old bereavement, and to my great satisfaction he invited me to the feast. His principal wife came into view puffing on a long cheroot, a pretty woman thirty years his junior whose grubby silk pantaloons in this supremely traditional setting hinted at new directions in which the Baliem might be heading.

Kulagaima, displayed in light filtered through the casuarinas, with its children gathered to swim among the leaves afloat in its wide, green pond, was the best of the valley. Elegaima, tucked away in the low hills to the north, was bare and arid. Here there were no people, no houses, only an abandoned and derelict mission, and the yellow river corkscrewing among black fields at the valley bottom.

'What are you going to show me?' I asked.

'Now you will see,' Namek said.

We left the car to fizz and splutter and walked through the coarse grass a half-mile down to a wood. This was unusual because all the lower branches of the trees, which would normally have been vulnerable to villagers in search of firewood, had remained intact. Numerous small birds sheltered among the trees, having taken up residence, it was to be supposed, in what they had come to regard as a safe haven. At our approach they swarmed away like bees. 'Is this one of those wusa woods you told me about?' I asked.

'This is wusa,' he said. 'Here I come to hide with my friends when the planes are in Wamena, but they find us when we come out for food. Four planes drop bombs, then when planes go, seven helicopters come. So there are twenty of us killed. They take me to Wamena and hold lighted cigarettes against my body.' An agonised rolling of the eyes accompanied the memory. 'I am the enemy,' he said. 'So they burn me.'

'So you have no reason to be particularly fond of the Indonesians,' I said.

There was a moment of silence while he mustered the sentences in English. 'They torture me,' he said, 'also I am blaming the Indonesians for other reason.'

'And what is that?'

I sensed what was coming. It was the common complaint of Dani that the Muslims – as most of the Indonesians were – prefer to carry out ritual ablutions in running water.

'Everyone shit in river,' he said.

It was arranged that I should arrive at Kulagaima for the dedication ceremony of the new church at 7.30 am. This I did, discovering that by this time the carnage was already at an end. Wherever I looked I saw pig-flesh on display, as inoffensive as the orderly prime cuts in an up-to-date butchery – and in this case on beds of freshly picked leaves. Girls had been stationed armed with palm fronds to fan away the blue dragonflies the meat attracted. The two Franciscan fathers in their vestments hovered in the background, seeming at first when I presented myself to be a little reserved, and it was hard to avoid the suspicion that they might not altogether have been happy at the presence of a Westerner at a church function of this particular kind.

The killing of the pigs had taken place in the garden of the new church, scrupulously tidied up for the occasion, and housing a simply knocked-together grandstand. What was strikingly different on this occasion from the routine of pig-feasts was that the womenfolk were not only permitted to be present, but were involved in various stages of the procedure.

The opposing sides, amounting to perhaps twenty or thirty warriors, veterans of the 1988 war who it was hoped would be finally reconciled at this time, faced each other across the garden with the meat piled between. What I found strange and in some way significant was that none wore ornaments: no shells, feathers or boar's tusks were to be seen. At one moment a brief altercation began, arms were waved and jeers exchanged, but this subsided at the Franciscans' approach.

The dedication service had been lengthy and the feasting that followed appeared likely to occupy much of the day, but a brief interlude of calm offered an opportunity to speak to the two Franciscans. Fathers Lieshout and Peters, by now the oldest European inhabitants of the Baliem, had arrived as young men in 1963, and had thus been witnesses of the many dramatic and sometimes bloody events that had transformed the life of the valley since that year. It was evident that their congregation was totally devoted to them. I could not help wondering if they could have been the same pastors whose converts in the early days could with difficulty be persuaded to leave the mission church, due to their belief that beneficial influences were absorbed through its seats?

Their presence on this occasion was benign and tolerant in the extreme, and I took the opportunity to sound them out on their attitude to what may seem the excesses of the Van Stone style of evangelism. 'We didn't burn the fetiches or destroy the sacred stones which are the symbols of their ancestors,' Father Lieshout said. 'That is not our task, but I know there are other churches who have another attitude. Some books say that Dani culture is bad, and only from the time the Gospel came in they became good people. We do not accept it. We did learn and we still learn a lot from these people. How to live together with other people that we forget already in Europe, we can find it here.'

On the subject of warfare he was adamant. 'War we cannot accept, and this is a ceremony of reconciliation. There is a problem. When they kill a man they take something, say his arrow, or some hair. This symbolises the dead man. They also call it aduarit, and they use it to exert influence via the dead men on their enemies. This is what we are working for – for the return of the aduarits they have taken. Only when this is done will there by lasting peace.'

The father managed a cautious smile. 'Now it is quieter. First the big men were shouting threats. Now they will eat together, everybody is feeling better. They are talking in a reasonable way. Perhaps someone will give back an aduarit. If that happens it would be a good thing. That would be a good thing. That would be a real success.'

This was the stage when shallow pits were being dug. Large round stones were collected to line them, and brushwood and branches carried in from the nearby forest for use in the cooking process. I was fascinated, once again, to observe the ingrained Dani taste for organisation and order displayed in these operations. Thus there were teams dealing with each separate activity; stones and combustible materials were collected by specialists of both sexes, who rushed to their work in all directions, leaping over walls and across ditches with the greatest possible verve and a continuous excited outcry.

With the pits lined with stones and the meat on them in position, the men drew back and the girls took over, arranging more stones over the meat, followed by a covering of brushwood and then branches for the pits, and transferring hot stones from one pit to another, using for this purpose split sticks employed as tongs. As the pits heated up, small explosions of grey smoke hurled stones into the air. Every explosion produced outcries of pretended alarm from the girls, and when one was struck with some force on the arm, the time had come for the men to take over.

It was also time for the girls to dress for the party, and with one accord they dropped everything and were off, athletes all of them, leaping the low stone wall of the church enclosure, dashing through the long grass of an uncultivated field into the trees of a spinney, and out of sight. I had observed that when not engaged in gardening drudgery they took every opportunity to burn up energy, and seemed quite unable to keep still.

Their passion for neatness, too, was remarkable. Muddy patches had appeared on the earth of the enclosure ravaged by so many feet, and a word of command sent the team racing to the fields in a hunt for dried grass to cover these, while a finer sort of grass mixed with some fragrant herb was spread over the grandstand seats.

Visitors drifted in, including a party of notables from a nearby village, all in conspicuously long penis sheaths, and with furled umbrellas hanging from their arms. What Namek called a 'silly man', dressed in an army battle blouse and peaked officer's cap, had wandered into sight, grimacing and saluting, and was treated with utmost courtesy by all present. Namek's second wife, a pretty 22-year-old, brought a touch of class to the proceeding, her ample bosom constrained in a tight brassière, worn with pleated skirt, green football socks and trainers. She had come with the girls who had done most of the dirty work so far. They were back now from their titivations, all in brassières, their bare skin wherever in reach covered with a festive scribble in many colours, and three pairs of dark spectacles between seven of them – the remainder having painted white spectacle frames round their eyes. Myself apart, the Franciscan fathers remained the only foreigners.

Now the men had entered into intense, competitive action. It was at a stage of cooking process before the fire was damped down by a thick cap of new grass and left to smoke, when all was flames and fury. Explosion followed explosion with heavy stones shot out in all directions, sometimes a distance of twenty yards before hitting the ground. Young men – still referred to in Dani terms as warriors – were on display in minor tests of courage. What was required of them was a maximum exposure to risk, and this was done by an unhurried approach to add more fuel to the fire, then, in the manner of a showy bullfighter who turns his back on the bull, a stylish and leisurely retreat to safety. In this way, once in a while, a warrior was brained, and we saw two men struck by stones, although they were able to keep their feet.

Nothing could have exceeded the excitement and with it the charm of this scene. The new church and its garden enclosure were overtopped by a majestic limestone cliff. From this it appeared that a recent earthquake had sheared away several thousand tons of its mass, to reveal a sparkling new surface in a precipice brilliantly striped and stained by vegetable juices released by the forest trees. Under this background the Dani girls touched up the coloured curlicues painted on foreheads and cheeks, examined the results in fragments of mirror, and chain-smoked long, thin local cigarettes. The men, in their best festive paint, attacked the enemy of the moment – the fire – cavorting, posturing and gesticulating defiance to cries of derision or applause. Shepherded by parents and friends, just out of range of the stone bombardment, irrepressibly smiling and overwhelming in their charm, the children of the tribe wandered on the lookout for susceptible strangers, like myself, to nestle up to.

Sociability was governed by a gentle protocol which might have drawn inspiration from a vicarage tea-party of old. Having charged about in all directions on fuel-gathering and other such errands, the young settled themselves within the church compound in decorous rows, maintaining a drone of polite, smiling conversation with their neighbours, punctuated in the case of both sexes by ritual and constant exchange of home-made cigarettes. There are parts of the world where the stranger must resign himself to being stared at – even to drawing a crowd. Papuan good manners permit no more than a quick, investigatory glance before the head is turned away. Young people coming from isolated foothill hamlets to Kulagaima for this party were likely to have seen few white faces before, but nobody looked twice in my direction, and a baby whose face crumpled with consternation at my appearance was instantly snatched away to be comforted out of view.

There was a determination to avoid messiness in the handling of the pork. A new contingent of lady helpers, their skin patterned in abstract blue designs, went the rounds with rectangles of meat held on glossy plantain leaves serving as plates. Portions varied with age, sex and status. Village patricians received double helpings which they brandished in each hand with an air of triumph before consumption. Fingers and mouths were constantly cleansed of grease with extremely fine hay-scented grass placed within easy reach, and those unsatisfied with the result trooped off to scrub themselves with a brush hanging by a chain over a fresh-water ditch.

Having arrived late and thus escaped the great holocaust of pigs that had started with the dawn, I had settled at Kulagaima to the enjoyment of a stimulating day. Nevertheless the celebration was a hybrid one. Men who had been roped in here from a world of miracles and ghosts were reduced by the pleasant pettiness of the occasion to a pretence of grumbling over the division of pork. The fathers had arrived at the best possible compromise, and amazingly, had come close to liberating the womenfolk for the day. Mitton and Gardner would have held up their hands in horror, taking the view that any breach in tribal custom weakens the culture that has enabled it to survive and presages its eventual collapse. They would certainly had disagreed with the fathers' peace-making, which was what the party was all about. 'War', Milton said, 'constitutes one of the major focuses of people's interest and energy.' He asked: 'An equal or even greater number perish from complications arising from the common cold, hence the death rate is not excessive.' Gardner, too, found ritual warfare on the whole a good thing.

Nevertheless, the Franciscans worked away at peaceful solutions which the anthropologists claimed the people in reality did not want. It was hard to believe that an end to their labours was in sight when in Wamena town itself at Easter in 1992 a brief battle was fought. Arrows flew through the air over the heads of the tourists on package deals from the orderly cities of the Netherlands, who until this experience might have found Irian Jaya unexciting compared, say, with Komodo and its dragons.

We left the party and set off along a path leading over walls and through ditches to the Wamena road. A slope climbed to a fronded backdrop under mountains blending with clouds. At the top of this rise, parting the tall grasses as though they had been curtains, two women moved into sight. At this distance one appeared as painted yellow, and as they came slowly down the slope towards us I realised that one was a woman in mourning and the other her attendant. The mourner wore only a *yokal* and was smeared all over from head to foot in yellow mud. Her companion was dressed in shapeless, dismal Western cast-offs, and a head-covering cowled like that worn by some unfamiliar order of nuns, although at close quarters this turned out to be made of sacking. Both these women held themselves in a stooping fashion, as if burdened by invisible loads. They carried digging sticks with sharp four-inch blades, used equally to cut root vegetables from the ground, or to beat off attempted rapes.

My impression was that these women were hoping to see a little of the celebrations without drawing attention to themselves. Namek signalled to them and they ducked back out of sight in a clump of ferns, where a moment later we found them. Namek spoke to them, and the attendant replied to his questions. Her charge had lost a brother killed in a skirmish, which entailed prolonged and complicated rituals of bereavement. Instead of smearing herself with mud at the time of the cremation –which, having dried on her body, would be left there until it fell off – the close relationship in this case required the mud to be added to daily until there was reason to believe that the ancestral spirits were satisfied. While in this early stage of mourning, the girl would be regarded by her community as suffering from a contagious sickness, a kind of emotional leprosy which, while curable, might retain its hold for months. The duty of the friend or neighbour who had agreed to act as her escort was to persuade her to take food, and to protect her, by carrying out the proper magical procedure, from attack by ghosts of the kind that battened upon grief. Mud-smearing came into this, too, because it served as a disguise from such phantoms, who despite their supernatural powers suffered from defective vision.

At this juncture it appeared that this ghastly maquillage was in need of touching up. The girl's breasts had been tied with cords to flatten them against her rib cage and the mud had flaked away from their upper surface, as it had at the elbows, ankles and wrists, through the flexing of muscles. These small defects seemed to be causing her concern, and her friend rummaged in her clothing to produce a pad of muddied leaves with which she dabbed at the exposed patches of skin, but with little improvement to the final result. Namek told me that the girl thought she was about twenty-five but such was the ageing effect of the mud that I would have believed her to be more than forty.

It was fortunate that the brother had been unmarried, for widows could expect harsher versions of the same treatment in such cases: more self-inflicted ugliness and more trouble with ghosts. Heinrich Harrer reports a kind of hysteria in his time, prompting widows to throw themselves from cliff tops into the Baliem Gorge, and this it was reported was still happening thirty years later.

It was an encounter that gave rise to a pause for reflection. Where we are saddened by death, the Danis are outraged. As part of the defences raised against sorrow, our funeral rites are brief and we have dispensed with all the old-fashioned theatricals of grief. As soon as possible the body is put out of sight, and we are left alone with our memories and a grave rarely to be revisited. Where a Western family will save up to send a son to a good school, its Dani equivalent in the past would make sacrifices to be able to mummify a father in the hope of keeping his remains in the house for 500 years.

Namek was inclined to disapprove of the government's ban on finger amputation. A single deft chop and the finger was gone, and with it, after a few hours, the pain of the amputation too. It acted as a safety-valve, relieved the mourner of ordeal by mud, and left her with something to show. Women who had lost fingers commanded special respect. He was convinced that a recent upturn in the number of suicides was in some part due to the ban.

We left the women to go on their way, but then turned to watch them through a screen of jungle tendrils and leaves. Once, as they supposed, out of our sight, they underwent an extraordinary change. They straightened up and their pace quickened. They still preferred to see rather than to be seen, for, descending the slope, they slipped speedily from the cover of ferns to the cover of bamboos, peering through stalks and fronds before skipping a few yards to the next vantage point – a kind of oriental ballet of evasion, with grief perhaps for a moment thrust out of mind.

EIGHTEEN

BACK IN THE spring of 1991 an item in a *Financial Times* someone had left on a train caught my eye. It recorded the success of an American mining company, Freeport Copper, which, following twenty years of what the newspaper described as almost unbelievable feats of engineering, found itself in possession of the largest copper mine in the world. The Ertzberg mountain in the highland of Irian Jaya, upon which so much technical innovation and engineering skill had been focused, was found to contain an uniquely vast ore body of copper, silver and gold. This, having been removed at the rate of 24,700 tonnes a day, left nothing of a once towering peak but an enormous hole. Now Freeport was reported to have hollowed out the neighbouring Grasberg mountain, two kilometres away, found also to be practically solid ore. As in the case of Ertzberg, problems were to be expected with overburden. This, in the specialised language of great mining corporations, is the mountain itself and its usual components of peaks, crags and forests which inhibit access to the ore. The fact was that colossal peaks minus their ore were being removed from the scene, and their remains – the overburden – dumped into the nearest valley. Soon the site of Grasberg, too, would be no more than a hole in the ground.

More important, more perturbing, was the news that the Indonesian government, in recognition of its outstanding achievements, had granted Freeport exclusive rights to a new mining concession 250 times larger than the existing one. This contract was for thirty years, nevertheless an exuberant Freeport spokesman expected that his company's operations would last well into the next century. The *Financial Times* article pointed out that the concession gave the company full access to mineral-rich mountains extending right across the country to the frontier with Papua New Guinea, and the reader was left in no doubt that Freeport would be extending its operations in that direction. To quote its 1991 annual report: 'We have completed preliminary surface and stream sampling in our new 6.5 million-acre exploration area where more than 6,000 rock and soil samples have been collected from thousands of sites.'

If not actually secretive in its operations, Freeport Indonesia might be said to have enshrouded them in extraordinary reticence, and it is perhaps natural that the world should wonder why this should have been. There is hardly a remoter place on earth than this mine, once no more than a mountain of copper, which, before the building of the road, was accessible only to a mountaineering enthusiast prepared to tackle a long trek interspersed with dangerous climbs. Pancak Jaya (5,039m.), lying a few miles to the south of the mine, is the highest peak between the Himalayas and the Andes, and similar, if slightly lesser, peaks cluster in the area. The 63-mile road built up from Amamapare on the south coast, passing occasionally along knife-edge ridges joining the peaks, is considered a marvel of road-building engineering. It is strictly private, its privacy being guarded by various checkpoints, and it is traversed only by company cars.

In a letter of 3 June 1992 from George A. Mealey, President of the parent company, Freeport McMoran of New Orleans, to Randall Hayes, Director of the conservationist organisation Rainforest Action Network, Mealey vigorously refutes a charge that his company's operations are not open to scrutiny. Between the years 1990 and 1992, Mealey points out, there have been 'at least 40 site visits'. There was a rumour that even journalists had been allowed to visit the mine. In my case the attempt to obtain the necessary sanction – organised by friends with long experience in this field – was prolonged and difficult, occupying four months in all. One was dealing not only with a company concerned with privacy, but the Indonesian government, with whom Freeport maintains a close relationship, and which shows signs of uneasiness at the presence in the country of foreigners other than bona fide tourists. Eventually a visit was agreed and a date fixed. I flew from Wamena back to Sentani, where I boarded a Boeing plane owned by the company for the flight to Timika, a hot little town on the edge of a swamp, where it was arranged that I should be met and driven up the celebrated road to the mining town, Tembagapura. Awaiting at the airport was Greg Probst, the PRO, and John Cutts, in charge of the Tembagapura Community Development Project. John had been born an American Indian and adopted at the age of two by a missionary. Before being taken on by Freeport he had spent most of his adult life among tribal people of the area, and spoke four of their languages. Both these men radiated interest and goodwill, and if, as was generally supposed, the company had decided the time had come to improve its image, they could not have sent more convincing emissaries than these.

A small fleet of company cars were lined up in the airport park, all of them Toyotas with the modifications necessary to cope with extraordinary journeys. Strict rules on driving are unavoidable in the company territory, including rigidly maintained speed limits, the use of lights – which are left on most of the time – and gears to be engaged at various points of the uphill and downhill drive. The first checkpoint is passed through at the airport perimeter with a quick scrutiny of the car and its passengers, and a tick on the register and an exchange of cordialities. Company employers treat each other with the courtesy more normally to be observed with the members of the armed forces than those in civilian life. Every drive up or down this extraordinary road, with its extreme gradients to be tackled in frequently adverse weather conditions, is part of a small shared adventure. Inconsiderate driving becomes an impossibility.

The lowlands we passed through in the vicinity of Timika, seeming to be an informal part of the Freeport territory, were hardly distinguishable from any rather poverty-stricken landscape anywhere in the tropical world. It was hot, untidy, and prey to the lassitudes of resignation and undernourishment. Timika underlined the difference between the hot country and the highlands. In the Baliem, energetic tribespeople displayed their largely naked but well-washed bodies. Here, where life moved at a snail's pace, they dressed in the shapeless international uniform of tropical clothes. This had been highlighted by charitable hand-outs of cast-offs. A girl wore a Victorian cape with a fancy-dress item of a gypsy's flounced flamenco skirt, and a man in grubby vest and slacks went about in a Mexican hat. It was an area scattered with big-bellied babies, tousled chickens and yellow dogs, and the sun's rays stabbed back from glossy leaves and the waters of the lagoons. There was hope in plenty for these people in the near future, John said, speaking with confidence and relish of company projects now afoot to better their lot. As things were, too much of the company's food had to be flown in from as far away as New Zealand, and the Baliem had failed them in the hoped-for vegetable supplies. Now, with the mine's continuous expansion, self-sufficiency was the goal in view, and he pointed at clearances in the straggling and shadeless secondary forest where the new future for Timika was about to dawn.

John knew all about these people. They were hunters and gatherers, as people down in the tropics always were, but at most times in the year there was little to hunt and gather so they lived rather miserably by fishing in the lagoons, eating the heads of the few fish they caught themselves, and selling the rest to the restaurant in Timika. The only problem was to persuade them to better themselves by becoming cultivators producing for the company, and in effect break them of age-old habits. I had read somewhere of the resettlement down in Timika of Amungme tribes-people displaced by the mine, and of their escape back to the mountains before they were picked up once more and sent back to Timika. A number of these were said to have died from malaria, which is a speciality of the region, and later, according to a Jakarta newspaper, 212 children of an unspecified tribe had succumbed to an epidemic. Were the people we saw here, I wondered, the survivors of the original Amungme? It was a matter to be gone into, I decided, perhaps at a later date.

There was a certain appropriateness in this approach along a preposterous road to a preposterous mine. There had been nothing quite like the mine on earth before, and the same could be said of the road. Not even the Incas of Peru had attempted a road of this kind, despite the millions of tons of rock shifted by their Stone-Age methods. This bull at a gate attack on the copper mountain called for audacity as well as a sense of adventure. The Pancak Jaya-Grasberg mountain complex is quite unlike the Alpine scenes with which we are familiar. There are no foothills. The peaks themselves rear up from the valley bed, bursting through the mists into the sky in the manner of the awesome mountain profiles painted by the Chinese artists of the past. They are packed closely together, and are described by geologists as young and dynamic, which is to say that they are only 3 million years old and are thrusting upwards at the incredible speed of about one inch a year. There was no way of squeezing a road through mountain gorges up to the 700-foot pinnacle of almost solid copper discovered by Jean Dozy, a Dutchman, in 1936. This being so, the road had to go over the top, and the engineers that took it on believed they were making road-building history.

What is different is that the Freeport road makes use of the nearly straight line of a ridge joining high peaks, and this was done by shaving away the sharp edge of the ridge until this was wide enough to allow the passage, first of one, then two cars. There is a point during the approach to this section of the road when it appears in the distance as a glistening thread drawn in the gloom through the mountain shapes and clouds. Cars, their lights on, crawl up and down, passing each other in endless procession. There are extreme gradients, bottle-necks and once in a while a lay-by where one could pull into the side and enjoy a moment of release from the drama. In the ridge area there are precipices on both sides. The road twists ahead like narrow braiding into the peaks, and the view over both edges is of great chasms of shadow from which the tops of lesser mountains soar up in rumpled folds. I asked Greg Probst if anyone ever went over the top, and he replied, 'Once in a while.' And did they ever survive? No, he said, not as far as he knew. Indeed, where we pulled in there was memorial stone to just such a tragedy. The previous year, a car carrying two nurses down to Timika had lost its brakes on the bend, and plunged into the abyss.

The stop provided an opportunity to examine the 120-kilometre-long slurry pipeline laid by the roadside. This carried the flow of concentrates which were the end product of herculean labours down to the company port of Amamapare on the Arafura coast, where it would be shipped away to Japan. It seemed surprising that the efforts of 10,000 men, the fleets of specialised vehicles, the squadrons of earth-movers tearing off the mountain-tops way up in the clouds, the mill's pulverisation of thousands of tons or rock, could be directed towards this visually mediocre end, and that so narrow a throat could disgorge so vast a treasure. Stopped for the second or third security check, where at a lower level a turning off to the west joined the company road, the explanation given was that this led to a block of rainforest about to be logged by a foreign concessionaire – a circumstance of which Greg and John showed that they thoroughly disapproved. The guards at the gate here were supposedly to exclude any possibility of piratical attacks by the loggers on the company's trees. Perhaps, in addition, although this was not mentioned, the security of the pipeline came into the question. In the troubles of 1977 it had been sabotaged, theoretically by local villagers in support of the OPM. It was another piece of disputed history which I was sure that Freeport, in its new mood of frankness, would be willing to clear up.

The final climb, with the Toyota's bonnet pointed at the sky, was into the level of Alpine tundra which in the mountains of Irian Jaya can take on aspects of spectacular arboreal agony. Here the invasion of moss had spread a species of netting over the vegetation through which stunted oaks and pines gesticulated with their distorted branches. Landscapes were weird and surrealistic. A grey, shining dome of rock arose like a tonsured head from suffocated lavender scrub, waterfalls piddled everywhere from rock faces. In one place a yellow smear spread on a distant mountain flank, and this, John said, was the sulphide content of a landslide, which were numerous and dangerous in this area of dynamic mountains.

Tembagapura, enclosed in this narrow valley, came suddenly into sight below. After the accounts I had heard, the view came as a disappointment, although John, parking in the space provided for its appreciation, clearly regarded it as memorable. Families from the town travelled up here in good weather for a refreshing glimpse, he said, of its order and beauty, but although I would have expected such an extraordinary human settlement to have impressed by its uniqueness, it failed to do so. Apart from the cliffs and peaks, it might have been Wamena viewed from the air.

Hemmed in though it was, the town was spreading up the lower slopes into whatever space could be found. Multi-storied buildings were going up in the background but the heart of the town was a matter of bungalows of identical size and shape, laid out in rows that awoke memories of a railway marshalling-yard or, at one point on the slope down to the town, of a mining settlement in the Peruvian Andes. This Peruvian similarity was heightened by the fact that almost all the few pedestrians we saw in the streets were small men in blue dungarees, yellow wellington boots and white miner's helmets. Most of them carried furled umbrellas and bent over slightly as if unable to free themselves psychologically from the constrictions of the mines. This was far from being the quintessential American small town of its description. It was at first sight very quiet, plain and withdrawn, and without any visible attempt to draw attention to itself, or control the overpowering theatricality of its surroundings. Apart from the slowly mooching little miners in the streets, the only sudden, and quite surprising sign of life we came upon, on turning a corner, was the spectacle of ranks of Indonesian children in Boy Scouts' and Girl Guides' uniforms, lined up in an early evening ceremony to salute the lowering of the Indonesian flag.

John delivered me to the company house where I was to lodge. Although a standard bungalow in a row, this proved to be spacious, comfortable and fitted with all conceivable household appliances. The windows were clean and the floors polished. There were calm pictures in good frames on the walls, and, to my huge satisfaction after a longish stay in a dry country, a shelf of Foster's beer from Australia, in a version containing practically no alcohol, which was all that was permissible in Tembagapura. Yellow wellingtons in assorted sizes stood by the door, a miner's padded jacket and helmet awaited me on a clothes peg, and a smiling Indonesian maid hovered in the background.

There was even a small front garden in which etiolated busy-lizzies strained towards the last of the light. Here John and I stood to take the measure of the weather. Today, he said, had been exceptionally good – that was for Tembagapura. Even as he spoke the few hunched-up little miners coming into sight opened their umbrellas, and cold, thin rain slightly perfumed with industrial workings began to fall about us.

Guidebook accounts of Tembagapura describe it as a typically prosperous American town, in which all that has been made familiar by the movies and come to be accepted as the American way of life, is accentuated almost to the point of caricature by its isolation. The picture is an imaginary one. In reality the atmosphere is austere, and there seems little at first sight in the way of entertainment, consumerism or gracious living to compensate for the bleakness of the physical environment. On all sides one encounters the stern virtues of our days. Everything in Tembagapura works.

Meals were taken in a canteen in which, as in every other area, company efficiency was reflected in the most trivial of details. A notice on the door said that breakfasts were served from 3 am. Early starts were the order of the day here. There were no roads apart from the one on which we travelled, and all journeys outside town had to be made by helicopter. By 5 am the lights were on in most windows, and at dawn the sky was full of the sound of the choppers pounding through the air. Normally the day's weather started with a show of promise, but by midday the slow signs of deterioration were to be detected, with mists gathering in the afternoon, and the start of a wetting at about four. All the streets were steep, and the evening rain kept them slippery. Company cars were available for most journeys of more than a hundred yards. During my short stay in the town I never saw anyone obviously exercising himself by going for a walk, and never saw an American wife on foot at all.

Like Wamena, Tembagapura would appear to have no centre, the nearest thing to one being a small shopping arcade containing an ill-stocked supermarket and a municipal office of a kind. Here a notice in English, although addressed to the Indonesian majority, and referring to the indigenous Amungme and the way they should be treated, refers to them a little contemptuously as 'the natives'. The town is dominated by a truly enormous sports complex, which at a distance resembles photographs of the Kaaba at Mecca. There are no dogs or cats to be seen in its streets.

With the rapid and successful spread of its mining activities, Tembagapura is expanding as fast as it can, with new bungalows jammed up against one another, and wild trees dangling their moss-clogged branches over rose-gardens newly hacked out of rock. Its latest population figure has jumped to 10,000, of which approximately 700 are American citizens and almost all the rest Indonesians. A handful of the Amungme, the original tribal occupants, were supposed to be tucked away in the holes and corners of the town, although I never saw anyone who by his dress or features I could identify as a tribal. When forced by circumstances to attend a clinic at the superbly equipped local hospital, I would have been certain that of the 200 or so persons attending for treatment, 100 per cent were Indonesians. The normal explanation for the non-employment of members of the original population is their lack of even the most basic of skills. It is generally accepted that recruitment of labour on the lower levels of proficiency is controlled by the Indonesian authorities who see it in their interests to organise the employment of as many immigrants as possible.

An endless wrangle has gone on between Freeport and its many critics over the circumstances by which it acquired the area of the mine and the extraordinary fact that the Amungme people, who previously lived by hunting and cultivating their crops where the mountains have been removed and Tembagapura built, should have been forced to surrender 10,000 hectares of their land for which nothing has been paid. This happened two years before the Indonesian occupation of West Papua had been legally ratified by the Act of Free Will. The Indonesian Constitution guarantees that 'The earth, the waters, along with the natural resources contained therein, shall be regulated by the government, and are to be used to promote the utmost welfare of the people'. The government also promises to respect traditional rights to land, but it is a promise that has rarely been kept. Legal quibbles, evasions and the manipulations of the law are used against tribal peoples like the Amungme who have been ousted from their lands. Yet how simple, how inexpensive it would have been for the company to have settled the whole affair on the spot with some sort of compensatory arrangement. How preferable such a solution would have been to throwing the dispossessed Amungme into the arms of the OPM resistance, thereby provoking the sabotaged pipeline, the 'Daisy Cluster' bombs said to have been used in retaliation by the Indonesian airforce against the Amungme village of Ilaga, and Amnesty International's scarifying report of prisoners held in the mine in steel containers, darkness and near-freezing temperatures.

This perhaps is the one area in which Freeport, whose engineering achievements have amazed the world, may be said to have revealed an Achilles heel of ineptitude, when a provision from its huge revenues small enough to escape notice in its balance sheet would have embellished its reputation, and put the matter right. But perhaps the government is at the back of its refusal to make reparation. Concessions have been granted to carry out logging operations in Indonesia wherever rainforest exists, all of which are bound to involve disputes over traditional rights, and the government is likely to avoid precedents, such as compensation to the Amungme, over rights many tribal peoples are certain to claim. While refusing to pay even small compensatory sums to those they have dispossessed, Freeport claims to have built schools 'so that the indigenous peoples can contrive to live where they are, while having the option to educate their children'. But as the Amungme have already been removed, the schools can be of no benefit.

All these minority people who have populated the innumerable islands of Indonesia and have developed their own separate languages and culture, are now to be persuaded or compelled to surrender to the central government the resources upon which they and their ancestors have lived.

At best they will become unskilled labourers working in mines, or in the plantations that are to replace the vanishing rainforests, or growing rice for the surplus population of Java dumped in their midst. Those like the Amungme who refused to accept this future can expect to be shoved away out of sight and forgotten. In this way the empire is consolidated.

NINETEEN

WE SQUEEZED INTO Greg's Toyota Special, and the last six miles of our journey to the mine was a charge up an impossible gradient and a final squeeze through a narrow tunnel which brought us to an absolute barrier at the foot of the peaks. At this point, fully disguised as miners in their working gear, we clambered into an iron belvedere from which the aerial tramcar is hauled into the newly levelled plateau in the sky at the centre of the drama. Peering into the abyss below, then up into the misted pinnacles ahead as the tramcar was lifted aloft, I recalled the pleasant qualms of childhood when subjected to some fairground adventure, and wondered if whoever planned this soaring approach nurtured a secret passion for the theatre.

The climb to about 13,000 feet takes an unnaturally prolonged four minutes. We got out, stiff in our miner's gear, breathing a little faster than usual, and blanched in the mist. Suddenly all the colours had gone, reduced to a bluish monochrome, and the meandering haphazard shapes of the familiar world were tamed by the simplicities of the mine. Two enormous mountains, the Ertzberg and the Grasberg, had stood close to each other, and their rugged profiles were now replaced by pale geometrical shapes. They had been mountains of limestone, with cores of igneous rock, and littered here, in a spread of soft white light among clearings of mist, was what was left of them, the 'overburden' which 130-ton earthmovers were tidying away along the perimeter. Thus in one corner of vision a ghostly step-pyramid had formed, and in another the dunes of a vaporous Sahara.

Enormous vehicles picked us up in their haloed headlights as they took shape, rumbled away and were blotted out. I looked down from the surrounding wall into the vast cavity from which someone had described the Ertzberg mountain as having been torn up by the roots. Greg thought it was a kilometre across. It was now full almost to the brim with countless millions of tons of water, the colour of Reckitt's blue, which would be put to some industrial use.

At this point Victor Holm, a senior mining engineer newly arrived from the States, took over; a man with a trick of quiet but convincing emphasis, and the expression of a High Churchman untroubled by doubt. 'I guess there's not much to see,' he said. 'Most of the action is underground these days. Ertzberg is kind of fading out but we still take fifteen thousand tonnes of ore a day out of the pit. You probably heard we're going to ninety thousand tonnes a day. Most of that's Grasberg. We have a two hundred and fifty-ton digger on its way from the States. That's the biggest in the world. Any of the kind we're using at this moment can pick up a twenty-five-ton mouthful of ore and dump it ready for the mill in under a minute, so can you figure how it will be when the big boys get to work. Know something? A single tyre for one of those sonofabitches costs forty thousand dollars. Give you some idea of the expenditure, when we actually make roads of them. Soon as a tyre shows signs of wear it goes into roadmaking. We're a godsend to the tyre industry.'

We had been swinging up and down the slopes in the fog and I had lost all sense of direction. 'Where does this road go to, Mr Holm?' I asked.

'Right now we're down in the Grasberg pit,' Holm said. 'We're probably about six hundred feet down in the mountain. There's a system of roads running round it at different depths, and it's quite possible to take a wrong turning and lose your way. Just imagine losing your way in a pit.'

'Like Dante's Inferno up in the sky,' I said.

He laughed. 'Well, maybe you're right,' he said. 'We aim to go down three thousand feet. Could be more if it turns out to be mineralised. That's one helluva hole.'

'What are those vehicles doing down there?' I asked. Earthmovers with blazing headlights were charging in one direction and another like a squadron of battle tanks.

'That's the Grasberg working level,' Holm said. 'The surface has been blasted to loosen it up, and now they're scooping away the ore. They go down nine metres at a time, then the charges go in to blast the next level.'

Holm manoeuvred past a hill of fog-shrouded rubble. 'Is all that ore?' I asked.

He picked up a lump of rock and handed it to me. It was very heavy, its surface veined with the glitter of metals fused in the volcano three million years ago. 'That yellow you see isn't gold,' he said, 'although there's a substantial gold content. The other stuff you were looking at was the overburden.'

'The original mountain,' I said.

'If you like,' he said. 'A general mix-up. Earth, rocks, vegetation and what have you.'

A few minutes earlier, while touring the perimeter with Greg, I had seen an earthmover snatch up a bit of useless scenery to which a small pine tree was still attached and rumble away with it out of sight. 'A bit of a headache for you,' I said.

'We have a problem,' Holm said. 'Two and a half billion tons of it.'

'You mean *million* tons,' I said.

'No, billion. We have one hell of a lot of overburden on our hands.'

'So what are you going to do?'

'Well, eventually push it into the next valley, and forget about it,' Holm said. 'What else can we do?'

'So what's the future of all this?' I asked.

'Rosy,' he said. 'Put it this way, we have high hopes. Mr Ward expects to have a dozen mines in the area, but the great question is what we'll come up with elsewhere. Most igneous rock is barren, but when metallisation exists it tends to occur in a belt. These mountains go all the way to Papua New Guinea where they've made encouraging assays. All I can say is the possibilities are limitless.'

'And will you be staying on here?' I asked.

'Well maybe and maybe not. Most of our people find seven or eight months is about right. The scene is very confined, and the wives who come here find it hard to take. They're usually warned that it's their duty to occupy themselves. They can go to sewing classes or sign up for watercolour painting. Everyone goes to church on Sunday and after that they go to each other's houses for any new video that happens to be about. The work is what counts, and outside that it's not much of a life.'

John Cutts was in constant attendance. He was an interesting man with a fine Sioux face, an excellent amateur anthropologist, flew alone in his microlite through these deep and land-locked valleys, and took the best videos of tribal ceremonies I had ever seen. He had had some accidental trouble with insurgents at a time when the OPM had been strong in the area, five years before. Villagers had implored him to come to their aid when guerillas had surrounded a post defended by five policemen – a circumstance setting off a panic among the villagers who had reason to fear a retributory attack by counter-insurgency aircraft. Rushing towards the post in the hope of persuading the OPM to hold their fire, John stopped a bullet in the upper arm which nearly carried away his shoulder. This proved to have been fired by the police, and he pulled up his shirt to reveal the hideous muscular turmoil caused by an armalite wound.

I would have said that John Cutts was incapable of a downright lie. His method of defending the company's position was to stage a diversion designed to draw away the attention from an unsatisfactory fact. John knew full well that those who took the difficult road to Tembagapura were likely to have a social or political axe to grind. The company had been charged with seizure of traditional land, of filling valleys with the wreckage of mountains, and polluting a major river, and that was what concerned them. Even Indonesian newspapers had been known to make reference to the wretched Amungmes living not quite out of sight in Tembagapura under plastic sheeting stretched across sticks in the fairly constant rain. John, as he was bound to, deftly avoided such topics.

In a letter to Freeport McMoran of New Orleans, Rainforest Action Network complains that 'most trips to the Tembagapura mine appear to be propaganda blitzes, designed to exhaust and astound the visitor – in all cases accompanied by Freeport representatives, in company vehicles and with company drivers'. 'Schedules', adds the writer, 'were tightly packed, so as not to allow for private interviews.' I myself was given a guided tour, probably similar in most respects to one provided until recently for visitors to the Soviet Union. It is hard to see how it could have been otherwise. No cars are available in Tembagapura other than somewhat specialised models adapted to deal with difficult conditions, and even were those to be available for general use, there are no roads other than the highway linking the mine with the coast. Travel otherwise can only be in one of the company's helicopters. To be able to conduct private interviews I would have had to arrive with an Amungme interpreter, who might not be allowed in, and would certainly have been hard to find. Schedules in my case were certainly not tightly packed. I was made welcome for as long as I was able to stay, which was one week. But all contacts are official. There is no investigation to be done.

A high spot of the visit was to the mine itself, a great engineering feat of our times, which when it is all over will inevitably leave one of the greatest messes on the face of the earth. No hesitation was shown in driving me all over it. It is there. Nothing can be done to cover it up. Holm's hunch that there might be more such mines to come was revealing indeed, if unintentionally so.

In Tembagapura I briefly succumbed to a long infection, which caused me to miss what must have been a pleasant interlude by way of a helicopter trip to a local feast. This was held in the village of Araonup where an assortment of tribals were celebrating the opening of a school. On his return John showed me a video of professional quality he had taken, and there was no doubt that all concerned were having a wonderful time. They ran about in all directions, garlanded with leaves, waving branches like Victorians on Palm Sunday, thereafter, by local custom, clubbing festive pigs to death before cooking them in the usual way. I was interested in the commentary accompanying the video, which came over as a set speech from a policy document issued by the Summer Institute of Linguistics, the largest and most powerful Protestant fundamentalist mission in the world. 'You can't sit here and protect little pockets of people, and think that you're doing them the privilege of protecting them from the outside world. It's changing, and it's going to change. What better way to help these people than to help them understand these changes, and maybe develop some skills they can market.'

The little pockets of people in this case are the Amungme. Fifteen years ago in Bolivia, where I had been sent by the *Observer* to investigate reports of the enslavement of forest Indians in the north, I was told to my astonishment at the Bolivian Ministry of the Interior that I would require the permission of Mr Victor Haltermen, Bolivian head of the S.I.L., before I could visit the area. The permission was not forthcoming. Mr Halterman came straight to the point. 'A number of Indians remain in forest areas designated for white occupation,' he said gently. 'They are a dangerous nuisance as it is, and they must go. Our task is to ease their passage.'

As a fundamentalist Mr Halterman agreed with the doctrinal statement warning of 'the unending punishment of the unsaved', which consigns to hell not only those millions brought up as Jews, Muslims, Hindus or Buddhists, but all the unimaginable multitudes of good and great men and women born into this world before the advent of Christ. 'I am a member of the S.I.L.,' Cutts admitted to me in our last interview, and he too – and most emphatically – was of Mr Halterman's fundamentalist view. It occurred to me how extraordinary it was that Indonesia, a Muslim state, with an enormous preponderance of non-Christians among its citizens, should support an organisation which assures so many of them that hell's fires await them beyond the grave.

This conversation took place on a natural rock platform above Tembagapura, to which people shut away in the depths of the valley would escape when they could to refresh themselves with a new view of a prosaic reality, transformed in the charm both of distance and a novel aspect.

John never failed to be impressed by the vista and its garnish of industrial romance. 'There's almost ten thousand people living in this town. It's just chiselled right out of the side of a mountain – you've got fourteen thousand-foot peaks up above these.'

The view was indeed majestic, all the more so in the strong, lugubrious colour-wash of evening light. Stubby fingers of cloud were reaching down through the peaks, and here and there the lights began to twinkle in the windows.

'It's expanding as fast as it can,' John said, referring to the town.

'Don't the Amungme regard these mountains as holy?' I asked.

He laughed it off. 'Let me say this,' he said. 'What's a mountain to them? These mountains are not even as valuable as a pandanus nut tree. When we go into an area and explain what the exploration programme is they say to us we're happy if you find a mine so we can experience some advancement in our area. We have an incubation programme to teach these people entrepreneurial skills. They feel like they want to be part of the changes they see.'

'And how is the exploration going? I hear the new lease goes most of the way to Papua New Guinea.'

'They've done a large project,' John said. He smiled unflagging enthusiasm. 'There have been a few spots they've decided to take a second look at.'

'I would have been happier to hear you say that what they have here already will take them a few years to digest,' I said. 'Victor Holm thought it might be the year 2000 before they get down three thousand feet to the bottom of Grasberg. I suppose a world collapse in the price of copper is the only hope.'

It was clear from John's expression that he was unable to take such remarks seriously. We walked together towards the car. Disappointingly the weather closed in on us a little before time. The houses in their rows slid beneath the mist, and there was the faintest of smells in the nostrils of industrially flavoured rain.

SELECT BIBLIOGRAPHY

Anti-Slavery Society, *West Papua: Plunder in Paradise*, Anti-Slavery Society Report No. 6, London, 1990

Carmel Budiardjo and Liem Soei Liong, *West Papua, The Obliteration of a People* in, *Tapol* (Bulletin of the Indonesia Human Rights Campaign), 1988

James Dunn, *Timor, A People Betrayed*, The Jacaranda Press, Queensland, Australia, 1983

Robert Gardner and Karl G. Heider, *Gardens of War*, André Deutsch, London, 1969

Karl G. Heider, *Under the Mountain Wall*, N. D.

Jill Jolliffe, *Timor – Terra Sagrenta O Jurnal*, Lisbon, 1989

Robert Mitton, *The Lost World of Irian Jaya*, Oxford University Press (Australia), 1985

Parliamentary Human Rights Group, House of Commons, *The Santa Cruz Massacre, Díli (East Timor), 12 November 1991*

Don Richardson, *Lords of the Earth*, Regal Books, California, 1989

John G. Taylor, *Indonesia's Forgotten War*, Zed Books, London, 1990

John G. Taylor, *The Indonesian Occupation of East Timor 1974–1989*, Catholic Institute for International Relations, London, 1990

Forbes Wilson, *The Conquest of the Copper Mountain*, Atheneum, New York, 1981